Education and
Development

Education and Development

Issues in the Analysis and Planning of Postcolonial Societies

Edited by

Lascelles Anderson
Harvard Graduate School of
Education

Douglas M. Windham
State University of New York at
Albany

LexingtonBooks
D.C. Heath and Company
Lexington, Massachusetts
Toronto

Library of Congress Cataloging in Publication Data

Main entry under title:

Education and development.

    Includes bibliographical references.
    Contents: The educational policies of postcolonial states / Philip
Foster—The political context of education in the developing world /
Marie Thourson Jones—Educational progress and economic
development / Gary S. Fields—[etc.]
    1. Underdeveloped areas—Education—Addresses, essays, lectures.
2. Underdeveloped areas—Addresses, essays, lectures. I. Anderson,
Lascelles. II. Windham, Douglas M.
LC2607.E38   370'.9172'4   81–47562
ISBN 0–669–04654–x   AACR2

Copyright © 1982 by D.C. Heath and Company

Published simultaneously in Canada

Printed in the United States of America

International Standard Book Number: 0–669–04654–x

Library of Congress Catalog Card Number: 81–47562

To Our Families:
My mother, Iris, and the memory of my father, Sidney;
Joan, Michelle, John, and Leslie Anderson

Jeannette, Karen, and Douglas Windham, Jr.

Contents

Acknowledgments

The editors and authors wish to acknowledge the invaluable and understanding assistance given by Margaret Zusky, Susan Lasser, and Kathy Benn of the editorial staff of Lexington Books, at all stages of the production of this volume.

Introduction

Typically, whenever a new work appears in a field that is already fairly well represented, authors seem to have a strong compulsion to justify the addition in terms of what the other contributions have failed to discuss. We do not compare this book with others on education and development but simply go straight to the intellectual circumstances surrounding the birth of the idea for it. We hope we will throw some light on as yet still insufficiently understood corners of a very complex set of issues in the process.

The research program identified in the early literature on the economics of education and human capital tended to make education into an instrument capable of being manipulated to achieve higher levels of economic development. That we have in recent years come to a sobering recognition of the real limitations of education as a singular development instrument at one and the same time speaks to the past, as well as to the future. The revolution in scientific thought necessary to usher in a new era of thinking, to use a Kuhnian notion, has not yet taken place. We do know, however, that the original research program no longer facilitates effective thinking about education's real potential as the development tool we once thought it to be and that we are faced with a task no less radical and sweeping than that of questioning the very assumptions on which the earlier research program was postulated.

One reason for the failure of the earlier view is quite certainly that education was not sufficiently understood to be endogenous to the total social system and could not by itself effect the achievement of some specific desired end. Thus, education by itself could not be manipulated to generate high growth rates since conditions necessary for growth lay in other directions; and educational reform in and of itself could not guarantee the fundamental reshaping of even education's own internal conditions any more than to some minimal degree, if at all.

To cover this history in detail is a major task that neither time nor space allowed. We decided instead to try to neatly categorize some central issues by adopting a problems approach. In the process we hope to at least touch on some points of deep sensitivity in the education-development nexus, to lay out our ideas, and by implication, to pinpoint the task ahead of us.

Since education is really only one sector or activity among a host of such sectors or activities in a country, the first step is to see what development theory has to say about aggregate patterns of growth and development. It is perhaps fair to say that the famous Harrod-Domar model was the intellectual basis of thinking about development issues during the first and second U.N. Development Decades. That model's basic thrust was growth. Major points of the theoretical structure included the following: (1) that capital accumulation is indispensable for the maintenance of full employment; (2) that capital accumulation expands productive capacity at the same time as it expands income; and (3) that real income should grow so that income in the following period would exceed that of the current period by an amount sufficient to absorb into production the new productive capacity created by accumulation.

The model was simple and easy to use, and it gave estimates of growth rather directly. It was particularly suitable for countries in which all sectors were growing at the same rate and when the important parameters of the model—namely, the savings rate and the capital-output ratios—were fairly stable. However, a fundamental problem arises when we come to deal with factors besides capital. This made the model somewhat unrealistic in the case of developing countries where the major inhibiting factors might not be capital at all, but labor, entrepreneurship, and the availability of an appropriate institutional framework. In short, the perspective on development afforded by the model was rather limited, confined as it was to situations in which the achievement of high growth rates through the infusion of liberal amounts of capital almost alone was possible.

That this perspective was somewhat misleading was soon recognized. Already the notion of total factor productivity had become familiar in discussion about growth and development, and the work on aggregate models of growth was already pointing to the part played by factors other than capital and labor—by implication, education in the real growth of nations. Thus, at the same time, as a recognition of the limitations of capital-induced patterns of growth developed, perhaps even as a result of it, a feeling emerged that education had a major role to play in any process of growth and development. That we have somehow come to question that too is the very essence of the dilemma we are trying to highlight. This, however, did not take place before a period of major growth in educational systems around the world had passed. Between 1950 and 1970, for example, enrollments in primary schools in the non-communist underdeveloped world jumped from 65 million to 202 million. In Africa, the rate of school attendance grew fastest, perhaps due to the low starting levels there. In secondary education, 7.6 million students were enrolled in the schools in developing countries in 1950. This figure grew to 18.2 million by 1960 and to 42 million by 1970. Even at the tertiary level, rates of expansion were phenomenal: from 940,000 for developing countries in 1950 to 5.6 million in 1970.

Growth of the system, however, never really succeeded in accomplishing real change. It soon became quite obvious that expansion of education systems was clearly not a sufficient condition for change, either in education or outside of it. Questions of distributive implications began to emerge at the same time as doubts concerning the efficacy of the tools used to support the phenomenal growth in educational systems in service of projected industrial demands for qualified manpower. Educational reform became, by implication, the way of dealing with these unsatisfactory elements in the profile of educational development. The questions that were raised were not easy to answer, and we are now witnessing a sober recognition of the deep intractability of elements that, up until now, had been regarded as moldable, in this direction or that, as a result of conscious policy efforts.

All policy, whether aimed at the resolution of relatively minor concerns or directed to issues of major importance, appears to have the same central core of elements—namely, a set of goals, however identified, and a set of constraints that inhibits the attainment of these goals in one way or the other. These two elements are tied together by a set of conditions that relates the attainment of the goals to the resources and constraints in ways that are either presumed to be known or can be determined. However, the formulation of policy is only one aspect of the policy problem; policy leads to effects that are desired, if the policy is properly conceived and executed, or to those that are dysfunctional and undesirable, if the policy were ill planned or poorly conceived. Educational policy, in the context of development, has had to wrestle with some rather difficult issues, and attempts to cover all of them would be impossible. We therefore address five problems that we see as the most pressing: (1) the need to achieve equality of educational opportunity and implications of different societal objectives for such equity; (2) the problem of limitations of available data for studying questions of education development and progress; (3) problems in the interface between education and the labor market; (4) the uneasy relation between received notions of planning and the philosophical underpinnings of criteria of free individual choice; and (5) the fundamental problem of the endogeneity of education either viewed nationally or in the wider context of the matrix of international forces.

Distribution

In recent years, a worldwide revolution has occurred in thinking about distributive questions of all kinds. In developed countries of a liberal democratic bent, this has taken the form of a shift away from the concerns of the welfare state toward a more-radical call for the creation of redistributive mechanisms. In the developing countries, this shift has either been telescoped into much shorter periods, or in some cases, the politics of development itself has served to bring into sharp relief the central questions of maldistribution of the resources and of opportunities and the urgent need for their necessary reshaping. In development education, this preoccupation has fostered great expectations about the possibility of achieving fundamental shifts in the pattern of opportunity, through provision of more, and in some cases different, kinds of education. Education has not been able to carry such a burden, however, not only because it represents only one part in a complicated nexus of social relationships defining rewards and benefits, and therefore not independent, separate, and powerful, but also because even within its own borders it has had to settle for less by way of its own internal reshaping in the direction of greater equity. The social-class composition of education, for example, has shown itself to be much more resistant to policies aimed at changing its associated biases than had hitherto been thought to be the case, and this resistance has resulted in many cases in a feeling of almost total hopelessness on the part of people and agencies whose job has been to deal with such problems and their eventual resolution.

Among the more-specific issues that embody redistributive concerns and objectives, we can point to the emphasis on nonformal education as a major one. Here the realization is that formal education, as it is usually known, will really be out of reach for many persons, due to any of a number of factors, and that it is perhaps better to try to reach these people through nontraditional lines than to leave them permanently out of the pool of recipients of some type of education.

However, nonformal education raises its own set of questions, and these are quite different from those that typically confront formal education. Thus, they require altogether new approaches, and it is only now that some consensus is emerging on how best to try to accomplish what is to be done. Basic criteria that international agencies now seem to see as necessary include the following: Programs should be functional, serving well-identified target groups; they should be constructed and operated as part of a broader total rural education-and-development effort; and they should be capable of replication. Additionally, high levels of managerial capability are a major requirement for the success of rural development programs. Ironically, this is where the need is perhaps greatest.

There is, however, a fundamental problem with which we have to reckon: Will nonformal education succeed in creating expectations of two types of education and thereby foster divergent views about the usefulness of these alternative modes? This issue has had to be raised constantly since it points to the real possibility of dysfunctionality in a most crucial area of educational policy that affects large numbers of people.

This issue is joined by the contribution of Colletta and Holsinger in chapter 8. They explore the many meanings of the term *nonformal* education and, in so doing, make a distinction between the three modes: (1) formal, (2) nonformal, and (3) informal education. Each one is associated with a different aspect of human development, with formal education being most appropriate to the transmission of knowledge, using the conventional technology of the classroom; nonformal education being most appropriate for the transmission of skills (in the earlier on-the-job-training sense); and informal education being most appropriate in the affective domain, in the transmission of attitudes. These authors discuss a broad range of issues relating to these categorizations and identify propositions, which we believe to be eminently testable once the proper facilitative research-design requirements are satisfied.

Equalizing outcomes represents only one aspect of the broader equality consideration, to be joined by the logically prior concern for appropriate considerations on the input side. Thus, achievement of reasonably equitable outcomes argues for the attainment of some minimally acceptable spread in the distribution of inputs. If the former is accepted as a fundamental tenet, then the question of access becomes crucial. It entails the recognition of biases caused by social-class background of students, and it means defining what equality of opportunity really means and by what means it can be secured. More attention must be placed on location of schools in relation to residential patterns; educational facilities must be as available to low-income and remote populations as they are to less-disadvantaged ones; and the scope and meaning of access must be broadened to include those persons who have already passed through the school system and who are now in the labor force, as the 1974 World Bank Sector Working Paper argues.

Heyneman's chapter 7 speaks to this complex of issues. Drawing on a substantial body of research to which he has contributed greatly, Heyneman discusses the Third World results of using the basic production-function model to study the relative impact of a typical set of independent variables on schooling outputs. He concludes that, contrary to the persistent results of weakness of the postulated independent variables on variance explained in developed-countries settings, the results from developing countries are much more hopeful. Such a conclusion argues powerfully against uncritical extrapolation of developed-world results into the social milieu of developing countries in this area of educational policy.

Data Availability

Any attempt to analyze educational systems is confronted immediately with the problem of data availability and its quality. Even if that problem does not exist, in the sense that base-level statistics are amply available and are of appreciable quality, the question still remains as to the way such data should be assembled in order to throw light on the real nature and dimensionality of educational systems. Data are clearly needed on the broad categories comprising inputs, outputs, and internal processes of the system under study. Output data typically are satisfied in the form of measures of knowledge acquired in schools, but since the evaluation of schooling requires the prior specification of the societal objectives sought by schooling, measures of equality of opportunity and other social-equity criteria are at least as important in affording judgment about schooling success. These will remain, as they are at present, open to continued refinement and modification as the analytic bases of these normative criteria become enriched.

Undoubtedly, the most abundantly available body of data on education systems in developing countries is that on input indicators. These typically include indicators of enrollment, teacher availability, capital-facility availability, and financial input and textbook availability. Chapter 3 by Fields and chapter 7 by Heyneman address this group of issues, although from somewhat different perspectives. Fields structures his analysis of data and its quality in terms of indicators of progress in, and commitment to, education. He argues for fine breakdowns of statistical data to allow for analysis of the distributional issues so much at the heart of the present debate, but he cautions against the use of composite indicators since the prior question as to what should be included is not yet adequately answered.

Heyneman surveys numerous studies on input availability, with special emphasis on teacher characteristics, the availability of textbooks and supplies, and costs. He concludes that, whereas access for all appears well within grasp, it only highlights the issue of resource quality and the resultant need to move on that front also if true equality of opportunity is to be achieved.

Planning

Perhaps no corner of the education-and-development enterprise has seen more skepticism and criticism than planning. This certainly runs counter to the most modest expectations of practitioners of the art, in the not-too-distant past, concerning the efficacy and robustness of the methods of their craft. At the same time, a wholesale withdrawal is occurring from the large and complex planning models of the 1960s and 1970s. One becomes faced also with a sober realization that planning takes place in a broader network of social and political forces whose resilience is largely

impervious to the play of policy choices that planners typically assume
to be efficacious. Finally there is the recognition that planning quite often
plays, or could play, into the hands of antidemocratic forces and forestall
the very outcomes presumably sought by planning. In short, planning
easily becomes a centrist activity, undercutting thrusts for democratic
participation and decentralization without which it loses its legitimacy
and deeper reason for being.

Whether planning's failures stem wholly from these or other more
imperfectly recognized constraints is a question addressed by the contributions of Anderson (chapter 4) and Windham (chapter 9). Windham
underscores what he calls the dilemmas of planning. Basing his critique
on the need for a deeper appreciation of the richness and variety of the
educational experiences, he counterposes the hopes of the central planner
with the realities of the individual decision-making unit. The insight for
this way of structuring the planning dilemma is to be found in the superior
flexibility of microunits when faced with appropriate information against
which to fashion their own responses. Planning founders, then, to the
extent that it frustrates this individual search for desirable outcomes by
pretending that it is in command of information it really does not have.
Windham's prescription is for refashioning planning decidedly in the
direction of decentralized decision making so as to assure more-appropriate adjudication of the conflict between microdesires and macro-ob-
jectives. Anderson argues for educational planning that recognizes the
inevitable shrinking of the opportunity sets that planners typically assume
when the impact of international forces and events on domestic choices
takes the form of adding powerful and new binding constraints to these
local opportunity sets.

Foster's wide-ranging chapter 1 complements the Windham argument
for making much greater use of microprice incentives to achieve desirable
outcomes in education-planning policy. In terms of structural changes,
he argues for a devolution of planning decisions away from central administration and toward those agencies that are capable of quicker response.
The argument holds with equal force with respect to education finance
where public subsidies make sense at the lower, not the higher, ends of
the educational ladder, given the severely competing demands on highly
constrained public treasuries in most postcolonial states.

Education and the Labor Market

High rates of unemployment are a pervasive feature of the development
scene. The statistics are fairly well known. What is not so clear, however,

is whether education has a clear and decisive role in the alleviation of such conditions.

Early work on educational planning of a manpower-planning variety conceptualized the function of education as equipping workers with skills, these skills being loosely thought of as being generated by school attendance for a specific number of years. The results of this approach to manpower and employment policy through education are already clear—namely, huge numbers of educated unemployed and massive schooling inflation in the labor market. These results could be blamed on the somewhat mechanistic view of the relation between education and employment, to be corrected by policies that were more deeply theoretically grounded.

In chapter 5, Chiswick speaks to this set of issues. Building on neoclassical human-capital notions, she makes a distinction between worker, or productivity, skills and allocative skills. The framework is a two-sector model with movement of workers from the traditional sector to the modern sector being a function of the net present values of education investment in the two sectors. It is now possible to pose several questions that stand at the heart of education and development policy in postcolonial states. Chiswick raises some of these. Her conclusion is that development is much more likely where planning agencies place greater emphasis on allocative rather than productive skills.

Anderson's chapter 4, on the impact of multinational corporations, moves into uncharted territory and underscores the real possibility of severe limitations on the external efficiency of schooling in postcolonial societies, at the same time as patterns of technology transfer place severe upper bounds on the creation of endogenous technical capability.

Education as Endogenous

Finally, in chapter 2, Jones surveys a rich literature in the politics of education in developing countries and successfully demonstrates the enormous complexity of that political context. In chapter 6, Palmer, taking a macroview of the impact of education on patterns of migration, identifies another dimension to the matrix of external linkages that is associated with education in the process of development. In chapter 10, Birdsall and Cochrane undertake a careful examination of the relationship between education and parental decision making. In so doing, they demonstrate the substantial usefulness of the model of household decision making in the context of developing countries.

We have cast this volume in a colonial/postcolonial framework in order to capture the education implications of the development process of emergence from patterns and institutions of external dominance. We hope we have been successful.

Education and Development

Part I
Social-Science Perspectives on Education and Development

1 The Educational Policies of Postcolonial States

Philip Foster

History frequently reminds us of the continuities rather than the discontinuities that characterize societies undergoing rapid social change. Even the most profound political revolutions leave untouched far more than they destroy, and this seems pertinent when we examine the educational policies pursued by postcolonial nations. No one doubts the profound symbolic importance of the transition from colonial rule to independence that has occurred since the end of World War II. Yet most of the educational issues that generate fervent contemporary debate find their origins in the colonial past. If we are to understand the present situation, we must first examine the colonial legacy—a task not always congenial to the ahistorical education planner. Political revolutions always create their own mythologies, and in the postcolonial states this process is very evident when we address educational matters. It is important for new nations to demonstrate that current policies constitute a radical break with the past, but in so doing, a certain amount of postcolonial fiction has been generated.

Education and the Colonial Heritage

In spite of a good deal of talk about colonial systems, I am increasingly skeptical that we can characterize any colonial power as having had any broad and consistent educational policies. In practice, edicts and ordinances on education emanating from the metropole had only a limited effect on what was happening in individual dependencies where local conditions and resources or the enthusiasms of particular governors or voluntary agencies were often decisive in determining educational development. Certainly, in terms of quantitative growth, no consistent themes emerge if we contrast the various colonial traditions. In some respects, French Gabon, for example, had more in common with the Gold Coast than it had with the francophonic territories of interior West Africa, and northern Nigeria looked very similar to neighboring Niger. Colonial affiliation was, therefore, a poor predictor of quantitative development,

3

and almost invariably throughout the colonial world, variations between territories were less than variations within them.

Moreover, if we ignore simple quantitative indicators of development and look at the content of the educational experience that was provided by colonial regimes, we are struck by the enormous diversity of practice that actually occurred. It is still believed that, insofar as colonial authorities evinced any interest in educational development, they were largely concerned with replicating metropolitan structures and curriculums within their dependencies. This was not often the case, however, and the colonial literature abounds with abortive attempts to adapt educational structure and content to what were perceived to be local conditions and realities. For example, nothing could be further from the truth than the statement that French policies were uncompromisingly assimilationist in aim. To be sure, the use of French as a medium of instruction was axiomatic throughout French territories, and there were, indeed, very real differences in this regard between British and French language policies. At the same time, local curriculums and structures were frequently very different from those of the mother country, and for example, the French showed little inclination to export the metropolitan lycée to the dependencies. In fact, one of the paradoxes of West African educational development was that, in francophonic territories, the system that emerged had little in common with that of the metropole while in neighboring British Africa, in spite of prolonged discussion about educational adaptation, the schools very much resembled their metropolitan counterparts in terms of structure and curriculum (largely as a result of pressure from Western-educated local elites).[1] It would be no exaggeration to say that, in many respects, the convergence between metropolitan and local systems has been greater in the postcolonial period in spite of much formal emphasis on a radical break with the colonial past.

Finally, although consistency was not a characteristic of colonial educational policies, this is not to suggest that these regimes had no ideas about educational planning or any views concerning the role that formal schooling might play in development. If we understand planning to mean simply the organization of the structure and content of educational systems to accord with perceived economic and political goals, then it is simply untrue that educational planning is a postindependence phenomenon. There was no shortage of reflection about planning issues throughout the colonial period, and plenty of efforts were made at local implementation. However indifferent colonial regimes were to the provision of formal schooling in the very early days of colonial penetration, it was not long before the sheer exigencies of colonial administration and the need to develop the colonial economies, while ensuring the loyalty of local populations, obliged them to consider educational objectives and strategies.

That such efforts were not necessarily inspired by a spirit of benevolence toward colonial populations is beside the point—it is always outcome, not motive, that is significant.

It is chastening to realize, therefore, that few educational issues are discussed in contemporary postcolonial states that were not foreshadowed in some way in the colonial literature. In quantitative terms, the relationship between the volume of educational outputs and employment in the modern sector was a matter of great concern, particularly in some French territories where crude attempts were made to match supply with effective demand. Many contemporary planners are (incorrectly in my view) exercised by the relationship between education, urbanization, and unemployment, but they can take comfort from the fact that this issue was not ignored by their colonial predecessors. Moreover, although the planners did not have at their command the techniques of cost-benefit and rate-of-return analysis, they often expressed strong views concerning the relative productivity of primary as opposed to secondary and higher education (for example nineteenth-century British India) and the advantages of general as opposed to technical, vocational, or agricultural schooling. Even the role of language policy as an instrument of political integration was debated, and in this matter one doubts whether any significant advance has been made since the colonial period.

Is there anything new? Quite obviously, the new postcolonial elites can initially command far more legitimacy than their colonial predecessors in the pursuit of national educational goals (because, indeed, colonial regimes were always damned if they did and damned if they did not). Hence the range of policy alternatives open to contemporary planners is ostensibly far greater. Though it is fashionable to assert that few such options are really available since the postcolonial states are part of an integrated world system, any examination of postindependence developments would suggest that these nations do, in fact, opt for different strategies.

Moreover, since 1960, the sheer volume and quality of empirical data that has examined the articulation between educational systems and the socioeconomic structures in which they are imbedded has grown apace. Contemporary planners simply know much more, and they command a body of technical expertise not available to early policymakers (whether the heirs of colonialism are wiser or more perceptive is quite another matter). Thus, we now understand more about the functioning of educational systems, and the failure of many colonial educational policies can often be attributed to the fact that colonial administrators were simply unaware of the functional nexus between education and the broad social and economic changes that they themselves had initiated.

There is some merit to the view that the colonial educational experience has put postcolonial regimes in a better position to identify educational strategies that will not work rather than having a clear notion of those that will. Even here, however, one is impressed by the degree to which planners persist in implementing policies that were manifest failures in the colonial period, perhaps in the belief that political independence changes all the parameters within which planning takes place. In practical terms, they frequently overstress the role played by ideology and political will while ignoring the profound structural and economic changes that began in the colonial period. The postcolonial era represents rather a deepening and an extension of these processes, and to ignore them is to ensure that the outcomes of educational planning will rarely coincide with national objectives.

Thus, in this synoptic chapter, it would be less profitable to examine the vagaries of particular postcolonial educational policies than to point to certain structural characteristics that are common to nearly all postcolonial societies, irrespective of particular local traditions, and that tend in turn to determine the broad pattern of educational development.

First, colonial hegemony was everywhere associated with the monetization of local economies and the replacement of largely subsistence by exchange activities. However, this process usually occurred at an uneven rate within individual territories, leading to substantial regional disparities in rates and levels of development. The corollary of monetization was the development of more-complex forms of occupational structure that far exceeded the limited division of labor prevailing in precolonial societies. The new occupations associated with colonial administration, industry, and commerce were characterized by substantial differences in status and income. Although the so-called modern sector of full-time wage or salaried employment comprised only a small proportion of the total labor force in colonial territories, it exercised a disproportionate influence over the aspirations of local populations. Moreover, in contrast to the situation in most colonial metropoles, full-time-employment opportunities were nearly everywhere dominated by government agencies. One of the indirect effects of this situation was to elevate the role of the state, and one of the true legacies of colonialism has been to create a form of statism, which assumes that development can only occur through the direct involvement of government in nearly all processes of social and economic change—a dictum that is as misguided as it is impossible to achieve, given the limited coercive and administrative capacities of most postcolonial regimes.

Along with the spread of a cash economy and the growth of more-complex occupational structures came the increasing urbanization of colonial populations. Town dwellers usually did not and still do not constitute more than a small minority of those populations in spite of massive rates of urban growth. Also, it must not be forgotten that in most nations substantial in-migration to the towns is paralleled by a degree of out-migration to rural areas; the boundaries between city and countryside are very permeable. Nonetheless, towns have often exerted a disproportionate influence over postcolonial-development strategies insofar as they normally consituted the foci of nationalist movements and as postcolonial leadership was initially drawn from the ranks of the Western-educated urban elite. Not surprisingly, in spite of much formal emphasis on the tasks of rural development, most postcolonial elites, until recently, have been less sensitive to the needs of the rural masses than to the demands of more-vociferous and politically volatile urban dwellers.

The processes of socioeconomic change that began in the colonial era had their educational analogues. The diffusion of schooling in most colonies was closely associated with the level of monetization of local economies and the development of towns and transport networks. There was a definite ecology to educational diffusion, and internal differentials in levels of economic development were paralleled by massive inequalities in the provison of education. Frequently, colonial regimes tended to favor particular ethnic or social minorities at the expense of others, but quantitative variations in the distribution of schooling usually tended to result from differentials in internal rates of economic change. Thus, although we now tend to see educational expansion as an independent variable in economic development, it is worth remembering that in the initial phase of growth the demand for, and the supply of, schooling tended to follow upon economic change; it was the cart rather than the horse in the process.

I would suggest that considerable inequalities in access to formal schooling (correlated with equally substantial rates of attrition and dropout) are a virtually inevitable feature of early patterns of educational development. Indeed, it can be argued that in economic terms they may not only be inevitable but desirable where short-term strategies suggest the concentration of resources in more rapidly developing sectors or regions. However, the long-term political consequences of uneven rates of change cannot be disregarded. As we have seen, one of the particular characteristics of colonial societies was that limited opportunities for full-time employment in the modern sector were dominated either by government or sometimes by large-scale expatriate enterprises. In most territories an enormous premium was placed upon the possession of educational qualifications in job recruitment into this sector, particularly insofar as alternative opportunities for occupational and social mobility were limited. Level of formal education was therefore a powerful predictor of subsequent status and income (perhaps even more so than in the metropoles themselves), and there can be little doubt that private rates of return to education were substantial in the colonial period. Where marked inequalities in education provision are linked to high rates of private return to education, this situation constitutes a potential focus for group antagonisms. The issue was often latent in the early colonial era but erupted toward its end and became the center of mounting conflict in many new states in the early postcolonial years.

Thus, minorities who had evinced little interest in schooling during much of the colonial period found themselves at a distinct disadvantage within the context of the new polities, and the struggle for a greater share of educational resources became a dominant issue. Although frequently interwoven, conflicts tended to take several forms. First, confrontation over equality of opportunity in access to schooling occurred along regional lines as between educational haves and have-nots while the rural majority pressed for educational parity with the urban minority. Political antagonisms were exacerbated where broad geographic differentials tended to coincide with ethnic and linguistic divisions. Such was frequently the case in sub-Saharan Africa and in India where the Rimland versus Heartland issue has been salient in educational politics since independence.[2]

A second, though less-frequent, source of tension emerged where minorities who had enjoyed high status in traditional precolonial society were able, in the colonial period, to command a disproportionate share of places in the educational system, particularly at secondary and tertiary levels. In British India, for example, the Brahmans and other twice-born castes were significantly overrepresented in higher education, and their preeminence has tended to persist. Thus, traditionally dominant minorities were able to maintain their status, even with the emergent social structure of modern India, in direct contrast to the situation in much of sub-Saharan Africa where the earliest beneficiaries of Western education were often indiviuals of low or marginal status.

Whether the situation in India was the result of systematic British policy is moot, but in other areas, colonial regimes explicitly based their educational strategies on the presumed social, economic, and cultural "needs" of different ethnic and linguistic groups. Malaysia is a classic example of the results of this type of policy. Although the British were concerned with extending a high-quality education (in English) to a tiny minority among the Malay ruling aristocracy, they were content to provide only a truncated rudimentary schooling (in Malay) to the rural mass— that is, education was to be adapted to the needs of the peasantry. Concurrently, the growing Chinese population was not only able to achieve commercial domination but also, largely through its own exertions, to take disproportionate advantage of educational opportunities at secondary and higher levels. The substantial imparities that resulted were politically containable in the colonial period, but group conflict inevitably erupted in the early years of independence. What appeared to be an enlightened colonial educational policy proved to be politically disastrous in the context of postindependence realities.[3]

Growth and Expansion in the Postcolonial Period

I have devoted particular attention to the forms of status-group conflict that emerged in the colonial years since I believe that the early educational policies of most of the new states were dominated by political issues. To be sure, national education plans usually included ritualistic paragraphs stressing the role of education as an instrument of economic development. However, educational policymakers in newly independent states had no more idea of the educational strategies needed to achieve this kind of objective than their counterparts in the developed world. Indeed, in the 1950s and early 1960s, no body of research or analysis existed that could provide adequate policy guidelines for educational planning designed to maximize economic growth. In practice, most postcolonial elites were content to assume that more education, of whatever level or type, was somehow conducive to economic progress, and not until the late 1960s and the 1970s was this early optimism replaced by a degree of skepticism about the whole role of formal education as a major instrument of economic transformation.

This skepticism did not matter much since in the early days the primary issues were political, not economic. Equality of opportunity in access to education and fair shares for all were the questions that exercised the masses to the point at which existing inequalities in educational provision became a basis for separatist movements that erupted in some states. Ironically, nearly all of the educational-planning literature during this early period is silent concerning the political parameters within which planning was to take place. Planning seemed to be seen largely as an exercise in technical expertise that involved the setting up of educational targets (the rationale for which was seldom clear since the objectives of policy were rarely explicit). However, these demographic exercises bore little relation to what was, in fact, happening in the political context, and few educational planners seemed to be aware of the small corpus of social-science literature that addressed these matters.

Thus, postcolonial elites were obliged willy nilly to respond to mass popular demand for education. Whether such policies had any economic rationale or not was irrelevant. The preeminence of the political obliged regimes to expand the supply of schooling and to attempt to reduce the most obvious educational inequalities based on regional, and ethnic, differences. In so doing, they exposed the relative futility of all forms of macroeducational planning based on demographic projections and the erection of regional or national targets. There is hardly an educational plan for this period whose targets and projections were not massively exceeded at the primary, secondary, and tertiary educational levels, and these early documents now constitute little more than quaint reminders of how misguided early planning strategies were. No educational plans could have been successful unless they had taken account of the political and economic causes of the educational explosion and included these as elements within planning strategies.

In any event, the period 1950–1970 witnessed a remarkable growth in formal-education provision in postcolonial states.[4] At the primary level, enrollments underwent a fourfold expansion in sub-Saharan Africa (excluding the Republic of South Africa), while in South and Southeast Asia they increased by a factor of three. To be sure, the rate of primary-school expansion has now peaked in the latter two areas, dropping from a quinquennial rate of growth of almost 40 percent in the period 1955 to 1960 to less than 20 percent in 1970–1975. However, the pace of expansion has not markedly diminished in sub-Saharan Africa, falling from 36 percent in 1955–1960 to only 33 percent in 1970–1975.

Increases at the postprimary level have been even more dramatic. In the secondary sector, the period 1950–1970 saw a thirteenfold increase in enrollments in sub-Saharan Africa and a ninefold expansion in South and Southeast Asia, with an overall quinquennial growth rate averaging 80 percent in the three regions. Once again, over the period 1970–1975, the rate of expansion dropped to about 35 percent in two Asian regions but still remained as high as 90 percent in sub-Saharan Africa.

Tertiary education witnessed the highest rate of increase in the early postcolonial period. Even if we allow for the small base in initial enrollments, the magnitude of the increase in the provision of university places was fiftyfold in sub-Saharan Africa, tenfold in South Asia, and sixfold in Southeast Asia during 1950–1970, with a gross quinquennial rate of increase approaching 100 percent. Even in the period 1970–1975 when the rate of expansion had dropped to about 20 percent in the Asian region, it still remained as high as 65 percent in the black African nations.

One could, of course, produce a plethora of materials documenting this educational explosion in greater detail. In themselves, they do no more than testify to the immense pressure that was placed upon new ruling elites to enhance educational provision. The increase was essentially demand driven, and retrospectively, one can only conclude that governments had very little option but to respond. To have done otherwise would have, in most cases, undermined their legitimacy, which was largely based on populistic rhetoric. Thus, educational development had a certain symbolic value in that it demonstrated to the citizenry that governments were making tangible efforts to fulfill the promises made during the preindependence period. However, now that growth has, for the most part, peaked, governments are in some position to assess the short- and medium-term consequences of their policies.

Some Unanticipated Consequences of Educational Development

Let us first take a look at the equality-of-educational-opportunity issue. Quite obviously, much contemporary discussion in the developed world concerning the meaning of the term is largely irrelevant to poorer nations.[5] In the less-developed world, the issue hinges largely on questions of gross access and continuance in schooling, and in this regard, postcolonial policies have not effected the massive transformations that were anticipated. To be sure, aggregate opportunities for entry into formal education have everywhere been enhanced and this has been no mean achievement. At the same time, this does not mean that relative disparities in access to schooling as between regions or social and ethnic groups have necessarily diminished. In other words, minorities that were able to establish early educational advantages in the colonial period are usually able to maintain them in the postcolonial years.

In geographical terms, the absolute gap between the most and least developed regions tends to increase rather than diminish in intermediate periods of growth. This has been particularly true where more-decentralized patterns of educational policymaking have been pursued, but even in ostensibly more-centralized systems, internal geographical disparities remain substantial. This is not to suggest that inequalities are always undesirable in themselves but rather that educational systems have not been able to fulfill the ostensible political objectives of postcolonial regimes.

Similarly, the use of explicit or implicit quota systems to rectify social or ethnic imbalances in access to education are rarely effective in the short term. Such strategies have a long history and more recently have been employed in India in the context of the Scheduled Caste controversy and in Malaysia in an attempt to reduce the more-obvious disparities in access to secondary and higher education as between Chinese and Malay. However, such policies (as elsewhere) are at best stopgap measures whose effects have been relatively limited. For example, in India, ethnic quotas assigned to the lower-caste groupings often remain unfilled, while in Malaysia the Chinese still dominate the most intellectually demanding segments of the educational systems.[6] In effect, the bases of social inequality in the new nations are not very rapidly affected by short-term strategies that focus on altering the life chances of minorities through the use of quotas.

It would be unnecessary to attempt to summarize once again the already massive body of findings from the postcolonial states that has demonstrated the substantial relationship that exists between level of academic achievement and the familial background of students as measured by variables such as level of paternal income, education, and occupation. Controversy over the significance of these findings dates back to the middle 1960s, but it would be difficult to conceive of any educational system in which a degree of status inheritance did not occur. In this sense, a great deal of contemporary theorizing about modes of social reproduction and the inheritance of cultural capital constitutes little more than the use of a rather pretentious nomenclature to describe a process with which sociologists have long been familiar. The real issue is, of course, given the present situation, whether the educational systems of the postcolonial states can be regarded as being closed and impermeable to the aspirations of the less privileged. I do not believe that the evidence suggests this is the case; under present conditions, gross inequalities do, indeed, exist but this is not to suggest that the schools have not functioned fairly effectively as instruments of social mobility in the postcolonial period. The fact that aggregate rates of mobility are low in many of the new states has less to do with the schools than with the low rate of structural change in economies that are developing but slowly, if at all. To this extent there is merit in the view that, if equality of opportunity is a national objective, then it is too much to expect the schools to achieve this goal without commensurate change taking place in the economies of the new states. At the most general level, this is a view that is often held by both radical and functionalist critics of development in these nations, though the solutions these groups would suggest are likely to be very different.

In short, then, it was not long before the new states discovered that massive rates of educational expansion, conjoined in some areas with specific strategies designed to assist underprivileged regions or groups, could not be expected to eradicate types of inequality that had their roots in the pattern of social change begun in the colonial period. In this they were in good company since even the developed nations with far more resources at their command have as yet found it difficult to transform the pattern of educational life chances of their various ethnic and class minorities. It would be an exaggeration to regard the problem as intractable, but it can be viewed as amenable to substantial solution over generations rather than decades.

However, quite apart from growing skepticism over the educational-opportunity issue, the new states found that growth in schooling had produced consequences that had not been anticipated. As we have seen, very little serious consideration was given to economic issues in the early postcolonial period, but politically inspired educational programs always have their economic corollaries and these could no longer be ignored. By the mid-1960s, in most new states, educational expenditures typically accounted for between 20 and 25 percent of the national budget and in some nations soaked up 5 percent or more of gross domestic product (GDP) (although why 5 percent should have been regarded by some agencies as a danger level was never clear and was, in itself, symptomatic of the mechanistic approach adopted by early educational planners). However, the sheer magnitude of expenditures was so great that for the first time hard questions began to be asked concerning the economic rationale for investment in schooling.

Further, these questions focused not only upon levels of aggregate expenditure on education but also upon the allocation of resources by sector and type of schooling. Could one, for example, justify prevailing levels of expenditure on tertiary education? Typically, enrollments at this level stood at 3 to 4 percent of total educational enrollments in most new states (less than 1 percent in sub-Saharan Africa) but usually accounted for between 17 and 20 percent of budgetary allocations for schooling. Similarly, the ratio of per capita public expenditures for secondary, as opposed to primary, schooling stood at approximately 3 to 1. Taken by themselves these figures meant little, but what is important about them is that the earlier generation of educational planners was not equipped to answer the questions they posed—that is, planners could generate data on costs, but they had given no real attention to the assessment of individual or social benefits.

Retrospectively, high rates of expansion at secondary and higher levels clearly were, in some instances, due to the egregious influence of expatriate advisors who argued that rates of economic development were, in large measure, dependent on the supply of high- and middle-level manpower.[7] Such views were fashionable in the developed world in the 1960s, and it was perhaps unavoidable that they would be exported. Though the pretensions of high-level-manpower planning have now largely been exploded, it is evident that its effect in some countries was to divert resources from lower to higher levels of education without any substantial justification for so doing.[8]

However, questions also began to be raised concerning the payoff to alternative forms of education within sectors. At the tertiary level, most new states had accorded higher priorities to expenditures on science, technology, and more vocationally oriented training programs. Paradoxically, while per capita expenditures in these areas remained high, as opposed to outlays on the humanities or social sciences, the proportion

of students in them typically fell. At the same time, at the secondary
level, the old controversy over vocational as opposed to general training
that had exercised an earlier generation of colonial administrators was
once more revived.

As far as primary education was concerned, the issue in most new
states tended to revolve around the whole question of what role formal
education could be expected to play in agricultural and rural development.
As we have noted, this issue was not salient in the early days of independence given the propensity of essentially urban-oriented elites to give
priority to industrial growth. This latter strategy had proved to be non-
viable in many new states by the mid-1960s, and attention was refocused
on problems of rural development. Ironically, the issue was raised in
substantially the same manner as it had been in the colonial years: were
rural primary schools to continue teaching primarily bookish subjects
(though what is particularly bookish about literacy or numeracy is difficult
to discern), or were they rather to focus upon curriculums specially designed for rural schools in which agriculture and rural science would play
a significant role? This once again demonstrated the propensity of educationists in the new states (as elsewhere) to perceive educational problems in curricular rather than economic or structural terms.

These controversies seemed very pertinent in view of the emerging
problems. In most states, sluggish rates of development meant that the
rate of expansion of full-time-job opportunities in the modern sector was
rarely commensurate with increased educational outputs. During the colonial period, a completed primary-school education was often sufficient
to obtain employment, but the effect of expansion was to rapidly raise
the minimal educational requirements for job access. Later, more highly
educated cohorts tended to displace the less-educated downward in the
occupational structure while it was believed that substantial levels of
unemployment existed among recent school leavers. The consequence
was that demand for education at higher levels continued to expand as
a result of competition for employment, leading to the supposed evils of
credentialism and the fashionably entitled diploma disease.[9]

In Africa, in particular, the problem of the unemployed primary-
school leavers received much attention due, in part, to the belief of ruling
elites that they constituted a potential source of political instability. It
was also believed that one of the primary effects of rural schooling was
to enhance the flow of migrants to the towns, thus contributing to higher
rates of urban unemployment and denuding the rural areas of educated
manpower.

Moreover, egalitarian sentiments were outraged by what seemed to
be a growing polarization of the occupational structures of the postcolonial
nations. The benefits of education, it was averred, has only accrued to

the few. On the one hand, a relatively small percentage of the labor force in the modern sector enjoyed superior conditions of employment, while on the other hand, the mass of the workers was absorbed into the informal, semisubsistence sector wherein the conditions of existence were marginal or even deteriorating—the so-called dual economy.

In view of these developments, some postcolonial regimes could hardly be blamed for experiencing a certain loss of nerve. Massive educational expansion appeared to be producing a series of undesirable side effects: Persistent inequalities in educational access remained while dysfunctionalities certainly seemed to exist between the educational system and the occupational structure. This apparently gloomy picture sometimes led to the view that direct controls should be placed on the rate of educational expansion—a strategy that would have been politically very difficult. Alternatively, a position favored by some educationists was that the problem was not quantitative but qualitative in nature. What was needed was not quantitative control but a change in the content of educational programs that would involve a resocialization of the school population to new political and economic realities.

It was not surprising, given this kind of climate, that some nations during the late 1960s and early 1970s had a brief flirtation (and it was hardly more than this) with the radical educational solutions exemplified by Cuba, Tanzania, and the People's Republic of China. How far policymakers were really influenced by these models is difficult to judge though their merits were frequently discussed at international conferences and debated in local universities. In any event, although Cuba's educational efforts have been quantitatively impressive, there is little evidence that they have made a substantial contribution to that country's overall development (in spite of the eulogies of expatriate enthusiasts).[10] Tanzania's policy of "Education for Self-Reliance," part of which is, ironically, derived from elements of earlier colonial educational policies, is manifestly experiencing difficulties, and in practice, its schools seem to look very much like schools in other postcolonial states. Finally, the devastating educational consequences of the Cultural Revolution are now so apparent that it would be only the boldest of educational planners who would perceive this as a viable policy option for the postcolonial nations.

Thus, the influence of radical models has been ephemeral, but there is no question that postcolonial states have now entered a period of uncertainty concerning their future educational strategies. With the exception of those laggard areas where rapid growth continues, the rate of educational expansion is tapering off. For better or worse, massive formal-education structures exist and it would be idle to assume that any radical transformation of these systems will occur. Indeed, this would be as unnecessary as it would be undesirable. Rather, what is needed is the development of a series of pragmatic strategies that can rectify some of their more-dysfunctional features.

New Directions in Educational Policy?

In earlier pages it was noted that in the 1950s and early 1960s, little research and theory could provide the basis for educational policies designed to maximize economic growth, but I would contend that since the late 1960s a sufficient volume of theoretical and empirical literature has emerged that can provide a sound basis for new and viable strategies.[11] Moreover, although political issues can never be disregarded in the realistic planning context, they have perhaps a little less salience than they had in the earlier period. This provides an opportunity to lay somewhat more emphasis on explicitly economic objectives.

Thus, since formal-education infrastructures are established, governments are now in a position to exercise some policy options that were initially not open to them. These options boil down to an attempt to relate educational development more directly to the operation of market forces and to remove the distortions of market signals that occurred as a result of earlier policies, combined with an effort to improve the internal efficiency of educational systems.

We proceed, on the assumption that the type of macroeducational planning (including high-level-manpower planning) that characterized the earlier stages of postcolonial educational growth is no longer appropriate in the present context. Such policies had currency as long as planners thought largely in terms of quantitative targets and outputs or where it was deemed necessary to localize the upper levels of the occupational structure as expatriate personnel departed. At that time, the issue of cost and efficiency was not paramount, but this is no longer the case.

The new strategies must, in my view, be micro rather than macro in nature and must be designed to enhance the role of individual decision making in the educational context. They are based on the application of human-capital theory in its broadest sense to matters of educational policy and rest upon what seem to be a series of more-cogent empirical findings concerning the functioning of education in postcolonial societies.

First, although the political response tended to dominate early educational policies in postcolonial states, it is evident that the demand for education was largely economic in origin. If private rates of return to schooling were high, then demand was bound to escalate. To suggest that the phenomenon was one of social demand is to imply that demand was inelastic and unrelated to either cost or future income considerations (in fact, in the later postcolonial period there is evidence that in some areas demand has already tapered off and that absolute enrollments had fallen as a probable result of diminishing private rates of return to individual investment).[12] Thus, although governments found it difficult to resist pressures for more schooling, it is also true that they compounded the problem whenever the provision of free education at all levels became an element of national educational policy since its effect was everywhere to enhance private rates of return.

The provision of free education at the primary level is now such an axiom in postcolonial states that there can be little expectation that such policies will be reversed. I have suggested elsewhere the desirability of more-decentralized systems that would give local agencies the right to levy fees.[13] However, Papua New Guinea has been the only newly independent country to experiment with decentralized strategies, and most postcolonial states seem committed to national policies in which the principle of free education at the primary level is unquestioned. However, since the evidence suggests that private and social rates of return are higher at the primary than at other levels, an economic argument can be advanced for the provision of free primary school along with the more-standard rationale based on the public need for a literate citizenry.[14] New states would, however, be most unwise if they conjoined the free with the compulsory. Legislation to make primary schooling compulsory cannot be enforced unless the overwhelming bulk of children is already in school. Moreover, the costs of enforcement would be enormous as would be any attempt to reduce dropout rates at the primary level. Postcolonial states would do well to avoid these two traditional red herrings.

It is apparent that in most states the primary level is the significant sector upon which major planning efforts must now concentrate. That sector impinges most directly on the lives of most citizens and their children, and it typically absorbs 50 percent of educational budgetary expenditures (probably too little). In suggesting this, however, we must clear our minds of a few misconceptions. In earlier pages, I have indicated that there is now a tendency to blame the primary schools for just about every pathological phenomenon evident in postcolonial societies—the flight from the land, urban migration, unemployment, and crime.[15] As we have seen, some observers believe that direct controls should be placed on the rate of school expansion. It could be concluded that, if things were really as bad as this, it would be better to abolish primary schools altogether.

These phenomena are real enough, but to assume that the schools cause them is erroneous. Doubtless, the propensity to migrate to urban areas is related to the level of formal education of individuals, but the educated typically constitute only a minority of urban migrants in postcolonial states.[16] Some existing evidence, moreover, shows that the taste of the educated for migration is diminishing in some nations while the gross rate of urban drift is also falling.[17] If a primary aim of policy is to check urban migration (and this is misguided in itself), then the answer must be to develop strategies that will improve the conditions of rural life vis-à-vis those in the towns. These policies may have education as a component, but this is secondary to a variety of other strategies that have nothing to do with schooling. However, it would be dangerous in the first place to assume that employment conditions have deteriorated in postcolonial states or that increased urban unemployment is associated with migration; there is evidence to suggest that this is not the case.[18]

In fact, a substantial proportion of the educated unemployed is not unemployed at all. To be sure, many have not been able to obtain full-time employment in the modern sector (though some do after an initial period of waiting), but most are either absorbed back onto the land or enter the informal sector of the exchange economy. With respect to the latter, it is simply not true that earnings are everywhere inferior to the highly paid formal sector although the mean is lower. There is a substantial overlap in earnings, with the mean level of income for the agricultural sector being less than that for the other two. In reality, the dual economy described earlier does not exist; there is simply a gradation from high-paying to low-paying jobs, with the bulk of workers concentrated at lower levels.[19]

Thus, a good deal of concern about the malfunctioning of educational systems is based upon erroneous assumptions. No one doubts the reality of poverty and underemployment in postcolonial states, but the schools per se have little to do with this. Would poverty and unemployment be diminished or disappear if the schools were abolished? This is arrant nonsense. We have noted, however, that an alternative view contends that current problems are not the result of schooling per se but a consequence of the dysfunctional curriculum in the schools. This raises once again the weary issue, dating from the colonial period, that the rural schools, in particular, should develop a curriculum based on local realities, which usually involve agriculture.[20] The effects of this, it is contended, would be to raise agricultural productivity, to reduce the drift from rural areas, and hence to diminish urban unemployment. Enough evidence now exists to suggest that this is a fallacious line of reasoning, and one would be reluctant to raise it were it not for the fact that variants of this prescription are still continually bruited in postcolonial states and that its most recent manifestation is in the community-schools program of Papua New Guinea. At this juncture, it can only be said that such policies have no economic viability and constitute a real threat to the aspirations of rural folk.

Strategies for rural development do not hinge essentially on schooling, but the evidence suggests that, insofar as formal primary education does make a contribution to rural development, it does so through the diffusion of literacy and numeracy. The principal task of the primary school in the developing countries (as in any country) is precisely to effect this. Given the realities of this level of schooling in poor nations, the most that can be hoped for is that young people acquire the basics of literacy and numeracy, a degree of general knowledge, and hopefully, some acquaintance with rudimentary science. The real problem with primary schools is that they attempt the task but that they currently do it poorly and inefficiently because in most postcolonial states a substantial proportion of youngsters leaves school without having achieved functional literacy. If they have not achieved this level, then it is difficult to discern what they have achieved (except perhaps a desire to ensure that their own future offspring will receive a better education, and this is in itself a desirable thing). It is sometimes suggested that a major consequence of primary schooling might be to engender attitudinal transformation. Children acquire, for example, modern attitudes that are more conducive to the acceptance of change and the requirements of development.[21] If this is the case, then so much the better, but until we know more about attitudinal effects of school experience (and we know little), this cannot become a realistic objective of policy. The principle objective at the primary-school level must be to discern which combination of inputs, commensurate with limited resources, is likely to achieve maximal cognitive gains for students, particularly in the areas of literacy and numeracy.

This rather stark statement opens up a whole agenda of research and planning that has direct policy implications. For example, do enhanced teacher inputs in terms of quantity and quality make much difference in the classroom? There is some evidence that teachers have more impact in less-developed than in developed countries, but this, in itself, does not necessarily suggest a concentration on the enhancement of teacher inputs. More significant gains at lower cost might be recorded through more large-scale production and diffusion of appropriate textbooks.[22] What is the cost-effectiveness and efficiency of audio-visual aids such as radio and television as supplements or alternatives to conventional classroom techniques? The evidence here is mixed although television is probably a poor bet in terms of the substantial programmatic infrastructure that is required—that is, local culture almost demands that content be specific, and development is therefore immensely costly.

One could continue in this vein from a consideration of projects designed to estimate the efficiency of small rural schools to others that would attempt to assess language-learning outcomes in multilingual societies where the political decision has been made to diffuse a national language. All these types of questions have one thing in common in that they are essentially micro-oriented and concerned with optimum allocation of limited resources. Obviously, these issues also preoccupy policymakers in developed nations, and in some cases, local planners may be obliged to depend on the exportation of policy-oriented findings from the developed world due to lack of local resources. However, this is sometimes a dangerous procedure, and a real need exists for the development of planning agencies that can either develop local research strategies or at least replicate studies effected elsewhere in local settings.

Thus, I suggest that the policy agenda in postcolonial states will begin to change; the tasks of sheer quantitative expansion are likely to occupy a less-major role in the future than attempts to effect a qualitative upgrading of primary schooling. The most sensible response to problems of quantitative growth might be to decentralize this type of decision to regional or district agencies, with central government's supplementing local resources where necessary while planning units concentrate their efforts on the type of policy-oriented research suggested in the previous paragraph.

A shift in policy and planning priorities would also seem desirable at the secondary and tertiary levels. Although the proportion of the relevant age cohort entering these sectors is still small in most nations (typically 8 percent and less than 2 percent respectively), unit costs remain high relative to primary education (by an average factor of 4 and 16) while social rates of return are usually lower. The problem is manifest at the tertiary level where real costs per university student stand at seven times those prevailing in the developed world relative to income per capita.[23] Undoubtedly, economies of scale can be effected through continuing expansion that is still proceeding apace. However, it is questionable whether the high priority accorded secondary and tertiary education by an earlier generation of manpower planners is justified. Moreover, the level of demand and rate of expansion at these levels is, in part, due to massive public subsidization of costs, the effect of which is to make a secondary and tertiary education profitable for the individual but less obviously so for society. Given an increasing body of data concerning the more socially selective composition of student bodies in the tertiary sector, there must be a presumption (supported in the relatively few empirical studies available) that the more-affluent rather than poorer segments of local populations benefit disproportionately from current modes of financing secondary and tertiary training.

A consideration of principles of equity and efficiency would suggest that both would be served by a greater devolution of costs from the public to the private sector because, even where economies of scale do occur, the aggregate burden on the public treasuries of poorer states will be substantial if rapid expansion continues. Clearly, planners will need to consider a series of options such as loans, graduate-education taxes, graduated fee scales based upon family income, and so forth. Even if the public burden is only marginally reduced, some contribution will have been made to the principle that those who benefit should make proportionate contribution to cost.

Unfortunately, one must recognize the immense institutional and political difficulties that stand in the way of such policies. Some predicate the existence of a relatively efficient tax system, which is rarely the case, while others, based on differential fees or student loans, may face organized opposition from students who still constitute volatile political constituencies in these nations. Attempts to introduce loan systems, for example, were summarily defeated in Nigeria and Ghana by this essentially self-seeking minority.[24] Rationally conceived policies are always at the mercy of the political in postcolonial states, and political skills, along with technical expertise, are required of local planners.

One does not feel optimistic, therefore, about the chances for policy changes of this nature in these nations. However, there is a greater opportunity of effecting reform in another context. As we have noted, early planning at secondary and higher levels tended to emphasize the importance of vocational subjects with a particular emphasis on science, technology, and agriculture, while at the same time, students showed some reluctance to enter these fields. What seemed to be an irrational preference for economics, the other social sciences, and the humanities on their part now seems to have sound empirical support. Recent research suggests that in developing countries costs are substantially lower in the latter fields while relative earnings are normally higher (with the exception of marginally greater earnings in medicine and engineering). Moreover, the social returns to training in the humanities and economics are frequently higher than for engineering and agriculture. Agriculture, in particular, is a very poor last.[25]

This would imply that most nations would do well to emphasize more-general education at secondary and tertiary levels and to be cautious in attempting to expand relatively high-cost vocational areas of study. Even where a need is manifest, as in the case of doctors, many countries should consider whether their interests are best served by the production of relatively few, highly trained, but high-cost, technicians or whether they should concentrate on an enhanced output of middle-level practitioners (a policy that served the Soviet Union well in its earlier period of development). We have used medicine as an example, but policy-makers must discern those areas of specific training that have a high payoff while they recognize that the formal secondary and tertiary system must largely concentrate upon training in the humanities, sciences, and social sciences.

This leads to a few observations on the whole relationship between general and vocational training and the linkage between the formal- and informal-education sectors in postcolonial states. During the 1960s, most educational planners seemed to be unaware that substantial and highly efficient informal-training networks already operated in most countries in complementary relationship to the formal-education systems.[26] Even if they were aware of this sector's existence, it did not seem to influence their strategies that tended to emphasize the vocational tasks of formal training. Although some authors early recognized the significance of the informal sector, its importance was not perceived until the 1970s when a new spate of literature on the topic emerged. Unfortunately, it has become (as I initially feared) the fashion of the 1970s in the same way that manpower planning was the vogue of the 1960s.[27] Further, much of this mainly descriptive literature has little implication for policy since it is extraordinarily difficult to evaluate any informal-educational system in a meaningful way.

Perhaps it is better that such evaluations are not undertaken. The informal sector emerges as a response to real market needs, and in these terms, it is efficient. Moreover, costs are either born by users or employers. It is questionable whether the state should involve itself in attempts to regulate, control, or even replicate activities in this sector when its priorities must lie in a different direction—namely, the provision of largely general training at all levels. Attempts to formalize the informal sector would be in direct contradiction of the forces that led to its development in the first place. Thus, although a useful symbiotic relationship usually develops between the formal- and informal-educational systems, attempts to define this more formally reflects in itself the statism of many educational planners.

Concluding Observation

This overview of the educational policies of postcolonial states has examined both their colonial roots and their changing emphases over time. Additionally, I have made some unashamedly prescriptive statements concerning the course that future policies might take. These statements do not suggest any massive restructuring of educational systems (it is too late for that) but rather involve a series of pragmatic strategies designed to enhance the efficiency of those systems and to relate them more directly to the marketplace. What has been difficult for many postcolonial regimes to recognize is that formal education is not a developmental panacea. Many of problems of developing nations do not find their origin in the educational system, and, for example, one frequently finds planners proclaiming educational solutions to dysfunctions that result from distortions in the market economy. When such solutions are unsuccessful, there is a tendency to indict the educational system, and in just over a decade, we have moved from a phase in which education can do no wrong to one in which it can do no right. This latter stance has led to some rather bizarre proposals for educational and societal transformation.

Such efforts are as unnecessary as they would be destructive because the educational achievements of most postcolonial states are real enough. A broad basis of literacy (perhaps one of the most critical contributing factors to development) has been created. Athough inequalities in access to schooling still exist, and will for generations, some of the most politically explosive imparities have been diminished while educational policymakers are gaining a clearer understanding of the relationships between schooling and the economic and stratification systems in which they are imbedded. Given their limited resources, the educational development of these states has been substantial, and at present, it is equally appropriate to recognize their accomplishments while drawing attention to the limitations of current policies.

Notes

1. Remi Clignet and Philip Foster, "Convergence and Divergence in Educational Development in Ghana and the Ivory Coast," in *Ghana and the Ivory Coast; Perspectives on Modernization,* ed. Philip Foster and Aristide Zolberg (Chicago: University of Chicago Press, 1971), pp. 265–291.

2. See Lloyd Rudolph and Susanne Rudolph, eds., *Education and Politics in India* (Cambridge: Harvard University Press, 1972), pp. 51–67.

3. For the best overview, see Bee-Lan Chan Wang, "Educational Reforms for National Integration: The West Malaysian Experience," *Comparative Education Review* 22 (October 1978): 464–479.

4. Computed from UNESCO, *Statistical Yearbook* (Paris, UNESCO 1963–1978/1979).

5. For the most succinct exposition of the various meanings that can be attached to the term, see Mary Jean Bowman, "Education and

Opportunity: Some Economic Perspectives," *Oxford Review of Education* 1 (1975):73–84.

6. Bee-Lan Chan Wang, "Government Intervention in Ethnic Stratification: Effects on the Distribution of Students among Fields of Study," *Comparative Education Review* 21 (February 1977):110–123.

7. The classic example is *Investment in Education,* Report of the Commission on Post School Certificate Higher Education in Nigeria (the Ashby Report) (Lagos: Federal Ministry of Education, 1960).

8. See B. Ahamad and M. Blaug, eds., *The Practice of Manpower Forecasting* (San Francisco: Jossey-Bass, 1973).

9. Ronald P. Dore, *The Diploma Disease* (London: Allen and Unwin, 1976).

10. For example, Martin Carnoy and J. Werthen, "Socialist Ideology and the Transformation of Cuban Education," in *Power and Ideology in Education,* ed. F. Karabel and A.H. Halsey (New York: Oxford University Press, 1977), pp. 573–587.

11. Basically, this literature stems from the contributions of the human-capital school, but in the context of the developing countries, the really seminal work was M. Blaug, R. Layard, and M. Woodhall, *The Causes of Graduate Unemployment in India* (New York: Penguin Press, 1969).

12. See, for example, K. Hinchcliffe, "The Unprofitability of Secondary Modern Schooling in the Western Region of Nigeria," *West African Journal of Education* (Ibadan) 14 (1970):180–182; and "A Comparative Analysis of Educational Development in Ghana and the Western Region of Nigeria," *Nigerian Journal of Social and Economic Studies* 12 (1970):103–113.

13. See Philip Foster, "Dilemmas of Educational Development: What We Might Learn from the Past," in *Education in Melanesia,* ed. J. Brammall (Canberra: Australian National University, 1976), pp. 15–38.

14. For a most comprehensive review of the rate-of-return literature, see G. Psacharopoulos, *Returns to Education* (San Francisco: Jossey-Bass, 1973).

15. See, for example, John Simmons, *The Education Dilemma: Policy Issues for Developing Countries in the 1980s* (New York: Pergamon Press, 1979), p. 14.

16. See R.H. Sabot, "Education, Income Distribution and Rates of Urbanization in Tanzania," mimeographed (Economic Research Bureau Paper 7216, University of Dar es Salaam, 1972).

17. Ibid.

18. See, for example, Peter Gregory, "An Assessment of Changes in Employment Conditions in Less Developed Countries," *Economic*

Development and Cultural Change 28 (July 1980): 673–700; and Amos Harley, Dorothy Fernandez, and Harbans Singh, "Migration and Employment in Peninsular Malaysia, 1970," *Economic Development and Cultural Change* 27 (April 1979):491–504.

19. See Gregory, "Assessment of Changes in Employment Conditions."

20. For what, it is to be hoped, will be a final and definitive discussion, at least in the African context, see John W. Hanson, "Is the School the Enemy of the Farm?" African Rural Economy Paper No. 22 (East Lansing: Michigan State University, Department of Agricultural Economics, 1980).

21. Donald B. Holsinger, "The Elementary School as Modernizer," *International Journal of Comparative Sociology* 14 (1974):180–202.

22. See L. Alexander and J. Simmons, "The Determinants of School Achievement in Developing Countries: The Educational Production Function," Working Paper No. 201 (Washington, D.C.: World Bank, March 1975); Stephen P. Heyneman, "Textbooks and Achievement: What We Know," Working Paper No. 298 (Washington, D.C.: World Bank, October 1978); and Thorsten Husen, L.J. Saha, and R. Noonan, "Teacher Training and Student Achievement in Less-Developed Countries," Working Paper No. 310 (Washington, D.C.: World Bank, December 1978).

23. G. Psacharopoulos, "The Economics of Higher Education in Developing Countries," Working Paper No. 439 (Washington, D.C.: World Bank, 1980).

24. For Ghana, see Peter Williams, "Lending for Learning: An Experiment in Ghana," *Minerva* 12 (July 1974):326–345.

25. Psacharopoulos, "Economics of Higher Education."

26. Perhaps a chapter of my own was among the first to draw attention to the importance of the informal sector. See Philip Foster, "The Vocational School Fallacy in Educational Planning," in *Education and Economic Development*, ed. Mary Jean Bowman and C. Arnold Anderson (Chicago: Aldine Publishing Company, 1965), p. 142. See Philip Foster and James R. Sheffield, eds., *Education and Rural Development* (London: Evans Bros., 1974), pp. 1–2.

27. See Foster and Sheffield, *Education and Rural Development*, p. 2.

2

The Political Context of Education in the Developing World

Marie Thourson Jones

It is puzzling that countries with apparently similar problems, similar school systems, similar resources, and even similar goals have very different experiences with educational policy. To give just one example, leaders of Morocco, Algeria, and Tunisia made similar commitments to encourage the study of science, mathematics, and technology in the mid-1960s. Fifteen years later, Algeria and Tunisia had moved much closer to their goals than Morocco. Factors that might be invoked to explain the Moroccan case by itself—a shortage of science teachers, the legacy of French education, and competing needs within the educational sector—were also present in Algeria and Tunisia. Why, then, should results be so different in Morocco?

The answer to this and to similar puzzles lies in analyzing policy-making processes—understood here as both the capacity and willingness to act. Through such processes, material shortages are transformed into real constraints and resources into real support, in part due to the ways their distribution is influenced political power, authority, and competition. More specifically, in the North African case described, competition among ministers, the nature of political opposition, and informal political style each affected choices made in educational policy.

Rather than elaborate one particular comparison, the purpose of this chapter is to analyze in general terms how politics is thought to affect educational policy. Case studies typically find greater political influence than multination surveys. In large part these differences originate in their respective methodologies, particularly in variables used and the way process is observed. The chapter argues that a more accurate assessment of influence requires bridging these methodologies with variables derived from a close examination of the processes they are supposed to represent. Thus, the second goal of this chapter is to discuss ways to analyze political factors, their weight, and their action. As a step in that direction, in-depth comparisons of a limited number of cases show potential for yielding more appropriate variables.

I would like to thank Arnold Anderson, Charles Bidwell, and John Craig for their helpful comments on this chapter.

Politics

Politics, political domain, and *political system* all refer to relationships
and processes whereby binding choices for the collectivity are made.
Gurr defines a political system as "a more or less institutionalized pattern
of authority relations between elected and appointed officials, on the one
hand, and citizens, on the other . . . [involving] the definition of [the
state's] goals, the regulation of its members' conduct, the allocation and
coordination of roles, and the allocation of valued goods and services
among its members."[1] Working from this definition and from the more
familiar definitions of Easton ("the authoritative allocation of values"[2])
and Lasswell ("who gets what, when, and how"[3]), to study politics is
to study how the distribution of power affects outcomes. For education,
as for any policy, the political context is important insofar as relationships
of power and authority condition which problems reach the public agenda,
how solutions are sought and chosen, and how legitimacy and other
resources are used to enforce decisions.

If the theoretical specification of political effects is relatively clear,
actual evidence is more ambiguous. In contrast to widespread agreement
on the salience of social and economic factors for policy, there is less
consensus on the significance of politics. Those who have worked on
educational reform often see political factors such as radical changes in
leadership or pressure from one ethnic group as central to explaining
educational change or its absence.[4] Some scholars have focused on political goals attached to schooling and on the manipulation of schools by
politicians in both colonial and postcolonial societies. Abernethy and
Coombe contend that "the political significance of education [implica-
tions of politics for education and vice versa] in contemporary societies
increases with the degree of change a society is undergoing."[5] Critics
of inequalities of access, resources, and outcomes in education often
blame these inequalities on economic or ethnic elites that dominate the
political apparatus.[6]

However, scholars who have analyzed statistics from a large number
of political units have had mixed results. Using enrollments or expenditures as measures of policy, they have found few statistically significant
relationships for their political variables. In most cases the statistical
contribution of political variables is smaller than that of socioeconomic
factors. In some cases, controlling for the latter dramatically decreases
the explanatory power of the former.[7] Although such studies do not
dispute that political processes exist, they suggest that, in the long run,
characteristics of the political system do not determine, or even have
much effect on, social policies. Rather, political institutions seeem to
convert socioeconomic resources and demands into policy without leaving

much distinctive imprint. Similar polities enact different policies; different polities generate similar ones.

These contrasting conclusions reflect, in part, differences in what constitutes explanation. In case studies of individual policies, one looks for an exercise of power that makes something happen that would not have happened otherwise. Multination surveys, however, demand a regular coincidence of political forms and policy. Because of such differences in perspective, analysts tend not to employ the same independent and dependent variables. Thus, to evaluate the effects of political factors, two questions are addressed in the following pages. First, what phenomena need to be explained? Second, how closely must actual processes be observed in order to account for their results?

Policies and Outcomes

Which outcomes are likely to bear the imprint of political factors? Policy studies concentrate on several connected but distinct categories of action, all labeled policy: statements of intent by officials; decisions published as laws and decrees; actual measures taken (budgets, construction of schools); and outcomes (enrollments, occupational attainment). These four categories are not ranked in order of absolute political impact; rather, different sorts of political exchanges take place at each level. This means that findings ought to differ according to the type of policy studied. For example, these four categories are ranked by their nearness to centralized authority and therefore vary in their dependence on compliance, cooperation, or congruent actions by autonomous private actors. Individual choices not fully controllable by political authorities should dilute the significance of regime characteristics for policy outcomes, the fourth category.

Indeed, one type of outcome—enrollment rates—has not shown strong relation to structural traits of national political systems.[8] This should not be surprising since expansion of schooling depends heavily on private demand to fill classrooms and, in some cases, to build them. Thus, one would expect socioeconomic variations across and within nations to have stronger effects than political features such as size of cabinet, one of the measures used by Meyer et al.[9] Moreover, the effects of political and socioeconomic development on enrollments have been diluted by internationalization of economic trends and of perceptions or misperceptions of education.[10]

Public expenditures as a measure of policy are less directly dependent on private decisions, though certainly constrained by national wealth. Verner found that variations in per capita expenditures correlated highly with gross national product (GNP) per capita ($r = .96$).[11] However, this particular variable raises another problem in measuring political effects—namely, that per capita figures do not capture real political issues as well as measures that express how much is spent relative to available funds and competing uses. Few would contend that an African country should spend as much per pupil as the United States or that failure to do so represents a political decision. On two measures that come closer to actual choices—expenditures as a percentage of GNP and of budget—political factors are not overshadowed by socioeconomic factors.[12]

Total expenditures may not be a reliable indicator of differences among regimes. Variations in budgets among nations do not bear any necessary or consistent relation to the substance of policy, except, perhaps, to policy on enrollments. In a ninety-nation survey, Clark broke down budget figures to relate them to specific policies. She compared one policy that affects the entire population (per capita expenditures on education) with another more likely to favor the elite (percentage of budget devoted to higher education). Her political variables correlated more highly with the latter distributional policy, outweighing the socioeconomic variables in that case.[13] Even so, correlations were not strong.

It is significant that studies of one, or a small number, of cases tend to select other, more-substantive problems for analysis than large surveys. They are more likely to look for political effects where political choices exist—for example, mechanisms to link schools to the economy, language of instruction, regional and ethnic distribution of classrooms, means for regulating access to higher education, and autonomy of schools. After all, researchers who choose this approach seek out controversy and debate, not routine and consensus. By focusing on such issues and by using a different methodology, they are more likely to find political explanations but perhaps also to overrepresent them. In contrast, multination surveys are likely to underrepresent political factors by studying routine, widely reported events or by choosing variables that represent outcomes. The problem is that neither today's hot issues nor routine decisions alone represent educational policy.

Other differences between the two approaches affect the likelihood of their discovering political causes. Case studies are often structured to compare results with stated goals, but they are less adequate for appraising what results might reasonably have been expected. Multinational surveys do hold up external standards of performance, at least implicitly, but in testing for regularities between political systems and educational programs, such surveys may fuse issues, goals, and capacity into one variable. The deviation of any one of these factors will weaken apparent correlations between politics and policy. It would be instructive to separate out educational problems from issues, issues from goals, and goals from capacity. One way to do this is to compare nations that had similar educational systems, problems, and resources twenty-five years ago but whose policies have diverged since then. such controlled comparisons provide a yardstick for contrasting different dimensions of policy and, as is argued later, for evaluating their causes. The North African example that introduced this chapter and Court's work on Kenya and Tanzania illustrate this approach.[14] Alternatively, the same country can be observed under different regimes, as in Fischer's study of Chile.[15]

To assess the effect of recent political factors on education, it is also necessary to control for the historical underpinnings of current practice. Previous policies create financial commitments (teachers' salaries), expectations (continued expansion), and organizations that may be difficult or costly to alter. In many cases, change is a more-valid indicator of policy than a single-time measurement. It seems quite obvious, for example, that French- or British-style school organization inherited from the colonial period still influences the structure of educational systems in many developing countries. The effect of postindependence politics would be evident only in departures from, or adherence to, the earlier model. Yet in trying to explain variations in the centralization (political incorporation) of education, Ramirez and Rubinson looked at the way schools were organized in 1965 without controlling for colonial legacies.[16] In effect, they tested whether the organization of school systems was the consequence of only contemporary levels of state dominance, centralization, and socioeconomic development.

It is not clear how much change is possible even under the most favorable political circumstances. In revolutionary societies, political factors that in other settings act as powerful brakes on reform are eliminated or attenuated. Instead, a new political elite, espousing a new ideology, takes over. The will to reform is strong, decision-making hierarchies change, and the capacity of the bureaucracy to resist innovation should be reduced. Revolutionary regimes tend to pursue two goals simultaneously—namely, equality of access to education and integration of young people into the economy. They may make impressive progress toward one or both objectives. However, experiences of the Soviet Union (1920s), China, Chile, and Tanzania suggest that, despite the reduction of political obstacles to reform, other factors still hamper successful change.[17] Revolution does not eliminate competition between education and other sectors for scarce resources. At the outset, educational issues may be neglected as leaders devote their attention to consolidating power or overhauling the economy. Schools do not necessarily enjoy higher priority than factories, especially in recruiting the workers, technicians, and engineers needed to teach children skills and attitudes appropriate to the work place. At upper reaches of the government this competition may take the form of personal clashes between egalitarians and economists. Revolution does not ensure harmony within the education sector. Over and above the obvious point that no one may know how to accomplish the new goals quickly, equality and training of cadres may dictate contrary allocations of talent and other resources. This clash is particularly evident over criteria for promoting students or use of students' limited time. Moreover, new elites are not immune to the desire to ensure that their own offspring have every advantage in competition for academic advancement. Also, despite changes in the political elite and upper ranks of the bureaucracy, there is a continuing need to enlist cooperation from individuals throughout society—teachers, students, parents, educational specialists, and others—who may not understand or accept the reforms. In other words, the degree of change possible is undoubtedly limited, probably in predictable ways. To discover such regularities, however, requires looking more closely at processes in order to disentangle different sorts of political variables and to chart more accurately their interpenetration with socioeconomic factors.

Models of Process: The Proximate Causes of Policy

Most definitions of politics make decisions the locus of inquiry and, by extension, ask how issues come to be placed on the agenda; goals set; solutions proposed, adopted, and implemented; and results evaluated. Politics is that type of process through which the distribution of power resources shapes a variety of outcomes. Policies and programs may also be arrived at through rational analysis or be designed to satisfy organizational needs. Undoubtedly the history of any policy will show a mixture of these transactions. In order to clarify the characteristics of these different processes the following sections review rational, bureaucratic, and political models of policymaking. Readers will recognize the influence of Allison in this formulation, but the distinctions made here do not follow his classification exactly.[18]

Rational Models

However one pictures an ideal policymaking process, there is widespread agreement that reality does not correspond. However, analysts disagree over whether such deviations are merely mistakes that can be eliminated with better information and organization or whether they are inherent in the fabric of policymaking. Rational models have no perfect counterparts in reality. Their function is to describe and improve the technical side of decision making. These models assume clear goals (preferably put in order of priority), a unified actor, and good (if not perfect) information. Implementation requires clearly formulated and transmitted instructions from policymakers to subordinates and field agents. Departures from this ideal are considered errors correctable by better information, more elaborate statistical models, and clearer lines of communication and authority. In reality, the mistakes that such improvements can solve are limited to cases in which goals themselves are not at issue. Though useful as an analytical fiction, the rational model has, unfortunately, also become a prescriptive ideology of planners.[19] For balance, it is important to consider why other factors inevitably have and even should have an impact on policy.

Bureaucratic Models

Analysts using bureaucratic or political perspectives take conflicting goals as a starting point and argue that management of, or competition over, allocation of scarce resources divorces policymaking from any rational model. In this sense, rationality describes the calculations of individual participants without being able to account for larger processes involving many actors with diverse preferences. The bureaucratic perspective is more limited than the political by its applicability to policies planned, chosen, of implemented through large hierarchical organizations. Still, since education is most often organized into systems transcending the individual school, this model helps to account for some educational policy.

Everyone has a favorite lament about excessive bureaucracy, the common theme being that bureaucracies hamper achievement of goals and may even produce effects contrary to objectives. On coming to office, Salvador Allende complained that twenty-seven different actions were necessary to place a new teacher in Chile.[20] Because of delays in approving purchase orders, the Ethiopian Ministry of Education ended up returning money to the Ministry of Finance, thereby compromising its ability to ask for larger budgets later.[21] In many countries, the rigidity of civil-service pay scales precludes incentives designed to lure experienced teachers to rural areas or to attract science graduates to teaching.[22] Proximate causes of such conditions may seem contradictory from case to case: for example, maintenance of fairness through a uniform personnel code, corruption (more rules generate more bribes), anticorruption (crosschecks to prevent embezzlement), shortages of qualified staff (everything has to be checked by top people), and excess of qualified staff (give them something to do). Each such explanation suggests that conditions related to running the organization rather than to educational objectives account for standard routines and regulations.

Scarce resources and complicated tasks seem particularly important in accounting for behavior in bureaucracies. Shortages of money, competent people, time, and information in the face of almost limitless possible uses give rise to routines and shortcuts aimed at economizing resources available to the organization. These simplifications can be seen in the way that information is collected and solutions explored. The satisficing model, for example, predicts that individuals will choose the first acceptable solution rather than the best and that the search for a solution begins with those alternatives closest to current practices.[23] As a result, changes are most likely to be incremental. In implementing policy, it is often necessary to act through many levels of organization, if not through several autonomous organizations. This imperative generates simplified, sometimes rigid, procedures in attempts to elicit uniform behavior and thus to avoid mistakes caused by misunderstanding or by too much discretion at lower levels. Mistakes due to poor adaptation of programs to individual circumstances are often the price.[24]

For individual participants, power and position also bear on their quotidian dealings. Bureaucratic roles and hierarchy determine how employees are judged and influence how they can deal effectively with peers, clients, superiors, subordinates, and assorted outsiders. A frequent practice is to act in ways that protect, perpetuate, and enlarge their unit, its routines, and autonomy. Hence politicians, administrators, and even technical specialists evaluate activities not only in terms of their effect on the problem being treated but also by their effect on the organization. Agents may resist, subvert, or remold policies in order to reduce their disruptiveness to established routines and divisions of power.

Of course, the strength of the unit may be viewed by participants as a prerequisite for solution of subtantive problems; whether it is is another matter entirely. Benveniste found that in the Mexican Ministry of Education superiors maintained their own power by limiting the autonomy of subordinates. This behavior enhanced their own roles as mediators and conciliators but discouraged subordinates from communicating across agency boundaries or building coalitions that might facilitate implementation. In 1965, the advent of overall planning in education increased the potential benefits of exchanging information and provided some people—those with larger political ambitions and those who believed in planning—with an issue around which to build coalitions. The possiblity of recognition balanced the risk that specific initiatives would be rejected by the minister of education.[25]

Control of information, in this example and others, is a key to protecting one's own position and organization. It is important—even instinctive—to try to limit what outsiders and superiors know about one's performance. The potential usefulness of information, defined of course, by what one perceives as necessary, is balanced off by the various costs of getting it—especially if the cooperation of other units is needed—and risks of its dissemination. Officials frequently end up relying on very gross statistics such as expenditures, enrollments, or passage rates as proxies for the goals of education, inaccurate as those proxies may be. In a recent study of the Mexican educational bureaucracy, for example, McGinn found that planners simply assumed that teachers were actually qualified, present, and following assigned lesson plans.[26] Perceptions of the hazards of information are not groundless. In Tunisia in the 1960s, criticisms of educational reforms were given solid ground when the Ministry of Planning began collecting and publishing statistics on failure rates and school leavers as alternative means of evaluating the performance of the educational system.[27]

Political Models

Another sort of resource shortage lies at the base of political models. The various actors—individuals, informal groups, organizations, and governmental agencies—have different objectives and perceptions of problems, solutions, likelihood of success, and reasonable trade-offs. Because there are never enough goods to satisfy preferences of all members of society, competition ensues to define issues and to gain priority for one's own ends in the allocation of available (marginal) resources. Rational decisions may be impossible given the absence of a standard by which to evaluate alternative goals and the indefiniteness of the goals themselves.[28] The result of this competition is more likely to be negotiated compromise than coherent policy. By paying attention to power, perceptions, and competition, this model accounts for change better than the bureaucratic approach with its emphasis on incremental movement and protection of organizational routine.

In models of political process, policies and outcomes are explained by acts of power meant to influence outcomes. The significance of power is based on two related propositions: (1) One's ability to influence policy depends on the allocation of power resources within the rules of a specific political system, and (2) who makes policy influences the kind of policy that emerges. Analysts differ in looking at decisions, nondecisions, or implementation, but they agree that formal decision-making structures should not be taken at face value. Research should elucidate who is included and excluded, what their perceptions and goals are, what political resources they possess, and how they act.

Many ordinary resources can be converted into political resources—for example, wealth and education as they are related to propensity to participate,[29] family ties, access to information, credentials, formal roles, and membership in large organizations. A person's use of resources is affected by general political structures and styles that shape both opportunities for participation and the legitimacy of citizens in the eyes of officials.

How is power exercised? A dominant school of analysis focuses on the level of general policy, explaining decisions with reference to the active, visible process of reconciling interests through competition and negotiation. The notion of openly competing interests and pressures may be viewed as a negative or positive force in education. Abernethy and Coombe note that short-term pressures may be so great as to impel policymakers to neglect long-term goals.[30] Some of the large multination surveys treat competition (measured by pluralism of parties) as a stimulus for educational expansion and for other policies responsive to the wishes of the citizenry. However, to assess the extent and importance of competition requires going beyond measures of voting and number of parties. Political systems differ in the degree to which policymaking is open to public scrutiny and in treatment of public disagreement. Just because conflict is not expressed in the same way as, say, in the United States and Europe does not mean that it does not occur. It is important to distinguish between style and substance since party rivalry is not the only sort of competition relevant to policy.

Even in the multiparty system the likelihood of observing open discord may depend on the moment of observation. Peters suggests that the importance of competition varies over the life cycle of a policy. At the beginning, programs reflect little more than preferences of the elite. Much later, when the policy is fully established, changes occur in the form of routine increments and adjustments. Broad public competition seems to show its strongest relationship to increases in expenditures during the middle period when the government or other political groups are mobilizing demand and before the programs are fully institutionalized.[31]

It would be interesting to test Peter's hypothesis in developing countries where, one suspects, rapid growth in expenditures on education has occurred even in the absence of party pluralism. Indeed, this particular measure seems most appropriate for a legislative model of policymaking. Whatever the effect of mobilization of demand on total level of expenditures, substantive policy tends to emanate from bureaucracies and international-aid agencies. Many, if not most, educational reforms originate within an elite or within ministries of education. Programs are often developed in the absence of—at best, the anticipation of—demand from the population from whom programs are intended. Thus, it would be important to investigate other arenas and other forms of competition and power to explain development of policy.

Competition may also appear insignificant where certain problems are deliberately excluded from public decision and therefore from access to public resources. These nondecisions are problems that do not get on the public agenda even though they are grievances expressed by part of the population.[32] It is usually acknowledged by scholars that the relative power of groups affects which solutions to problems will be considered by officials. Students of nondecisions insist that the avenues by which problems themselves reach the agenda are not neutral. These, too, depend on the power and legitimacy of those with demands and on the will and ability of incumbents to exclude them.

Large numbers and broad categories of citizens may not even try to influence collective policies because they cannot, because they do not feel it realistic to try, or because they do not formulate their wishes in terms of a larger political setting. Some citizens may choose instead to adjust programs to their own needs at the point of implementation. In this sense, the archetypal political act in many countries may not be voting but visiting the headmaster to get a child reinstated in school. Acts of bureaucratic resistance described earlier may likewise involve exercises of power. That individuals try to alter policy in small ways helps to explain why even elites who prevail in policy planning will not prevail to the same degree in practice.

The autonomy of citizens and their capacity to make independent decisions can exert a significant passive effect on the realization of goals. Governments face the problem of figuring out what sorts of policies people will go along with automatically or else how to gain their compliance at low cost. This problem is complicated by considerable uncertainty about the reaction of the public to programs that originate with intellectuals, bureaucracies, or international-aid agencies, often in the absence of an expressed demand from potential clients. Even the most authoritarian government rarely has sufficient power to force acceptance of all decisions.

In her study of Chile, Fischer found that the widespread appeal of reforms under Frei, especially the expansion of schooling, aided acceptance of the package despite some resistance from older teachers to changes in curriculum, exams, and inspection.[33] By contrast, in a study of reform under the military government in Peru, Cleaves found that officials were less able to mobilize support for their educational programs than for agricultural reforms. Whereas agricultural reforms were complementary and cumulative, educational changes revolved around discrete issues such as bilingualism and university reform. Hence, it was harder to build a coalition that could overcome the opposition of important groups to specific proposals. Of particular importance was parents' neutrality on, or opposition to, bilingual education, based in part on their fears that it would limit their children's futures. While some resistance to the reforms was based on educational rationales, other objections were rooted in seemingly tangential goals. The teachers' union opposed the government in principle and student leaders feared that organizational changes would diminish their constituencies.[34]

The degree to which it is necessary for officials to build coalitions of support—that is, the degree to which automatic compliance cannot be assumed—varies from issue to issue. On the whole, coalitions for enforcement will be most essential where citizens' autonomy or alternatives are greatest. Elmore's warning that, in the United States, public policies are not "the only—or even the major—influence on the behavior of people engaged in the process" may be applied with caution to other societies.[35] Educational and political institutions help define the zones of discretion that citizens enjoy. States with virtually no private schooling would seem to have an easier time enforcing decisions because children are captive; they have nowhere else to go.[36] Even if parents can decide no more than whether to enroll their children, to let them continue, and to send them to one track or another, the sum of their choices may thwart policymakers' goals. Schooling of girls in the Middle East and vocational schools everywhere bear witness to this phenomenon. In places where communities control schools or where private schools abound, the problem of enforcing national policies is more complex, although some observers would argue that schools are then more responsive to local preferences. Harambee schools in Kenya reflect intense local demand for schooling and social mobility, while in the aggregate they aggravate the inflation of credentials and expectations.

Autonomy, concentration of authority, and participation in decision-making are themselves issues in educational policy. From the nearly universal battles over the autonomy of universities to Allende's attempt to give power to people's committees, this issue is rooted in a conviction that who makes policy is important to results. Moreover, control of schools is a political resource to be used in other contexts. Indian politicians are not alone in having discovered that ability to create schools and colleges is a powerful vote getter.[37] Here, as in other cases, many goals pursued with respect to education have little to do with learning per se.

The proposition that who makes policy shapes its content is most frequently based on the premise that different groups will have different interests and perceptions predictable on the basis of their position in society. Membership in a socioeconomic class, ethnic group, or corporate organization is associated with one's goals and values to the degree that it affects flows of information.[38] It is also thought to summarize one's connections to the rest of society. Cross-national regularities in perceptions and goals of similar groups have been fairly well documented. Teachers' unions tend to take their strongest stands on issues of pay and professional standing. Groups at the university oppose infringements on their autonomy. Parents tend to prefer academic to technical education for their children. Such similarities are not universal, however. Linguistic minorities, for example, differ in their assessments of, and attitudes toward, education in the vernacular. There are advantages in assuming that interests can be inferred from the identities of groups, but the internal coherence of such groups and the connection between social position and policy stands is still open to empirical verification.

An individual's formal role in policymaking can affect his perceptions and interests independently of group identities. As discussed earlier, protection and expansion of authority in the bureaucracy often affect the development of policy. Even where bureaucratic politicking is insignificant, educational policy made in bureaucracies is colored by technical knowledge, specialized information, and external reference groups. The importance of evaluating technical influences on policy is based on observations that many initiatives for educational change originate within bureaucracies, that specialists do frame alternative choices, and that technical language may be picked up by others to lend legitimacy to programs. Even assuming rational procedures in a search for solutions, specialists from different disciplines bring different techniques and standards to their tasks. It is no surprise that curricular specialists and economists may come up with quite different diagnoses of problems. Neither might evaluate problems much differenty than a counterpart from another country. The rapid diffusion of faddish and serious notions about education or models for planning is facilitated by foreign training, visiting foreign consultants, and international-aid agencies. It is then reinforced by reference groups and standards that local specialists derive from the international community.

Any discussion of policymaking in developing countries must include various international and foreign agencies or their representatives as independent actors whose power resources sometimes overwhelm those of local participants. Offers of aid for designated programs are often sufficient to alter local educational priorities, for better or worse. Colonial and quasi-colonial situations present striking examples of schools imposed from outside without particular sensitivity to local culture, custom, or values.[39] Such compulsion is far less frequent than more-complicated paths of influence. Foreign agencies may oppose one another on a given issue and find local allies to aid them. Local officials attempt to manipulate international agencies as well as the reverse. Host governments may treat unconfirmed social-scientific models (for example, manpower planning) as remedies and may demand that its specialists be taught these techniques. In short, the perceptions, goals, resources, and operations of outside groups should be analyzed like those of any other participants.

In the case of domestic and foreign actors alike, distance between those who make decisions and those for whom policy is devised is thought to affect the choices made. This proposition is evident in debates over the relative merits of centralization and decentralization.[40] Skeptical about expertise, advocates of decentralization argue that those closest to the problem are best able to find workable solutions, that participation in decision making increases commitment to their success, and that greater local autonomy gives citizens a more-realistic sense of the costs and benefits of education. The result is supposed to be policy that is more responsive to local needs and therefore more likely to be carried out correctly. Partisans of central control are more likely to claim priority for national goals such as integration and social justice. They may argue that local power structures and regional inequalities of wealth would impede policies meant to equalize opportunities for citizens throughout the country. The absence of uniform programs and standards is pictured as an open door to the use of more-ascriptive criteria in hiring. More important, central authorities anticipate (not without reason) that one day they will end up dealing with the consequences of local choices such as escalating costs, the composition of the labor force, demand for entrance to national universities, and even political unrest. Because most studies have concentrated on politics at the national level, the effects of different distributions of authority are still unclear.

In sum, to study process is to seek out information on the actors, goals, perceptions, resources, information, and organizational settings that surround the issues, programs, and outcomes. Ideally, the researcher examines exercises of choice and influence directly, but in practice, it is often necessary to infer them from other information. Moreover, even if one begins with an interest in specific decisions, it quickly becomes apparent that programs and outcomes can rarely be understood as a series of clearly formulated choices among alternatives. What passes for policy often turns out to be the result of uncoordinated decisions at many levels of society and accretions of incidental measures and errors. For all their complexity, however, outcomes are not random or unpredictable. Studies of policy and political process should investigate why and how results occur without either adopting participants' interpretations or assuming that all effects are necessarily intended. McGinn and his colleagues found that Mexican bureaucrats had neither the knowledge nor information to be able to design schools specifically to reduce social inequalities.[41] This is not to deny that such inequalities do occur, but their findings suggest that attention must be directed to examining wider political arenas and to placing political institutions into proper perspective.

Properties of Political Systems

Serious methodological problems exist in the study of political processes. Sufficiently detailed and accurate information is difficult to obtain. Even when available, such data are time consuming to analyze, and this problem usually limits the researcher to one or a few case studies, typically in one country. Generalizations to other countries are risky, and even in the country under study, patterns and broader influences may not emerge clearly from the idiosyncratic detail. The understanding of the politics of education would be greatly facilitated if manifest features of the political system more or less summed up the processes taking place and thus allowed broad multinational analysis.

This is precisely what is attempted in some of the large surveys. Political variables are usually chosen for their presumed relationship to processes through which power is exercised. Unfortunately, the multination studies often employ variables that are simply available for a large number of countries without checking the specific political dynamic of each of the countries being compared. Whether multiparty systems everywhere indicate constructive competition over policy rather than either underlying consensus or unproductive stalemates is rarely verified. Also, it is not clearly established that similar political phenomena will everywhere find expression in the same structural form. Competition may certainly be expressed through a plurality of parties, but the absence of parties does not necessarily mean absence of competition. In other cases, the measure used may be potentially interesting even if it does not have the meaning attributed to it. Ramirez and Rubinson's variable for "state power and authority" (government revenue/GDP) does show relative domination of the economy by the state but says nothing about power to get anything done.[42] Relationships between government revenue/GDP and centralization of education or, in another case, between size of the cabinet and enrollments are intriguing.[43] Yet it is neither clear what such relationships stand for nor obvious in the studies cited that all essential processes have been included.

How can researchers infuse variables with meaning beyond their literal sense and ensure that relevant factors are tested? The problem is to specify variables that capture adequately the elements of the presumed processes, including how structures facilitate or hamper the actions of

groups and shape their interests. There is no inherent contradiction between looking at processes and comparing large numbers of countries;
even their differing standards of explanation can be reconciled. However,
bringing these two approaches closer together requires greater attention
to identifying fundamental processes and to determining whether they
take the same form everywhere.

There is no perfect way to do this, but at this stage, comparative case
studies offer promise as a means for identifying significant relationships
and processes, evaluating the connection between variables and their
referents, and respecifying important variables. Comparisons of countries
or regimes should be designed to accentuate some factors thought to
affect policy, while holding others constant. For example, a common
linguistic and religious heritage, the shared experience of French rule,
and differences in recent political history make Morocco, Algeria, and
Tunisia a natural group within which to analyze educational reform. Their
policies do not always follow expected lines. Reforms of higher education
in Tunisia are neither so different from those of Algeria nor so similar
to those in Morocco as one might have expected from economic organization and political rhetoric. Analysis of how reforms are made in each
country helps to explain such apparent anomalies. In this way, new factors
may emerge, such as the importance of economic ministers, or new
measures may be produced for political will, distribution of power, and
governmental complexity.

Other natural units for comparison can be established based on culture, history, ideology, or level of natural resources. Fischer's study of
Chile under Frei, Allende, and the junta maximized ideological change
in order to observe its effect but instead found that the interplay of groups
was at least as important in explaining policy. As suggested earlier,
comparisons of revolutionary regimes offer fertile ground for inspecting
the effect of certain political changes on education and for identifying
the constraints that continue to bound reforms.

Finally, through small comparisons, variables can be respecified for
further study. If both capitalist and socialist regimes have large-scale
programs of vocational education, it is worth knowing whether this is
due to similarities that override ideological differences or whether the
dependent variable is inappropriate. It may turn out, for example, that
size of enrollment in such programs is not an important difference, while
criteria for access and availability of later training are. Issues that are
significant in local policy debates or in their long-term effects must be
sorted out from less-instructive variables.

It is doubtful whether this approach, or any other, will find politics
to be uniquely determinant of educational programs and outcomes.
Rather, by drawing case studies and multinational surveys closer together

in their underlying assumptions, it is possible to arrive at a surer understanding of exactly what effects and limits political factors have. Previous studies suggest that ideology, distribution of power, and organization each influences policy independently. How, where, and why they do—and how we know that they do—are the tantalizing questions yet to be settled.

Notes

1. Ted Robert Gurr, "A Conceptual System of Political Indicators," in *Indicator Systems for Political, Economic and Social Analysis,* ed. Charles Lewis Taylor (Cambridge, Mass.: Oelgeschlager, Gunn and Hain, 1980), p. 137.

2. David Easton, *A Framework for Political Analysis* (Englewood Cliffs, N.J.: Prentice-Hall, 1965), p. 50.

3. Harold D. Lasswell, *Politics: Who Gets What, When, How?* (New York: McGraw-Hill, 1936).

4. R.G. Havelock and A.M. Huberman, *Solving Educational Problems: The Theory and Reality of Innovation in Developing Countries* (New York: Praeger, 1978), pp. 72–73.

5. David Abernethy and Trevor Coombe, "Education and Politics in Developing Countries," *Harvard Educational Review* 35 (1965):287. See also Abernethy, *The Political Dilemma of Popular Education: An African Case* (Stanford, Calif.: Stanford University Press, 1969).

6. Dan C. Hazen, "The Politics of Schooling in the Nonliterate Third World: The Case of Highland Peru," *History of Education Quarterly* 18 (1978):419–443; and George Primov, "The School as an Obstacle to Structural Integration among Peruvian Indians," *Education and Urban Society* 10 (1978):209–222.

7. John W. Foley, "A Comparative Study of the Determinants of Public Policies," Occasional Paper No. 9 (Ithaca: Program in Urban and Regional Studies, Cornell University, 1978), chapter 6 and conclusion; and Joyce Matthews Munns, "The Environment, Politics, and Policy Literature: A Critique and Reformulation," *Western Political Quarterly* 28 (1975):646–667.

8. Joel G. Verner, "Socioeconomic Environment, Political System, and Educational Policy Outcomes: A Comparative Analysis of 102 Countries," *Comparative Politics* 11 (1979):179.

9. John W. Meyer, Francisco O. Ramirez, Richard Rubinson, John Boli-Pennett, "The World Educational Revolution, 1950–70," in *National Development and the World System: Educational, Economic, and*

Political Change, 1950–1970, eds. John Meyer and Michael T. Hannan (Chicago: University of Chicago Press, 1979), p. 54.

10. Ibid., pp. 37–55; and John E. Craig, "On the Development of Educational Systems," *American Journal of Education* 89 (1981): 189–211.

11. Verner, "Socioeconomic Environment," p. 173.

12. Ibid., p. 179; and Walter I. Garms, Jr., "The Correlates of Educational Effort: A Multivariate Analysis," *Comparative Education Review* 12 (1968):281–299.

13. Jill Clark, "Correlates of Educational Policy Priorities in Developing Nations," *Comparative Education Review* 20 (1976):129–139.

14. David Court, "The Education System as a Response to Inequality in Tanzania and Kenya," *Journal of Modern African Studies* 14 (1976):661–690; and Marie Thourson Jones, "Higher Education in North Africa: A Political Explanation of Recent Policy" (Paper presented to the Twenty-fifth Annual Conference of the Comparative and International Education Society, Tallahassee, Fla., March 1981).

15. Kathleen B. Fischer, *Political Ideology and Educational Reform in Chile, 1964–1976,* Studies on Social Processes and Change, vol. 46 (Los Angeles: UCLA Latin American Studies Center, 1979).

16. Francisco O. Ramirez and Richard Rubinson, "Creating Members: The Political Incorporation and Expansion of Public Education," in *National Development and the World System: Educational, Economic, and Political Change, 1950–1970,* ed. John Meyer and Michael T. Hannan (Chicago: University of Chicago Press, 1979), pp. 75–76.

17. Martin K. Whyte, "Educational Reform: China in the 1970s and Russia in the 1920's," *Comparative Education Review* 18 (1974): 112–128; Jerome Karabel and A.H. Halsey, *Power and Ideology in Education* (New York: Oxford University Press, 1977), part VI; Ronald Dore, *The Diploma Disease* (Berkeley: University of California Press, 1976); and Fischer, *Political Ideology.*

18. Graham Allison, *Essence of Decision* (Boston: Little, Brown, 1971).

19. Guy Benveniste, *Bureaucracy and National Planning: A Sociological Case Study in Mexico* (New York: Praeger, 1970), pp. 14–22.

20. Cited in Fischer, *Political Ideology,* p. 68.

21. Teshome G. Wagaw, *Education in Ethiopia* (Ann Arbor: University of Michigan Press, 1979), p. 179.

22. Ibid., pp. 128–130, 162–164.

23. James March and Herbert Simon, *Organizations* (New York: John Wiley & Sons, 1958), pp. 140–141; and Charles Lindblom, "The Science of 'Muddling Through'," *Public Administration Review* 19 (1959):79–88.

24. Richard Elmore, "Organizational Models of Social Program Implementation," *Public Policy* 26 (1978):185–228.

25. Benveniste, *Bureaucracy and National Planning,* pp. 56–59, 95–97.

26. Noel McGinn, Susan Street, and Guillermo Orozco, "Theories of the State and the Reality of Decision-Making in Mexican Education" (Paper delivered to the Twenty-fifth Annual Conference of the Comparative and International Education Society, Tallahassee, Fla., March 1981).

27. Marie Thourson Jones, "Public Influence on Government Policy: Family Planning and Manpower Development in Tunisia" (Ph.D. diss., Princeton University, 1979), pp. 255–256.

28. Maurice Kogan, *The Politics of Educational Change* (Manchester: Manchester University Press, 1978), pp. 15–20; and Andre Benoit, "A Note on Decision-Making Processes in the Politics of Education," *Comparative Education Review* 19 (1975):155–168.

29. Sidney Verba, Norman H. Nie, and Jae-on Kim, *Participation and Political Equality: A Seven-Nation Comparison* (Cambridge: Cambridge University Press, 1978), chapter 4.

30. Abernethy and Coombe, "Education and Politics," p. 288.

31. B. Guy Peters, "Non-Additive Models for Policy Research: A Longitudinal Evaluation, *Western Political Quarterly* 28 (1975):542-547.

32. Peter Bachrach and Morton Baratz, "Two Faces of Power," *American Political Science Review* 56 (1962):947–952; and Frederick Frey, "On Issues and Non-Issues in the Study of Power," *American Political Science Review* 65 (1971):1081–1101.

33. Fischer, *Political Ideology,* p. 54.

34. Peter Cleaves, "Implementation of the Agrarian and Educational Reforms in Peru," University of Texas Technical Papers Series No. 8 (Austin: Institute of Latin American Studies, 1977).

35. Richard Elmore, "Backward Mapping: Implementation Research and Policy Decisions," *Political Science Quarterly* 94 (1979–1980):604.

36. On schools as monopolies, see John Pincus, "Incentives for Innovation in the Public Schools," in *Social Program Implementation,* eds. Walter Williams and Richard Elmore (New York: Academic Press, 1976), pp. 43–76.

37. Harold Gould, "Educational Structures and Political Processes in Faizabad District, Uttar Pradesh," in *Education and Politics in India,* eds. Susanne Hoeber Rudolph and Lloyd I. Rudolph (Cambridge: Harvard University Press, 1972), pp. 94–120.

38. John E. Craig, "Expansion of Education," *Review of Research in Education* 9 (1981).

39. Noel F. McGinn et al., *Education and Development in Korea* (Cambridge: Council on East Asian Studies, Harvard University, 1980).

40. Philip Foster et al., "Dilemmas of Educational Development: A Symposium," *Comparative Education Review* 19 (1975):375–433.

41. McGinn, Street, and Orozco, "Mexican Education."

42. Ramirez and Rubinson, "Creating Members," p. 76.

43. Verner, "Socioeconomic Environment," p. 177.

3 Educational Progress and Economic Development

Gary S. Fields

Many development agencies seek to channel economic assistance to those less-developed countries (LDCs) and activities that will help the poor to achieve a better life (this phraseology is from the U.S. Foreign Assistance Act as amended in 1975). Education is an important indicator of countries' performance. This chapter examines the suitability of alternative education indicators as guides for planning and evaluating countries' progress and commitment toward increasing the participation of the poor in development.

Both the short- and long-term benefits of education must enter into an analysis of education's contribution to development.[1] Education is a valued component of present consumption because it has the essential characteristics of merit goods.[2] However, the case for expanding education is even stronger if it can be shown that educational investment pays off in enhancing future productive activity. The tools of cost-benefit analysis, used appropriately, may help to evaluate the investment potential of education. Likewise, economic analysis may help to gauge the consumption value of education vis-à-vis other alternative uses of resources.

In economic terms, it is possible for a society to have too much education. Education has an opportunity cost—for example, the cost of having more schools may be fewer hospital beds or less food supplementation for the poor. This example illustrates two important features of merit goods: (1) Like other economic goods and services, merit goods are costly to produce, and (2) some merit goods may be valued more highly than others. Economic analysis can be of great value in forcing each decision maker to weigh (either implicitly or explicitly) the benefits of more education against the costs (both direct and in terms of other projects foregone).

Education, I believe, is a lower-order-merit good—that is, life itself, health, nutrition, clothing, and shelter are higher priorities. Poor countries may postpone the provision of education until such time as their people

An earlier version of this chapter was prepared for the U.S. Agency for International Development. I am pleased to acknowledge the helpful research assistance of Douglas Marcouiller and the valuable comments by John Eriksson and Richard Shortlidge.

are well fed, well housed, and well clothed. If this is the case, any measure of educational performance is an insufficient index of the economic well-being of the poor. The preferred indicators of educational progress and commitment, whatever they may be, are useful only in conjunction with indicators in other areas.[3]

The remainder of this chapter is organized as follows. The next section briefly highlights some of the major lessons from studies of educational performance in developing countries. The following four sections consider various indicators of educational progress and commitment that have been suggested, the availability of data to measure them, the indications they give on educational performance in five LDCs, and the possibilities of improving future reporting of these indicators. The seventh section and the accompanying appendix present a critique and reformulation of the social-cost-benefit approach to evaluating education's past performance and planning education for the future. The last section summarizes the main results.

Lessons from Studies of Educational Performance in LDCs

In many countries, a veritable education explosion has occurred.[4] More people are receiving more education than ever before. UNESCO publishes data on the growth of education at various levels throughout the world. School enrollments have increased faster than population growth. Higher education has expanded most rapidly. LDCs have achieved higher rates of educational growth than developed countries.

Often, unemployment befalls relatively well-educated individuals (high-school graduates and even some with college degrees). Numerous studies have shown that the unemployed are relatively well educated.[5] The highest unemployment rates are found in the intermediate-education categories. The causes of unemployment and underemployment among the educated have been extensively debated. Among the arguments are inappropriateness of the type of education received, creation of false hopes by the educational system, low quality of education, inability of the economy and the labor market to create enough jobs that utilize the skills of the educated, and unemployment as part of a process of rational search by the educated for the best jobs.

Educational opportunities are unequally distributed geographically. In most LDCs, a much higher proportion of urban children is able to attend school than the proportion of rural children. Some regions have virtually no upper-level schools or well-educated persons. Within a country, school quality frequently varies substantially from one area to another.

Educational opportunities are unequally distributed according to parents' socioeconomic status, but educational systems are far from closed to the children of the poor. Some observers argue that educational systems are stratified so as to exclude the children of the poor, while others characterize LDCs' educational systems as vehicles for social mobility. The truth most likely is located about midway between the two extremes.

Where studies of school finance are available, they indicate that, although the poor receive a disproportionately small share of the benefits of education, they also pay a disproportionately small share of the costs. The benefits to the poor are limited by inadequate access to education, while the costs paid by the poor are reduced by the lower taxes they pay. Evidence on this point is available in studies of countries as diverse as the United States (Hansen and Weisbrod 1970), Colombia (Jallade 1974), Brazil (Jallade 1977), and Kenya (Fields 1975). Jallade's study of Colombia goes one step further, showing that the ratio of benefits of education to costs is highest for low-income families and that it decreases steadily as income rises.

When educational systems expand, some poor children are drawn into the enlarging school systems. Innumerable instances at the regional, or even village, level could be cited. We lack information, however, on the extent to which the children of the poor rather than the middle or upper classes benefit from the provision of additional spaces. The lack of information is particularly acute at the secondary and higher levels.

Educational growth tends to occur contemporaneously with economic growth. Two kinds of evidence are available: cross section and time series.[6] The pattern that emerges from cross-section evidence is that high-income countries tend to have higher educational enrollments. In the time-series evidence, at the primary and secondary levels, enrollment tends to grow fastest in the faster-growing countries. However, the association is not a close one. The literature on the relationship between educational growth and economic growth is plagued by a persistent difficulty—namely, the problem of causation. Educational growth causes economic growth and economic growth permits educational growth, but the relative importance of these two simultaneous effects has not yet been demonstrated satisfactorily.

Others with more faith in social-rate-of-return studies than I would use the findings of these studies to argue that more national and international resources should go toward the provision of education, particularly primary education, in LDCs. I agree with this policy conclusion but not because the social-rate-of-return studies have convinced me.

**Conceptual Suitability of Indicators of Educational
Progress and Commitment**

Various indicators of educational progress and commitment have been
proposed, and following are my assessments of some of them.[7]

School-Enrollment Rates

Enrollment rates refer to the fraction of school-aged children who are
enrolled in school. I believe these rates are the best single indicator of
progress. They show how many children actually have access to schools,
data on which is particularly important at the primary level. This reflects
both the existence of spaces in school and parents' ability to pay fees and
to forgo their children's labor. School enrollments are regularly measurable at low cost. Nearly always, enrollment rates are broken down by
level of schooling. This breakdown permits us to distinguish between
primary education (which many regard as a basic human right and which
is most relevant to the target group—the poor) and other levels. Other
breakdowns for which data are sometimes available are by sex and by
geographic location. These breakdowns may reveal alarming instances
of inequality of opportunity. In the case of geographic breakdowns, however, even in countries where the poor are concentrated in particular
geographic areas, there is no assurance from regional data that in fact the
poor in poor areas are the recipients of education. An even better breakdown of school-enrollment rates would be by socioeconomic status of
parents, since socioeconomic distribution is a much better indicator of
the extent to which the recipients of education are the poor, but such
status is an elusive concept that is not easily measured.[8] Enrollment rates
are also meaningful indicators of commitment. Care must be exercised
in interpreting enrollment data as a sign of commitment, though, since
it is hard to tell whether the commitment is by private individuals seeking
personal gain for themselves and their children or by a concerned public
sector. For many reasons, some of which have nothing to do with society's
commitment to education for the poor or lack thereof, parents of high
socioeconomic status are more likely to acquire more education for their
children.

Recipients of Nonschooling Education

Numbers of recipients of nonschooling-education indicate the participation of the population in less-formal-educational programs. Included in

this group are recipients of apprenticeship, adult education, on-the-job-training, extension, and other forms of continuing education. Rarely are these broken down below the national level. Conceptually, they are good measures of progress, since they show how many persons have access to learning opportunities outside of schools. Some difficulty of interpretation exists since nonschooling education may either complement or substitute for schooling, and this may vary from one country to another. There is also a measurement problem in defining who is a recipient. Nonetheless, this is a promising area on which little research has been done to date.

School-Completion Ratios

School-completion ratios are calculated as the percentage of the labor force or adult population that has completed various schooling levels. As a measure of progress, these ratios are valuable in showing the stock of educated persons. Of particular interest is the proportion of primary-school completers. Breakdowns by location and sex and often tabulated. The limitations of completion ratios are that they are restricted to formal-schooling attainments and are very slow to change, even if rapid progress is being made for the young generation.

Literacy and Numeracy Rates

Literacy and numeracy rates refer to the proportions of adults who can read, write, and perform simple arithmetic operations—that is, they reflect the cumulative acquisition of skills. These measures are especially relevant to poverty groups, though the applicability only up to a basic level is also a limitation. Conceptually, literacy and numeracy are not easily defined, which leads some observers to reject these measures, but I would say that the definitional problem is surmountable with a certain degree of arbitrariness applied consistently over time. Literacy and numeracy rates can and should be used as indicators of progress.

Educational-Expenditure and -Finance Data

These data tell what quantity of private resources and how much of the government's budget and national income are spent on education. They also indicate how the educational system is financed (for example, whether it is out of tax revenues, student fees, and so on). Expenditure information is the single best indicator of commitment to education, though it is not entirely free of difficulties. One need only look briefly at the position of the United States at the top of the spending scale to realize that school expenditures depend in large part on a country's ability to pay. For intertemporal comparisons within a country, information on total expenditure needs to be supplemented by other data to show that more spending results in better-quality or higher-quantity education rather than, say, using the additional education budget to raise salaries of existing teachers without expanding enrollments. For international comparisons, observers must remember the great differences across countries in public versus private financing, central-government versus state and local responsibility, differential importance of private and parochial schools, and varying practices with respect to tuition and fees.

Conceptually, school-finance data may also be good indicators of commitment—for example, abolition of fees, reliance on more progressive taxes, and equalization of quality across districts and regions. However, users of school-finance data must be sensitive to secondary effects such as, if the public sector assumes a greater share of school costs, who pays the taxes to finance the government? Of course, the determinants of any public-finance system are many and complex. It is unlikely that school-finance information will be readily tabulated in an internationally consistent form, but even if it were, educational-finance issues are of secondary importance compared with production-function kinds of concerns.

Rate of Return to Education

The rate of return to education is the percentage increment in income that society realizes on its educational investments. Those who have faith in markets and in the technical prowess of economists say that social rates of return to education are guides to the efficiency of resource allocation patterns. On this view, educational systems are thought to be performing efficiently when social rates of return are equalized across various educational levels since it is inefficient for a dollar invested one place to earn more than a dollar invested elsewhere. To more-agnostic analysts, however, a high rate of return to education might mean any number of things: for example, that society is wisely spending resources in a high-payoff area, that more expenditure is needed until diminishing returns drive the marginal rate of return on education down to the social-discount rate, that the apparently high social rate of return to education is a mirage due to unjustifiable wage premiums received by highly educated workers, or that the rate of return to education may be high privately but not socially because the better educated are hired preferentially, bumping the less educated into lower-level jobs or unemployment. Because of these ambiguities of interpretation, I do not see that data on rates of return to education, taken by themselves, are of much use as an indication of either progress or commitment in the field of education.

Summary

The various arguments presented in the preceding sections are outlined in table 3–1. In summary, several indicators of progress in the education sector appear to be conceptually satisfactory to a greater or lesser degree: school-enrollment rates, nonschooling-education recipients, school-completion ratios, literacy and numeracy rates, and educational spending, each of these broken down, insofar as possible by schooling category, sex, geographic location, and parents' socioeconomic status. These same measures are much more difficult to interpret as indicators of commitment, but they still may be of some value. Of these, literacy and numeracy rates and rates of enrollment in primary education may be the best indicators of educational progress for the poor, and expenditure data may be the best indicator of commitment.

Data Availability on Educational Indicators

School-Enrollment Rates

The most accessible compilation of enrollment rates is the *Statistical Yearbook* series published by UNESCO. Primary- and secondary-school gross-enrollment ratios are given for about 140 countries, most of which are available on an annual basis. Three types of secondary education are distinguished: (1) general (academic or composite), (2) teacher preparation, and (3) other vocational or technical. For tertiary education, gross-enrollment ratios are published for a somewhat lesser group of countries (130) on a less-regular basis. Net primary- and secondary-school-enrollment rates are given sporadically for about 80 countries. In many cases, enrollment information is disaggregated by sex. Hence, good data are available for school enrollments broken down by level of schooling and by sex. However, breakdowns by parents' socioeconomic status, region, or other correlates of poverty cannot be undertaken.

Recipients of Nonschooling Education

Among the types of nonschooling education of interest are adult education, on-the-job training, agricultural extension, learning by radio, and

Table 3–1
Appropriateness of Various Indicators of Educational Progress

Indicator	Appropriateness as Indicator of Progress	Appropriateness as Indicator of Commitment
School-enrollment rates	Shows how many persons actually have access to schools, which reflects existence of spaces in school and parents' ability to pay fees and to forego their children's labor.	Difficult to interpret since a country may be committed to education but may choose to tend to other social concerns first.
Nonschooling education	Shows how many persons have access to education outside of schools; problem of interpretation since nonschooling education may either complement or substitute for schooling.	(same as above)
School-completion ratios	Shows stock of educated persons, but it is limited to formal schooling.	(same as above)
Literacy and numeracy rates	Reflects cumulative acquisition of skills, especially useful for poverty groups but applicable only up to a basic level.	(same as above)
Educational-expenditure and finance data	Use of expenditure data relies on the assumption that more spending results in more education in terms of quantity or quality; this may be invalid (for example, if additional spending is used to raise salaries of existing teachers). Finance data alone can tell little about progress (for example, if public sector assumes a greater share of school costs, who pays the taxes to finance the public sector?).	(same as above)
Rate of return to education	What it signals is not clear. High rate of return to education may mean society is spending resources in a high-payoff area, or more expenditure is needed (until diminishing returns drive marginal rate of return down to social-discount rate), result is spurious due to unjustifiable wage premiums received by highly educated workers, or rate of return to education may be high because better-educated are hired preferentially, bumping less-educated into lower-level jobs or into unemployment.	What it signals is not clear.

Table 3–1 continued

Indicator	Appropriateness as Indicator of Progress	Appropriateness as Indicator of Commitment
Breakdown by schooling category	Necessary.	Interpretation is questionable since it is hard to know in general and without study which level of education is most valuable per dollar expended in a given society.
Breakdown by sex	Important, since within a society, one sex may be favored at the expense of the other.	(Same remarks as for progress)
Breakdown by geographic location	Useful as guide to equality of opportunity; helpful if poor are concentrated in certain geographic areas; no assurance that the poor in poor areas are the recipients.	(Same remarks as for progress)
Breakdown by socioeconomic status	Socioeconomic status is best indicator of extent to which recipients of education are the poor.	Care must be exercised since there are many reasons why high socioeconomic-status parents are more likely to acquire more education for their children, and these reasons may have nothing to do with society's commitment to education for the poor.

so on. I have, however, reached the conclusion after an extensive search, that data on flows through nonschooling education are simply unavailable in any general source (though they may be available in local or country data sources). UNESCO does publish annual data on the number of radio receivers per 1,000 inhabitants in each of 150 countries, but it does not give any indication of the spread of radio to the poor or the use of radio for purposes of education rather than entertainment.

School-Completion Ratios

School-completion ratios are available for 134 countries and territories in the UNESCO yearbook, of which most have data for more than one year. The availability of these data corresponds to infrequent (for example, decennial) population censuses.

Literacy and Numeracy Rates

The 1980 UNESCO yearbook contains a special table (table 1.3) that is a "complete inventory of data on illiteracy from 1945 onwards held by the UNESCO Office of Statistics." Literacy data are not published regularly, but this one table summarizes all of the postwar censuses with literacy information. Figures are published for 158 countries and territories; 95 countries have at least two data points separated by between five and twenty years. Usually, both the number of illiterates and illiteracy rates are shown. Sometimes data are disaggregated according to sex. race, language, or other population subgroups.

Two features of the literacy rates bear mention: (1) There is no regular periodicity, and (2) literacy is not defined in a consistent fashion, either internationally or intertemporally.

Numeracy rates are not usually collected or regularly published.

Educational-Expenditure and -Finance Data

Information on educational expenditure is available in the UNESCO yearbook. The data include:

Total public expenditure on education: current versus capital, as percentage of GNP, and, as percentage of total public expenditure (available for 160 countries and territories);

Current expenditure by use (administration, teachers, and so on) (about 120 countries and territories);

Current expenditure by level of education, broken down by primary, secondary, and tertiary education; some include figures for special or adult programs (about 120 countries and territories);

Capital expenditure by level of education (available for 110 countries).

No compilation of educational-finance data is published.

Rates of Return to Education

Rates of return to education are available for many countries but only in scattered ad hoc studies for irregular dates.[9] Changes over time have not been measured.

Breakdowns

Breakdown by educational level is usually available on an annual basis for most countries in the world.

Typically, literacy and completion rates are broken down by sex. Enrollment rates are not broken down by sex by UNESCO.

Geographic information is often found in individual countries' census volumes or statistical-data books. It is not, however, centrally compiled in a readily usable form.

Data on parents' socioeconomic status can be derived from only a handful of special-purpose, one-time studies.

Summary

A quick and ready view of educational-sector performance can be obtained for a large number of countries. Enrollment and expenditure data are compiled annually. For the other indicators, accurate and reliable data are available for a single point in time or scattered intervals. The only indicators that might conceivably be used to evaluate short-term changes in education indicators are

Total school-enrollment rates,

School-enrollment rates by school level,

School-enrollment rates by sex,

Total government-expenditure data on education,

Government-expenditure data on education by school level.

For assessing educational changes over longer periods, say, decades, many countries also have data on:

Total school-completion ratios,

School-completion ratios by school level,

School-completion ratios by sex,

Total literacy rates,

Literacy rates by sex.

In the short run, other indicators, whatever their merits and limitations, can be used only in an ad hoc fashion on a case-by-case basis. The availability of data on the various indicators is sketched in table 3–2.

Education Indicators in Selected Countries

It is interesting to examine the evidence on educational indicators in countries with reasonably well-understood development histories.

Table 3–2
Availability of Data to Measure Various Indicators of Educational Progress

Indicator	Available for a Single Point in Time?	Available on a Regular Basis over Time?
School-enrollment rates	Yes, in most countries, in compilations of educational statistics	Yes, in most countries, in compilations of educational statistics
Nonschooling education	Yes, in many countries, from ad hoc studies	No, with few exceptions, not generally available on a regular basis
School-completion ratios	Yes, in many countries, from censuses or household surveys	Available for scattered dates but not annually
Literacy and numeracy rates	Yes, in many countries, from censuses or household surveys	Available for scattered dates but not annually
Educational-expenditure and finance data	Expenditure data: Yes, in most countries, for public spending, from government budgets; Finance data: No, except for a few countries with ad hoc studies	Expenditure data: yes, in most countries, for public spending, from government budgets. Finance data: No
Rate of return to education	Yes, in many countries, from ad hoc studies	No, except for a few countries at irregular intervals
Breakdown by schooling category	Yes, where the above are available, it is according to level of schooling	Yes, where the above are available, it is according to level of schooling
Breakdown by sex	Yes, in most countries, in compilations of educational statistics	Yes, in most countries, in compilations of educational statistics
Breakdown by geographic location	Yes, where the above are available, in many countries, although not usually in compilations of educational statistics	Yes, where the above are available, in many countries, although not usually in compilations of educational statistics
Breakdown by socioeconomic status of parents	No, except in a few countries with ad hoc studies	No, except in a few countries with ad hoc studies

In a previous study (Fields 1980), I examined development progress and commitment in six LDCs.

In brief, their development histories are as follows:

Brazil, 1960–1970	Moderately high economic growth, rising inequality, falling absolute poverty;
Costa Rica, 1961–1971	Rapid economic growth, falling inequality, falling absolute poverty;
India, 1960/1961–1968/1969	Very little economic growth, slightly falling inequality, rising absolute poverty;
Philippines, 1961–1971	Rapid economic growth, rising inequality, constant absolute poverty;
Sri Lanka, 1953–1971	Slow economic growth, falling inequality, falling absolute poverty;
Taiwan, 1964–1972	Rapid economic growth, falling inequality, falling absolute poverty.

Educational data for these countries, except Taiwan, are taken from The UNESCO *Statistical Yearbook*. Selected information for the other five countries appears in table 3–3.

When one thinks of educational progress in poor countries, one thinks immediately of literacy. In each of the five countries, the literacy rate went up, though in four of the five, the number illiterate increased.[10] In these countries, literacy data were collected only at eight-to-ten-year intervals. No relationship between the countries' development performances and changes in their literacy rates is apparent over these intervals.

The second set of data refers to the highest level of schooling achieved by persons over the age of twenty-five. Costa Rica had the highest completion ratio, as may be expected from its relatively high per capita income. Contrary to expectations, Sri Lanka and the Philippines had lower proportions without schooling than Brazil despite being much poorer than Brazil. Information on schooling attainments is collected only infrequently, but over the intervals for which we have information, the data are intriguing—the greatest reductions in the proportions without schooling are found in the high-growth countries. Whether this is suggestive of a more-general association, and whether the observed relationship is cause or effect, are fundamentally important questions that are open to further investigation.

The third piece of information is educational distribution by sex. Costa Rica is the country with greatest parity—that is, literacy rates and

Table 3–3
Educational Change in Five LDCs

Indicator	Costa Rica	Brazil	India	Philippines	Sri Lanka
Illiterates over 15 years old (million) [females in brackets]	1963: 0.11 [.055]; 1973: 0.12 [.062]	1961: 16.8ª [8.5]; 1971: 18.1 [10]	1961: 187 [109]; 1971: 212 [124]	1958: 3.1 [2.3]; 1960: 4.1 [2.1]; 1970: 3.6	1963: 1.5 [1.1]; 1971: 1.7 [1.2]
Illiteracy rate (percentage) [females in brackets]	1963: 16 [16.5]; 1973: 11.6 [11.8]	1960: 39 [55.8]; 1970: 33.8 [36.9]	1961: 72.2 [86.8]; 1971: 66.6 [81.1]	1958: 25.1 [30.5]; 1960: 28.1 [19.1]; 1970: 17.4	1963: 24.9 [36.3]; 1971: 22.4 [31.5]
Highest educational level reached by population over 25 years old (percentage of total) [females in brackets]					
No schooling	1963: 20.6 [20.6]; 1973: 16.1 [16]	1950: 65.3 [69.6]; 1970: 42.6 [46.5]	1961: 75.5 [90]; 1971: 72.2 [86.6]	1960: 33.5 [37.3]; 1970: 19.8 [22.2]	1963: 32.3 [46.7]; 1971: 29.5 [40.9]
Partial primary schooling	1963: 49.1 [49.2]; 1973: 49.1 [49.8]	1950: 15.9 [12.9]; 1970: 26.7 [24.1]	1961: 15.8 [6.7]; 1971: 22.7 [11.7]	1960: 49.7 [48.9]; 1970: 56.4 [57.2]	1963: 39.6 [32.1]; 1971: 23.5 [20.5]
Complete primary (only)	1963: 19.6 [19.7]; 1973: 17.8 [17.7]	1950: 13.9 [13.5]; 1970: 19.4 [19]	1961: 6.3 [2.7]; 1971: N.A. [N.A.]	1960: N.A. [N.A.]; 1970: N.A. [N.A.]	1963: 6.9 [5.1]; 1971: 35.4 [28.2]
Residual (those with some secondary or higher)	1963: 10.7 [7.7]; 1973: 17 [6.5]	1950: 4.9 [0.8]; 1970: 11.3 [5.2]	1961: 2.5 [0.6]; 1971: 5 [1.6]	1960: 16.8 [13.8]; 1970: 23.8 [20.6]	1963: 21.1 [16.1]; 1971: 11.7 [10.4]
Definition of primary (number of years)	6	8^b	5	6	5
Gross-enrollment ratios					
Primary	1960: 0.94; 1970: 1.10	1960: 0.95; 1970: 0.83	1960: 0.4; 1970: 0.6	1960: 0.95; 1970: 1.14	1960: 0.95; 1970: 0.99
Secondary	1960: 0.21; 1970: 0.28	1960: 0.11; 1970: 0.27	1960: 0.2; 1970: 3	1960: 0.26; 1970: 0.50	1960: 0.27; 1970: 0.51
Higher	1960: 0.05	1960: 0.02	1960: 0.0; 4	1960: 0.13	1960: 0.01
Educational expenditure (current and capital) as a percentage of all public expenditure	1965: 26.1; 1972: 29.1	1965: 11.9; 1974: 15.2	1965: N.A.; 1975: 26.2	1965: N.A.; 1975: 9.4^e	1965: 15; 1973: 12.2
Educational expenditure (current and capital as a percentage of GNP)	1965: 4.6; 1972: 5.5	1965: 2.9; 1970: 2.9	1965: 2.6^d; 1970: 2.8^d	1965: 2.5; 1975: 1.6^e	1965: 4.5; 1973: 3.6

Current public educational expenditure by level

Level	A 1965	A 1970	A 1973	B 1965	B 1970	B 1973	C 1970	C 1975	D 1965	D 1973
Primary and preprimary	60.4	51.2	45.5	23.3d	22.4d	47.2	83.2e,g	80.0e,g	62.8g	34.6
Secondary	16.7	18.9	16.9	42.1d	42.5d	32.1	3.9e,g	8.0e,g	25.1g	53.6
Higher	11.5	10.5	23.6	23.1d	24.6d	13.9	6.6e,g	5.4e,g	5.4g	7.5
Not distributed	11	19.4	14	10.2d	9.2d	4.4	6.3e,g	6.6e,g	4.9g	4.4

Current public educational expenditure per pupil by level. For primary level, primary in 1965 has index value = 1. For higher levels, primary in the given year has index value = 1.

Level	A 1965	A 1970	A (N.A.)	B 1965	B 1970	C (N.A.)	D 1965	D 1970
Primary	1	1.3	N.A.	1	1	N.A.	1	1
Secondary	1.9	2.2	N.A.	4.9	4.9	N.A.	2.5	2.7
Higher	7.5	4.7	N.A.	46.7	35.7	N.A.	13.2	23.6

Sources: UNESCO, *Statistical Yearbook 1976*, tables 1.3, 1.4, 3.1, 3.2, 6.1, 6.3, 6.5.

aRefers to illiterates over 13, not 15, years old in 1963.
bAfter 1971.
cTotal enrollment (of whatever age) divided by total population in the specified age group.
dIncludes some private expenditure on private education.
eCentral government only.
fMinistry of Education only.
gEstimate.
N.A. Not available.

educational attainments are nearly the same for the two sexes. Disparities are greater in Brazil and the Philippines. The largest differences are in India and Sri Lanka. The pattern in these five countries is for equality of educational opportunity by sex to increase with level of GNP per capita. This reflects partly parents' discriminating in favor of their sons in poor countries and partly cultural differences in the particular countries considered here.

Fourth, we have statistics on enrollment ratios. UNESCO distinguishes *gross* and *net* ratios. The gross primary-school-enrollment ratio is the total primary-school enrollment (regardless of the age of students) divided by the population of primary-school age. The gross ratio can rise above one if there are many repeaters. The gross rates are reported annually. The net ratio eliminates from the enrollment figures those students who are not in the usual age category. These data are available for just a few countries at irregular dates and are not reproduced here. The gross enrollment data show a very mixed group of countries—Costa Rica, the Philippines, and Sri Lanka—in which the gross primary-school-enrollment ratio rose and approached or exceeded 1. Primary-school enrollments rose in India too, though with a smaller proportion of the school-aged population involved. The reported decline in primary enrollments in Brazil is anomalous in a fast-growing country but consistent with the unevenness of the Brazilian development model.

Finally, information is available on educational expenditure. Looking first at educational expenditure as a percentage of the government budget and of GNP, only Costa Rica's rose in both categories. In Brazil the share of educational expenditure in the national budget increased, but it remained the same percentage of GNP. In countries with two very different development histories—the Philippines and Sri Lanka—education lost out relatively. Turning to the composition of educational expenditures, divergent patterns also emerge. In Costa Rica, Sri Lanka, and to a lesser extent, the Philippines, a relative redirection of educational expenditures occurred away from primary, and in favor of secondary, education. Only in India did the share going to primary education rise. The last piece of educational-expenditure data is relative cost of different levels. That measure shows a rising relative cost of higher education in Sri Lanka and a falling relative cost in Costa Rica and India. India, though, continues to have the highest ratio of higher-to-primary education expenditures.

Note, finally, the categories for which we do not have data: recipients of apprenticeship and other nonschool education, numeracy rates, education-finance data, rates of return to education, breakdown by geographic location, and breakdown by socioeconomic status of parents.

Table 3–4 presents my qualitative judgment of changes over time in

Table 3–4
Relative Educational Performance in Five LDCs

Indicator of Educational Performance	Costa Rica	Brazil	India	Philippines	Sri Lanka
			Country		
Literacy rate					
Level	Good	Fair	Poor	Good	Good
Change	Good	Good	Fair	Good	Poor
Parity by sex	Good	Fair	Poor	Fair	Poor
Highest educational level reached					
No schooling, level	Good	Poor	Poor	Good	Good
No schooling, change	Good	Good	Poor	Good	Poor
Parity by sex	Good	Fair	Poor	Fair	Poor
Enrollment rate, primary					
Level	Good	Fair	Poor	Good	Good
Educational expenditures					
As percentage of GNP, change	Good	Fair	Fair	Poor	Poor
Share of primary, change	Poor	N.A.	Good	Poor	Poor
Higher relative to primary, change	Good	N.A.	Good	N.A.	Poor

Note: N.A. means not available.

the various education indicators. This information helps us to reach an overall assessment of comparative educational performance in these five countries. Despite a certain inevitable degree of arbitrariness, the results are suggestive of countries' educational performances.

Three countries' experiences are more or less as expected. Costa Rica looks most favorable, which is consistent with its favorable GNP level and growth and income-distribution records. India's essentially poor performance is consistent with its overall poverty and record of nongrowth. Brazil's record of aggregate educational growth with widening disparities parallels developments on the income-distribution front.

The educational record of the other two countries was somewhat unanticipated given their income-distribution experiences. On the one hand, the Philippines did relatively well in educational terms despite its poor income-distribution record. On the other hand, Sri Lanka exhibited less educational progress than might have been expected from its income-distribution performance. In both cases, the education results are in closer accord with GNP performance (high in the Philippines, low in Sri Lanka) than with income-distribution performance.

From this examination of five countries' education and development performances, no unambiguously favorable or unfavorable cases appear; no obvious instance of commitment or lack thereof is located. It is interesting that what seems to emerge is a closer relationship between educational performance and aggregate economic growth than between educational performance and distribution (in terms of either relative inequality or absolute poverty). This relationship suggests that countries may make substantial progress in education when, and only when, they can afford to. It also calls into question the value of educational performance—at least as measured by the available indicators—as a guide to countries' commitment toward raising the economic status of the poor. These speculations are just that—speculations—and require more-rigorous formulation and testing on more-extensive data sets. Such an analysis merits close attention in future studies of education and development.

Toward Improved Data Availability and New Indicators

How can improved data for assessing educational progress and commitment be provided? The following paragraphs present my recommendations.

1. *Reduce Reporting Delays.* Some of the indicators of educational performance described in preceding sections are conceptually clear and

easily calculable. In fact, these are largely the indicators for which accurate information is already frequently available on a regular basis. In some countries, the usefulness of these indicators is limited by reporting delays. Technical or financial assistance to speed the processing of such data would be helpful.

2. *Develop Standardized Measures.* Both within and across countries, concepts vary and measurement procedures differ. More-useful information could be gotten without much difficulty in the future if measures were standardized—for example, literacy and numeracy rates. One simple but effective technique for measuring literacy in a survey situation is to hand a person a card that reads, "Write your name here." If the respondent writes his name, he is said to be literate. While this is overly simplified and does not reflect functional literacy as closely as one might like, it has the great virtue of easy administration. Perhaps more-sophisticated tests could be devised, not only for literacy but also for numeracy and other skills. Standard questions like this could be made a part of every future population survey or census.

3. *Improve upon the Measurement of Nonschooling Education.* School data, being easiest to obtain, are most often published. Surveys often produce valuable data on literacy or other educational achievements. However, in recognition of the failures of some adult-literacy programs and the successes of some nonliteracy-based skill programs such as agricultural extension and radio education, efforts need also to be made to measure nonschooling education and skill acquisition. People might be asked whether they had participated in a formal training program, been visited by a government extension officer, or regularly listened to educational radio. As with literacy and numeracy rates, standardized questions on nonschooling education could be integrated into future survey efforts.

4. *Cross Classify Existing Measures by Socioeconomic Status.* Measures like school-enrollment ratios or literacy rates do not tell us to what extent the poor benefit from educational programs unless these data are broken down by recipients' socioeconomic status. Educational information from household surveys can and should be tabulated in relation to such socioeconomic status measures as family income, parents' occupation, parents' education, and (in the case of farm families) land and cattle ownership. For example, households in an income-distribution survey could be classified according to their socioeconomic status into quintile groupings; the school-attendance patterns of each quintile's children could then be tabulated. As an indicator of education's contribution to development, it is at least as important to have information on which particular families benefit from education as it is to know how many have benefited. From the perspective of using educational data in antipoverty

planning, the lack of socioeconomic-status detail is the most serious deficiency in the available education data.

5. *Do Not Publish Conceptually Difficult Data.* Some indicators require sophisticated users for successful implementation. An example is social-rate-of-return analysis. Anyone with graduate training in economics can calculate social rates of return to different levels of education. Few, however, know how to modify rate-of-return calculations according to particular local circumstances so as to produce meaningful data. Unfortunately, in the field of education, social programs and policies can and have been misdirected by listening to high-sounding social-cost-benefit calculations made by pseudo–social scientists. In this area, a little education in economics is worse than none. Any attempt to procure social rates of return for a large number of countries on a regular and timely basis can be expected to produce little useful information.

6. *Do Not Construct a Composite Index of Educational Performance.* We do not yet have a firm enough basis for deciding which factors to include and which to omit. Any attempt to assign weights to the included factors would be unsatisfactorily arbitrary. Then too, we do not have internationally comparable data with which to measure the included factors. In the present state of our knowledge, too much information would be lost and too little gained from a composite index to warrant its use.

Social-Cost-Benefit Analysis in Educational Planning

The basic idea of social-cost-benefit analysis in education is to relate the present value of the stream of social costs of additional education to the present value of additional social benefits. As a criterion for social decision making, cost-benefit analysis follows a familiar and basically sound economic principle—namely, that society should allocate resources to the activity that offers the greatest marginal social benefit (defined broadly) per dollar expended.

The essential requirement for project-planning and -appraisal procedures in education as in other fields is that they be sensitive to improvements in living conditions and to unfulfilled needs of the poor. Social-cost-benefit analysis can be a helpful tool in evaluating the extent to which a particular country's educational program has contributed, or will contribute, to the development effort.

A good, thorough social-cost-benefit analysis would be based at least on the following features:

Statement of Objectives. The country's development goals should be clearly stated. Presumably, many countries' lists of objectives would give first priority to the alleviation of absolute economic misery.

Forecast of Beneficiaries. In the usual course of things, programs are justified on the basis of number of beneficiaries. Also important here is a characterization of the beneficiaries in terms of socioeconomic status. It should be shown that the beneficiaries are drawn from the target group; fears that educational expansion cater to the elites should be allayed.

Projecting Size of Benefits. To assess the economic benefits from a proposed program, projections are needed on what the newly educated persons will do. What type of work will they find, and how much will they earn from it? How much more productive with education than without will they be at that work? Are other persons without education likely to be displaced, and if so, what will they do instead? Education officials and manpower planners need to work hand in hand in this area.

Magnitude of Costs. Both the direct costs of education and the opportunity costs must be figured in. Often, for an educational project, the relevant comparison is with the costs of some other educational project—for example, the opportunity cost of educating one additional student for one year at a university is X fewer elementary-school pupils.

Incidence of Costs. School fees are typically a fraction of the total cost. The incidence of fees and foregone earnings parallels the incidence of benefits. However, the incidence of other direct costs must also be estimated. In this area, features of the tax structure such as its progressivity or regressivity and overall budget surplus or deficit enter. It is probably the case in many LDCs that taxpayers as a whole, including many poor families, help to subsidize the education of the few, drawn disproportionately from the middle and upper classes.

Other Social Benefits. In concentrating here on the economic benefits, other noneconomic social benefits should not be disregarded. These benefits should be considered, even though they probably cannot be precisely quantified.

Compared with the preceding list, cost-benefit analysis of education as actually practiced is strikingly deficient. Table 3–5 describes what usually is done. It should be evident that the so-called social rates of return to investment in education leave a great deal to be desired. As conventionally computed, the average private and social rates of return neither ask the right questions nor measure the right phenomena.

Table 3–5
Cost-Benefit Analysis of Education in Practice

Aspect of Cost-Benefit Analysis	Usual Treatment in Literature
Stating objectives	Presumed goal in most cost-benefit studies is to raise output, not reduce poverty; these may conflict; education's potential contribution to poverty reduction is frequently not discussed directly.
Forecasting beneficiaries	Number of beneficiaries usually is taken into account; composition of beneficiaries is usually ignored.
Projecting size of benefits	Usually assumes that marginal benefits equal average benefit; this is unjustifiable in a labor-surplus context.
Quantifying magnitude of costs	Does a good job.
Estimating incidence of costs	Sometimes it enters as an afterthought but most frequently is ignored.
Considering other social benefits	Sometimes it is done; may be used to override cost-benefit circulations.

Conclusions

In this chapter, I have considered various aspects of education as an indicator of countries' progress and commitment toward helping the poor toward a better life and as a guide to development planning. I now draw together the findings and implications of the study.

Education is a lesser-order indicator of development performance. U.S. law specifies several specific indicators of development performance: promoting greater equality of income distribution, reducing rates of unemployment and underemployment, reducing infant mortalilty, controlling population growth, and increasing agricultural productivity. Of these, progress toward greater equality of income distribution through the alleviation of absolute poverty could be singled out as the most important indicator of development progress. I would place education alongside increasing productive employment and reducing infant mortality and ahead of improving agricultural productivity and limiting population. Used in conjunction with these other indicators, educational information is helpful in gauging countries' development performance. Like the other second-order indicators, however, education-sector performance should not be used alone.

The usual kinds of educational indicators provide useful information. The familiar indicators all measure the number of individuals who are receiving education at present or who received education in the past. We may reasonably presume that the poor benefit from educational growth, but direct evidence on the matter is scarce.

Considering the conceptual appropriateness of the various indicators and the availability of data for measuring them in LDCs, there are several applicable indicators of educational progress and commitment for which published data are available.

Data on access of the poor to education and changes in that access over time are available only in special studies for a limited number of countries. This kind of information cannot be used to measure educational performance or to allocate foreign assistance among countries. Future data-gathering efforts should give high priority to identifying the beneficiaries of education by socioeconomic level. In the few instances for which this information is already available, it should be used on a case-by-case basis.

In an examination of various educational indicators in five LDCs, no consistent pattern emerged. Each country did well according to some indicators, poorly according to others. Rapidly growing countries registered the greatest educational progress. The relationships between indicators of educational performance and of income distribution were weaker.

The reporting of data for assessing educational performance can be improved in a number of ways including reducing reporting delays, developing standardized measures, improving upon the measurement of nonschooling education, and cross classifying existing measures by socioeconomic status. It would not be helpful at the present time to publish data on certain hard-to-interpret measures such as social rates of return to education or to attempt to build a composite index of educational performance.

Education analysts, both in LDC governments and in foreign-assistance agencies, need to conduct more-sophisticated cost-benefit studies of education's contribution to development, paying particular attention to education's role in alleviating poverty. Yes, societies can have too much education, even when too much is very little, if they spend more for education on the margin than the least educated person is able to contribute to social and economic objectives. While cost-benefit analyses should consider the multiplicity of development objectives in LDCs, upgrading the economic position of the poor should be paramount. The information needed to evaluate existing education programs includes data on numbers of recipients, who they are (in terms of socioeconomic status), how much it costs to educate them, who pays the costs, what type of work they do after completing their education, and how much that work pays off to society. Rarely do cost-benefit studies even attempt to deal with the majority of these concerns.

To be a useful tool for deciding on aid allocation, cost-benefit analyses must accurately reflect actual labor-market circumstances. Educational planning should take full account of employment gains and wage improvements in contributing to the alleviation of poverty. Some of these improvements may be long term through creation of a high-level scientific and technical infrastructure that will increase economic growth, employ some of the poor in more-productive and better-paying jobs, and stimulate the demand for goods produced by those left behind in traditional sectors. Others may be shorter term, producing immediate agricultural extension and on-the-job training, rapid improvements in adult education, and widespread gains in literacy among children. It is vital that the labor-market and antipoverty effects of educational programs be justified quantitatively and in relation to other alternative uses of resources and not just in the abstract. To come to a sound decision on which among the myriad of possible programs are most worthy of support, it is not sufficient to merely list but not evaluate the presumed benefits of education or to omit mention of opportunity costs.

Additional foreign assistance should not be granted solely on the basis of demonstrated progress and commitment in the field of education. Countries may have succeeded in the past and may continue to do so precisely because they are already advancing rapidly and can afford to devote resources to education. Use of educational indicators as criteria for allocating foreign assistance would be expected to create incentives, but they may not be the right ones. Some countries might misrepresent or even deliberately falsify data if the figures may be the basis for higher aid. In this case, countries' progress and commitment in the field of education will become virtually unmeasurable. Even more dangerous would be if countries actually do something unjustified to get more aid. For example, suppose an aid agency offered to match countries' new technical-education expenditures dollar for dollar. It is easy to imagine resources' being shifted from agriculture and health to education. This might be appropriate in one country and disastrous in another. No responsible decision maker can really claim to know which is the most effective use of resources in general. Until we know what policies work under which sets of circumstances, educational progress and commitment should be used as criteria for allocating aid only with the greatest care.

Notes

1. The landmark volume on education's role in development is that of Anderson and Bowman (1966).
2. Economists define merit goods as products and services that are of inherent value to society and that merit scarce public resources because the private sector does not provide enough of them.

3. This is not true of social indicators that relate to higher-order wants. Increasing absolute incomes of the poorest is, I submit, a higher-order indicator that may be treated by itself. Other higher-order indicators such as the upgrading of dietary standards in malnourished societies, reductions in infant mortality, declining morbidity, and increased longevity need not be considered in relation to other measures either. For these, more is preferred to less.

4. In the interests of brevity, much supporting documentation from an earlier draft of this chapter is omitted.

5. This literature is surveyed in Turnham (1971) and Psacharopoulos (1978).

6. The cross-sectional approach is frequently associated with Harbison. See Harbison and Myers (1964) and Harbison (1973). Time-series information may be found in the UNESCO *Statistical Yearbooks*.

7. In addition, other indicators, not treated here, include number of teachers, teacher-student ratios, dropout rates, and breakdowns of enrollments by age.

8. An additional difficulty is that socioeconomic-status data probably cannot be gotten reliably from school data but would require a supplementary household survey.

9. The evidence through the early 1970s is synthesized by Psacharopoulos (1973).

10. I am uncertain about the reliability of the Philippines data since it is inconceivable that the number illiterate could have increased from three to four million in just two years (1958–1960).

References

Anderson, C. Arnold, and Bowman, Mary Jean. *Education and Economic Development*. Chicago: Aldine, 1966.

Fields, Gary S. "Private and Social Returns to Education in Labour Surplus Economies." *Eastern Africa Economic Review*, June 1972, pp. 41–62.

———. "Higher Education and Income Distribution in a Less Developed Country." *Oxford Economic Papers*, July 1975, pp. 245–259.

———. *Poverty, Inequality, and Development*. Cambridge and New York: Cambridge University Press, 1980.

———. "Education and Income Distribution in Developing Countries: A Review of the Literature." In *Education and Income*, Working Paper No. 402. Washington, D.C.: World Bank, July 1980.

Hansen, W. Lee, and Weisbrod, Burton. *Benefits, Costs, and Finance of Public Higher Education.* Chicago: Markham Publishing Company, 1970.

Harbison, Frederick H. *Human Resources as the Wealth of Nations.* New York: Oxford University Press, 1973.

Harbison, Frederick H., and Myers, Charles A. *Education, Manpower and Economic Growth: Strategies of Human Resource Development.* New York: McGraw-Hill, 1964.

Jallade, J.P. "Public Expenditures on Education and Income Distribution in Colombia," Occasional Paper No. 18. Washington, D.C.: World Bank, 1974.

———. "Basic Education and Income Inequality in Brazil: The Long Term View," Working Paper No. 268. Washington, D.C.: World Bank, June 1977.

Psacharopoulos, George. *Returns to Education.* San Francisco: Jossey-Bass, 1973.

———. "Inequalities in Education and Employment: A Review of Key Issues with Emphasis on LDC's," Working Document No. IIEP.S49/8A. Paris: International Institute for Educational Planning, October 1978.

Turnham, David. *The Employment Problem in Less Developed Countries: A Review of Evidence.* Paris: Organization for Economic Cooperation and Development, 1971.

**Part II
Issues in the Analysis of
Planning and Development**

4

The Multinational Corporation and Educational Relevance in Developing Countries

Lascelles Anderson

Education provision has come to be evaluated in recent years along two efficiency dimensions: internal and external. While internal refers to the extent to which the system minimizes cost to meet a specified output objective, in the traditional economic sense, external has applied to the degree to which the education establishment, broadly conceived, succeeds in preparing people for the world of work. It, properly, also connotes the degree of interface of training needs and training supplied both in an out of school, since formal schooling alone is insufficient for the optimal provision of the requisite skills in the scale and time frames thrown up by continually changing technologies. This second sense of efficiency is therefore a much more-diffuse issue and much less amenable to the formal application of microeconomic theoretical insights on efficient resource allocation. I shall use the term *educational relevance* to refer to what has up to now been regarded as external efficiency.

It is reasonable to expect that, in an economy in which the rate and kinds of change of technology depend only, or to a large extent, on the domestic economy itself, the linkage between the educational system and the economy can be presumed to be achieved with minimal effort, all other factors remaining constant. However, when the rate of technological change becomes imposed, as, for example, by the sudden introduction of techniques of production that bear little resemblance to the emerging needs of the mass economy or the trend of technological change consistent with some notion of self-upgrading technology, strains can be expected to be felt in the relation between the educational system and the economy, and educational relevance is somewhat undermined. How the educational systems and policy in the receiving economies adjust and respond to these strains has never been examined fully. It is believed that the adjustment processes are complex and difficult, and when, as is the case, the multinational corporation is the means for such transfers of technology, these difficulties could constitute serious constraints on the articulation and execution of educational-cum-manpower policy in the typically less-developed country.

It is somewhat puzzling, therefore, that despite the importance of the growing transnational character of commerce and industry, studies of the environment within which schooling takes place—hence, in which the educational processes are known to act and to be acted upon—continue to be couched in mostly national terms. In this sense, the appropriate opportunity set facing education planners is somewhat improperly specified given the enlargement of the set of constraints occasioned by the pervasiveness of external linkages. Thus, while it is natural for a first perspective on the domain of policy affecting educational relevance in developing countries to be defined and evaluated in purely national terms and within national boundaries, it appears crucial that only with the inclusion of an international focus will the broad forces that shape national parameters come more fully into view and a more realistic appraisal of educational external efficiency in LDC be achieved.

One quite legitimate system level of analysis, therefore, is expressible in terms of purely national parameters; another, perhaps more-powerful, system level at which to conceptualize the interconnection between education and the economy is the level that is now increasingly being called the "world system." This development of the post–World War II period identifies a complex that takes account of the increasing internationalization of production processes. Peculiar to it is a growing division of labor along geographical lines, with the leading edges of technological advance concentrated in a few countries and with production increasingly carried on in areas often far removed from the locations of the central-control functions of the corporation. The multinational corporation becomes the major new factor in this structural transformation (Bornschier 1980) and constitutes a new and decisive independent variable, generating a broad range of strains and dislocations within host developing countries (Biersteker 1978, 1980; Frank 1980). That such a perspective argues for a broader approach in viewing the usual problems of development is already fairly well documented (Meyer and Hannon 1979; Bornschier 1980; Fröbel 1978).

What is not so well understood, however, because of the almost total absence of systematic investigation, is the impact of this recent development on the educational and training systems and outcomes in developing countries. Existing surveys of the subject, which are very few anyway, have found the literature to be both sparse and lacking a consistent theoretical base (Cartapanis, Experton, and Fuguet, 1977). This chapter accordingly represents a beginning attempt at an understanding and articulation of some of the critical dimensions of such multinational-corporation-induced effects on LDC education systems and policy by searching for an appropriate framework within which to assess the issues normally discussed in the literature.

The proper subject matter of this chapter is enormously wide. For example, it would be important to assess the impact of the multinational corporation broadly on the social processes of host countries, hence in areas both within and outside of production. However, this ambitious objective would extend the scope of the chapter well beyond acceptable lengths. I believe that it is possible to undertake a much less-ambitious task and yet to provide a meaningful perspective from which to view the many and varied issues that are identified in the interface of the two sets of interest—namely, multinational corporations and LDC educational relevance.

The chapter addresses two basic questions: (1) Does multinational-corporation penetration in LDCs have any tendency to weaken possibilities for appropriate factor utilization, especially under condition of excess labor, thereby reducing educational relevance? (2) Does the multinational corporation affect the technology-generating institutions like education and research and development (R&D) and, by implication, technology policy by the way technology is transferred, and if so, how? What are the implications to flow from these? Accordingly, the ensuing argument is organized in the following three areas: (1) a review of the theoretical arguments posed for understanding the growth of the multinational corporation in the post–World War II period as a way of deriving behavioral postulates, (2) technical choice in developing countries in the context of this internalization of capital, and (3) technology transfer and its potential effects on education and training outcomes in developing countries. As a preliminary exercise, a brief review of patterns of multinational-corporation expansion establishes the numerical dimensions of the setting.

Patterns of Multinational-Corporation Expansion

The enormous growth of the net flow of financial resources from the developed countries to the developing countries from 1960 to 1978 can be clearly observed from table 4–1. Private flows to the developing countries from the industrial countries, which averaged under $3.2 billion between 1960 and 1965, doubled the latter part of the 1960s and reached an estimated $32.8 billion by 1978. Of that total, private direct investment, which averaged $1.79 billion in the early 1960s, reached $9.47 billion by 1978. Rates of growth were 13.8 and 9.7 percent respectively. Multinational corporations account for the major portion of these private-direct-investment flows, understood to mean flows of equity and loan capital between parent company and overseas affiliate. If it is further

Table 4–1
Net Private Flow of Financial Resources to LDCs from Industrial Countries, 1960–1978

Flow	1960–1965 (average)	1966–1977 (average)	1972	1973	1974	1975	1976	1977	1978
Private flows[a]	3.19	6.02	8.33	9.46	7.33	22.15	20.87	29.99	32.82
Direct investment	1.79	2.90	4.23	4.72	1.12	10.49	7.82	8.79	9.47
Other flows[b]	5.87	7.44	11.12	13.20	14.72	17.95	18.39	19.50	23.81
Total net flows	9.06	13.46	19.45	22.66	22.05	40.10	39.26	49.49	56.63

Source: Isaiah Frank, *Foreign Enterprise in Developing Countries.* (Baltimore: Johns Hopkins University Press, 1980), p. 10.

[a]Includes direct investment, bilateral portfolio flows, multilateral portfolio flows, and export credits.
[b]Includes development assistance and official flows and grants by private voluntary agencies.

understood that these figures for direct investment usually understate the true measures of those flows due to increasing volume of service flows that move between parent and affiliate, the published data on these flows represent something of a lower limit to the truer magnitudes of all flows of private direct investment.

While international capital flows in substantial volume are not a new phenomenon, what distinguishes the post-1945 pattern from the one that characterized movements of international capital in the late-nineteenth and early-twentieth centuries is the substantially increased scope of ownership and control in the modern period. Earlier capital flows were largely portfolio investments, reflecting the existence of interest-rate differentials between countries. In the modern period, these flows represent the growth of control through the ownership of enterprises for the purpose of production. In this sense, there is a marked qualitative difference between the two periods in respect of this aspect of the internationalization of capital (Södersten 1970).

The fundamental shifts in the nature of direct foreign investment just referred to represent merely one aspect, however, of a broader set of qualitative changes that have been and are taking place. If these flows are observed sectorially, important new dimensions of these broad structural changes also are revealed. For example, in the twenty years beginning about the middle 1950s, U.S. direct investments have shifted from a preponderance in the extractive sector to near parity as between extractive and manufacturing, while between 1971 and 1978, similar shifts can be observed for direct investment from Japan and Germany, two other important sources of direct-investment flows (Vaupel and Curhan 1974; Reuber 1973; Frank 1980). While the data on total stocks and flows are extremely difficult to reconcile over time and between sectors, it seems clear that direct foreign investment in extractive industries is declining while that in manufacturing and services continues to increase substantially. Tables 4–2 and 4–3 give some indication of the sectorial distribution of direct foreign investment from industrial countries in developing countries. What the figures reveal is that, although direct foreign investment in petroleum and mining is still fairly large, flows into manufacturing and services account for nearly 60 percent of direct-foreign-investment flows during the 1965–1972 period. Major target areas for these flows are Latin America, where U.S. direct foreign investment predominates, and Asia, which represents the predominant presence of Japan. Regionally, major shifts have occurred in petroleum, where flows of direct foreign investment have moved from Latin America to Africa. While the percentage of stock of mining investment was just over 10 percent in 1970, flows into mining were under 8 percent during the period 1965–1972. Manufacturing and services are clearly the major benefi-

Table 4–2

Sectional Distribution of Flows of Foreign Direct Investment in LDCs, 1965–1972

Sector	Latin America	Europe	Africa	Mideast	Asia	Total
Petroleum	4.7	1	12.5	8	7.1	33.3
Mining	2.6	0.2	2.4	—	2.4	7.6
Manufacturing	20.2	6.2	3.5	0.7	6.7	37.3
Services	10.2	3.4	3.3	0.7	4.2	21.8
Total	37.7	10.8	21.7	9.4	20.4	100

Source: Isaiah, Frank, *Foreign Enterprise in Developing Countries* (Baltimore: Johns Hopkins University Press, 1980), p. 20.

Table 4–3

Sectional and Regional Distribution of Stock of Foreign Direct Investment in LDCs, 1970

(percent)

Sector	Latin America	Europe	Africa	Mideast	Asia	Total in Sector
Petroleum	24.2	16	43.4	91.4	23.2	33.3
Mining	10.6	4	18.4	—	7.1	10.3
Manufacturing	37.9	60	17.1	5.7	32.1	31.5
Service	27.3	20	21.1	2.9	37.5	24.9
Total Regional Distribution	50.8	6.4	19.5	9	14.4	100.1

Source: United Nations. *Transnational Corporations in World Development: A Reexamination. New York: 1978.*

Note: Services include shipping, trade, banking, tourism, and consultancy and investment in agribusiness.

ciaries in the many and varied shifts that have been taking place. This result is particularly significant and is shown to have decisive implications for many of the issues to be raised later on.

Having surveyed in summary fashion trends in the recent history of multinational-corporation penetration of LDCs, it remains for me to connect that with the central concerns of the chapter. My fundamental hypothesis about the relation governing the interface of the multinational firm and education is that such a relation can most effectively be found by assessing the long-run behavior of the firm through an appraisal of the reason for the internationalization of production. This in turn should lead to implications of such desiderata for the evaluation of firms' behavior in a variety of areas and, hence, for a better assessment of policy implications of the multinational-corporation/LDC education linkage. The next section is devoted to a consideration of this issue.

Theoretical Arguments on the Multinational Corporation

If multinational corporations are perceived to represent the existence of competitive advantage, then their growth must necessarily be associated with the existence of market imperfections, since no advantage would normally attach to individual firms in perfect competition. These advantages can be either location specific or ownership specific (Buckley and Casson 1976). Among the more-obvious location-specific factors are those of relative costs of production, market characteristics such as host-country size, and growth of relevant markets; degree of competition; and trade barriers, which are erected, for example, to effect a policy of import substitution as has been the case in many developing countries (Hood and Young 1979). Ownership advantages refer to factors the firm may exploit to its advantage and over which it has virtually complete control. These would normally include technological superiority, managerial capacity, and financial flexibility, and they tend to give rise to market imperfections of one kind or another. Thus, market imperfections will develop, and be reflected, in product differentiation, technological advances protected by patents and other use restrictions, special skill advantages possessed by management, and access to relevant capital markets. In recent years a proliferation of arguments has developed, to explain the growth of direct foreign investment and some of the subtle changes taking place among the investment flows and among regions. We now examine these specific theories.

Product-Cycle Theories

One of the earliest full-blown theories propounded to explain the growth of direct foreign investment is the product-cycle theory of Vernon (1966). Strikingly similar to that developed by Hirsch (1967), the product-cycle theory argues that the production life of a product consists of three stages: (1) the new-product stage, (2) the maturing-product stage, (3) the standardization stage. Low price elasticity of demand is characteristic of the first period due to monopoly advantages accruing to the innovating firm. In this stage, the main force supporting demand is increasing per capita incomes. On the supply side, labor shortage is the key innovating factor. Due to the need, in this innovating stage, for close cooperation between the various functions of production, research, and marketing, production takes place in close proximity to the market. The product in this stage is also not yet highly differentiated.

The second stage, the maturing product, is the period at which less-efficient producers fall by the wayside and the product becomes more standardized. Foreign markets now enter the picture, but mainly as export target areas. Exports continue as long as the marginal cost of production, together with marginal transport costs, are less than the average cost of production in the foreign market.

The final stage, the standardized product stage, is that in which incomes abroad plus low production costs move in favor of foreign investment. There is much less need for product innovation, and price competition emerges as a major consideration. Clearly at this stage, production is moved to locations of low labor cost, hence to the developing countries where labor, needed for standardized and simple production processes typically is in great supply.

Vernon has substantially modified this position on the product-cycle theory in recent years (1971; 1979), where the emphasis has shifted to oligopolistic behavior on the part of firms. Three phases again characterize the product cycle, but now these are identified with (1) innovation-based oligopoly, in which innovations need not be only labor saving but land and material saving; (2) mature oligopoly, in which the aggressive moves by a firm in any particular market are responded to by rivals in an attempt at generating a kind of oligopolistic equilibrium, at least in market shares; and (3) senescent oligopoly, in which producers locate according to geographical cost differentials and scale economies, which were important entry barriers in the earlier stages but which have ceased to be effective as such.

The Vernon theory, at least the earlier version, is highly successful in predicting the earlier phases of the growth of direct foreign investment. Whether it explains the recent trends as well is questionable. In this regard, the more-fundamental aspect of multinational-firm behavior that has to be explained is simultaneous worldwide-production strategy as opposed to time-phased shifts from home production to exports and then to foreign production. In the more-recent version of the product-cycle theory, the joining of locational and ownership advantages is brought much more to the center and constitutes the decisive factor in the choice between exports and foreign production. Thus, where locational advantages indicate that foreign production would be more appropriate, that becomes the clear choice. If, however, domestic-production costs are sufficiently lower and home markets sufficiently robust, firms may most likely choose to produce at home and then export.

In this latter form, the product-cycle theory can be shown to have strong similarity to an earlier theory propounded by Hymer (1960), but it does not yet provide us with a sufficiently broad framework within which to assess firm actions in the critical areas of our concern—namely, labor training and other education-related impacts.

Monopolistic-Advantage Theory

The truly seminal work on the theoretical underpinnings of the multi-national corporation and the growth of direct foreign investment was done by Stephen Hymer (1960). The fundamental question Hymer addressed was why it was that expatriate firms could successfully compete with local firms in the markets of the host country. For Hymer, local firms expand in order to exploit ownership advantages such as monopoly position. Expansion is the preferred mode of servicing foreign markets since the market in knowledge is highly imperfect and since the firm can better appropriate the rent accruing to it by its specific advantages by producing abroad as well as at home.

This theory, which is also usually associated with the work of Kindleberger, places the emphasis squarely on ownership advantages in conjunction with market imperfections and opens the way for the interesting generalizations of this position that were to come later. Thus Johnson (1970) extended the notion of ownership advantage to those goods that best can be exploited costlessly by subsidiaries, advantages having the characteristics of public goods within the firm, and among which is the public good, skill. Other contributions to the broad-ownership-advantage thesis include those of Caves (1971), who bases his position on the ability of the firm to differentiate products and to reap advantages from earlier product development, and Hirsch (1974), whose thesis rests on the advantages generated by past R&D expenditures.[1]

Internalization Theory

The major integrative advance in the theory of the multinational firm came with the work of Buckley and Casson (1976). Building on the emerging positions just identified—namely, market imperfections and ownership advantage—they managed to erect a theory, the analytic foundations of which date back to the seminal work of Coase (1937) on the theory of the origin of the firm. The basic premise of market imperfection, now extended to include not only markets in final products but significantly also markets in intermediate products, is used to suggest that when a firm enjoys advantages over its competition, in the face of these market imperfections, it will internalize the exploitation of these advantages rather than externalize them, as would be the case with licensing, management contracting, or the like.

It is sufficient to summarize the Buckley and Casson internalization theory. Returning to the argument of Coase (1937) on the reasons for the development of the firm, the Buckley and Casson theory is based on the notion that, under a well-known set of conditions, markets are the most efficient means of coordinating a set of interdependent activities. An important implication of this argument is that where external markets are perceived to be inefficient for whatever reason, there will be attempts to internalize these markets. This argument holds, with even more force, when markets are totally nonexistent. However, internalization involves costs as well as generates benefits. The optimal level of internalization is defined at that point at which the costs and benefits of internalization are equalized at the margin.

Market imperfections that induce internalization include the existence of long time lags in the face of th : absence of appropriate futures markets, the impossibility of discriminatory pricing to maximize benefits of monopoly position in external markets, unstable bargaining positions resulting from concentration of power, inequality of information as between buyer and seller concerning a product, and market imperfections generated by governments' actions. Where these characteristics are strong, inducements to internalize are in turn strong. For our purposes, the relevant intermediate products that exhibit these characteristics include highly skilled labor, specialized knowledge in the form of information produced by costly R&D, and high-level managerial technology. Because these intermediate products have the characteristics of public goods within the firm, the optimal method of exploiting them will be through vertical integration through the multinational enterprise. It is an important implication, therefore, that in an age of highly vertically integrated firms and of very costly internally generated knowledge and skills, by training or otherwise, research- and training-intensive industries will tend to be organized multinationally. Thus, the essential characteristics of the multinational firm are to be found not so much in the concept of multinationality but rather in the logically prior concept of internalization, and the factors that lead to its occurrence.

In summary, the multinational corporation will be concerned to internalize operations due to the imperfections in the market for knowledge. A major aspect of this new knowledge creation is a result of R&D and is embodied in the technical and high-level managerial skills that result from investment in knowledge creation and organization style in large research-intensive firms. Firms will normally finance such investments themselves, but since the new knowledge is embodied either in products or skills, firms will be unable to be assured of the full appropriation of the benefits of such investments unless workers do not quit or join other firms (Magee 1977). Given the potential loss of competitive advantage to indigenous or nonindigenous local-rival firms, multinational firms may be unwilling to invest too heavily in either the training of nonproprietaryskilled workers or managerial training beyond what is perceived to be minimally necessary.

Additionally, since R&D is a critical function in the process of knowledge creation, these firms will not be encouraged to open up R&D to local workers and trainable personnel, leaving whatever is required to be generated almost exclusively internally. Similarly high-level skills can be expected to be normally supplied from the firms' internal-labor market, given the condition of worldwide sourcing in intermediate products characteristic of their operation. What is the evidence on this and what might be the implications to flow from it for LDCs?

All the available evidence points to the absence of much basis for R&D's being undertaken by multinational corporations in the host country. A study by Creamer (1976) documents the negligible share of R&D from U.S. overseas affiliates. He estimates that 1.8 percent of total U.S. overseas R&D was found in the LDCs, and while this amount had grown to 3.3 percent by 1972, it was still quite small. Wionczek (1976) found that R&D done in Latin America is designed not so much to change products to fit tastes but, on the contrary, to change tastes to fit with preexisting products.

Other studies confirm this tendency toward R&D centralization, a condition that is fully consistent with the internalization thesis advanced earlier. Thus, Rubinstein (1962) finds that multinational corporations tend to adopt either the centralized approach or a more-decentralized one in which the basic research is still done at the center but in which applied research is done in departmental laboratories. Baranson (1973) notes that multinationals do not find compelling reasons for changing their R&D activities to suit the needs of LDCs, and Aroaz (1980), studying the Mexican situation in science and technology, also finds very weak links between R&D efforts and the system of higher learning, and the contribution of the former to the latter is considered quite small.

In his recent study of multinational firms in developing countries, Frank (1980) confirms that they do not normally have R&D facilities in LDCs, though some adaptation and quality control work is done locally. Reasons for this include unavailability of personnel, unfavorable scale economies, and product-standardization requirements that would rule out the necessity or even the wisdom of duplicate facilities for conducting R&D. Inadequacy of internal market size also appears to be an important inhibiting factor.

Lack of R&D activity as well as inadequate levels of it will be reflected in tenuous connections between the major technology-generating institutions in the society (including most important, tertiary education) and the commercial and industrial sectors. Increasing irrelevance of higher education to the emerging and leading edges of technological advance is in these circumstances are extremely likely prospect. Additionally, if the ability and possibility to do R&D is in any way related to the development of an indigenous technical and problem-solving capability, then multinational tendencies just identified would seem to imply a truncation of much critical development capacity in LDCs. Two results follow: first, that whatever R&D does develop would likely link the LDC in a new dependent relationship with the originators of available technical know-how; and second, there is a strong possibility that technologies employed in LDCs will tend, in a sense, to be inappropriate if the technology-generating institutions—namely, education and R&D—are only marginally connected to the needs of the broad mass of the population (Reedy 1979).

Technical Choice by Multinational Firms and the Employment Problem

Given that the fundamental characteristic governing the internationalization of production considered from the microeconomic position of the firm is the drive toward internalization in resource utilization, the multinational firm's behavior in respect of technical choice and factor proportions should also be understandable within that context. Consequently strong conclusions on the comparative behavior of multinational corporations and indigenous firms may be expected only within the analytic framework identified with the internalization thesis. This issue is important due to the high and rising levels of unemployment characteristic of many LDCs in the face of the equally rapid growth in the rate of industrialization measured through the growth of direct foreign investment.

This brings to the fore the famous choice-of-techniques question that has dominated a rather large part of the development literature in recent years. Curiously enough, however, the early literature—that associated with Buchanan (1945), Polak (1943), Kahn (1951), Chenery (1953), and Galenson and Leibenstein (1955)—cannot be shown to be particularly relevant to the practical concerns of developing countries or to the issues that are in burning need of resolution. Bagchi (1978) provides an excellent review of that literature, including an examination of the work of Dobb (1955, 1956, 1960) and Sen (1957, 1968), and has drawn sharp attention to what he calls the misplaced problematic in that part of the literature.

Essentially, appropriate technical choices in the context of development spring from a complex variety of sources and conditions and are not necessarily satisfied by purely engineering or technical specifications relating to golden ages or other concepts of balanced growth. Much of the early discussion was concerned with choices between growth and full employment, saw the issue of technical choice as almost solely a choice between labor and capital, and paid scant attention to the social forces and institutional frameworks within which such choices are actually made. For example, to assume an objective of growth, implying the condition of surplus maximization purely at the technical level, presumes that all the surplus generated would be invested. This need not be the case, however, since such surplus could go instead toward conspicuous consumption of a relatively narrow and favored section of the population. Additionally, the part that capital intensity plays in the mechanism of social control is not even mentioned, but such a potentiality surely exists, and it has far-reaching long-term implications for the nature of the emerging society, let alone the implied structure and function of schooling.

Whether multinational corporations choose highly capital-intensive techniques uniformly over other technical choices is clearly an empirical question, but given the argument for internalization, it is highly likely that, in fact, strong incentives do exist for such a tendency. At any rate, the factors that would lead to any particular pattern of technical choices are obviously far removed from the tidy theoretical models associated with that early literature on choice of techniques, and they must be evaluated in that broader context of relevant forces.

High R&D content of the firm's output is a striking feature of the typical multinational firm (Buckley and Casson 1976). Additionally, the firm is usually vertically integrated, practices worldwide sourcing, internalizes markets for products for which external markets do not exist or cannot be expected to allow for the full appropriation of monopoly rents, is associated with highly differentiated products, and tends to be high-level-manpower and skill intensive in its various production-process stages. The firm is also knowledge intensive and will want to protect the investments that produce that product. The multinational firm is also large and reflects ownership characteristics of the home-country economic environments. One home-country characteristic that may be expected to be pervasive is the high degree of capital intensity associated with goods and services appropriate to high-income areas. If the multinational firm produces goods, the argument goes, with the technology it knows best, then there will likely be a tendency to narrow substitution possibilities in the context of developing countries for these multinational firms. The empirical question, then, is to determine whether in fact technical fixity is observed in the operations of these firms and in what direction such fixity is biased.

**Empirical Studies of Capital Intensity of Multinational
Firms**

Numerous studies have been conducted to assess the truth of the proposition relating the multinational firm operating in developing countries
with high capital intensity and usually inappropriate technology.[2] The
results tend in general to be inconclusive. For example, take the proposition that the technical choice of the multinational firm is a function
of its size and other structural features such as technologically determined
narrow range for available technologies. One way to examine that proposition would be to assess the degree of factor substitution that is evi-
denced by multinational firms in a wide variety of industries.

Recall that the elasticity of substitution is the feature of the production
function to be observed in this case, and then observe that most of the
studies available do not support the argument for fixed technological
choices. Daniels's (1969) study of seventeen two-digit industries in developing countries found elasticities ranging from 0.4 to 1. Bruton (1972)
observed two-digit industries in Mexico, as well as in twenty-two other
developing countries, and found substitution elasticities ranging from 0.6
to 1 and 0.5 to 1.2 respectively. In 1973, Witte (1973) studied Mexico
and Peru and found similar results. Tyler (1974) studied twenty-two
industries in Brazil and found elasticities of substitution of from 0.44 to
2.67, while Pack (1976), using firm-level data in six industry groups
observed elasticities of 0.24 to 3.7. Gershenberg and Ryan (1978), looking at Uganda data, found elasticities on multinationals of 0.9942 and,
for indigenous firms, 0.3899. The evidence does seem to support the
conclusion of an appreciable range of substitution possibilities and responsiveness to relative prices by multinational firms. The rather complete
survey of this issue by White (1979) confirms this broad conclusion.

However, capital intensity and technological fixity may not be observed very well at the level of the industry if the claim is sustained that
many different products make up an industry and that it is really choice
of product and the variability among them that determine variability of
technical choice (Stewart 1977; Kaplinsky 1977). Hence, demand patterns
and income distribution are as important as independent variables in any
assessment of variability of technical choice. Thus, while these studies
point to sensitivity on the part of multinational firms to relative prices
of capital and labor, a finer identification of products might well serve
to reduce the perceived measures of the elasticity of substitution. Multinational firms might then be observed in fact to behave differently in
terms of capital intensity from indigenous firms, given more-powerful
tests used to discriminate between them. Additionally, multinational firms

may be expected to be more highly concentrated in high capital-intensive products and industries than indigenous firms.

This suggests is that, in the face of unlimited labor supplies, technologies employed by multinational firms may economize on labor and therefore may not succeed in reducing high levels of unemployment. Multinational-corporation penetration of LDCs is likely to be associated with highly inappropriate factor intensities, and this implies intensification of conditions of structural unemployment (Bornschier 1980).

Local educational institutions and planning are successful in these circumstances to the extent that they exhibit a high degree of flexibility and are capable of responding to the signals from the labor market with reasonable speed. However, in the face of rapidly changing skill requirements and an increasing detail in skill types, they will surely be hard pressed to match demand with the output of such skills. Major transformations in educational policy will be necessary to confront successfully this combination of circumstances. LDC educational authorities have been characteristically slow in shaping up to these demands for revamping curriculum content in the face of these pervasive factors that are changing the technological profile of their respective countries. The patterns of educational reform that can be pointed to do not support much optimism. To expect much improvement in the external efficiency of a schooling in this context is to overlook the pervasive reasons for the underutilization of labor resulting from the technological choices made in the industrial branches, by the multinational corporation, themselves such an important and still growing part of the industrial profile of developing countries.

The world-system model facilitates identification of yet another dimension of the cluster of problems associated with multinational-corporation penetration. LDCs desirous of competing in such a system (on the assumption that barriers do not exist to frustrate such an eventuality) must adopt the front-line technology in use. Such an eventuality will force a reordering of priority levels between full employment as opposed to industrial growth, reduce production-technology variability as perceived by the multinational firm, result in policy conflicts between employment and export goals, and will likely by implication slant educational policy away from maintaining optimal relevance of schooling to the objective of internal social reconstruction.

Technology Behavior of the Multinational Corporation

The preceding discussion has served to identify the factors that tend to foster a bias in favor of capital intensity for multinational firms. It has also been suggested, however, that the empirical work relating to this question might not have constituted powerful enough tests to effectively discriminate between multinational and other firms in the choice of factor intensity in developing countries. This leaves open the possibility that, in fact, technical choices are more limited than they appear, and decidedly so in the direction of capital intensity with its negative implications for large-scale labor absorption and an implied upper limit on educational relevance.

This problem represents only one aspect of wider set of conditions leading to marginalization in LDC education and training, to be joined by an equally powerful tendency on the part of multinational firms in the area of technology transfer to limit the accessibility of the flow of the information contained in the transferred technology to an extent determined by its own considerations for privacy and the garnering of monopoly rents. Again, the precise level will depend on the equating of marginal gains and costs of opening up R&D and technology to host-country workers. The evidence seems to suggest, however, that the costs of such a free flow of information are perceived to be much greater than the benefits at the margin (Frank 1980). In this final section, I pose some questions to flow from these and identify additional education-policy implications that most likely will follow.

Technology Transfer

Technology transfer is an enormously complex subject, spanning questions of statistical evaluation, forms of technology transfer, political postures regarding forms of transfer, the effect of transfers on receiving and giving economies, and the social implications of technology transfer. For our purposes, the central issue is none of these, but rather a twofold concern: (1) How does the multinational corporation transfer technology to LDCs, and implicitly, what options does the typical LDC have in the importation of advanced technology; and (2) what implications do these have for education and training functions within the LDC itself?

If we define technology as being embodied not only in plants but also in designs and capacities, technology transfer can be accomplished in a variety of ways. Girvan (1979) categorizes these as falling into three groups: (1) direct foreign investment, licensing for production, or supply of management-related technology under contract; (2) transfers consummated through technical assistance, consultancy, or turnkey plants; and (3) transfers through training at home or abroad and through individual acquisition of knowledge. Other classifications are available, but the important fact is the dominance of the multinational corporation, and in some cases, multilateral-aid agencies, in the transfer process. One important question that follows from this raises further questions about the restrictions that multinational corporations place on the patterns of technical development in the typical LDC, under such conditions of dominance.

Following Evenson and Binswanger (1978), technology transfer can be profitably conceived of in two dimensions—namely, in three phases involving three options. The three phases coincide with those referred to previously—namely, material transfer, design transfer (or transfer in the form of blueprints and so on), and capacity transfer, or transfer through the medium of scientific know-how. The receiving country has three options—namely, direct transfer, adaptive research, or comprehensive research. The critical question then relates to the factors that predispose to any specific phase-option combination.

Choices actually made reflect the relative bargaining strengths of both parties in negotiation. In this context, the evidence does not support the assertion of much strength on the part of the typical LDC, although some of that might be changing. For example, Biersteker (1980) has shown that, although Nigeria has managed to erect some rather stringent policies aimed at indigenization, multinational corporations have been successful in largely neutralizing the main thrusts of such policies. Developing countries would in all likelihood place greater emphasis on both adaptive and comprehensive research among the transfer options as a way of guaranteeing appropriate technologies. Such a choice is clear also as a way of fostering local technical capability in order to overcome growing technological dependence. Unbundling technology packages as a way out of this dilemma is not likely to occur either, given the normative and historical conditions precipitating internalization of production. It would run counter to multinational-corporation objectives and so cannot ordinarily be realistically hoped for, given the relative strength of the typical LDC in the bargaining process, especially regarding technology transfer in manufacturing sectors and industries. The case of Mexico, as shown by Sercovich (1980), is in every sense similar to that of Nigeria.

It is quite understandable, therefore, that the market for transfer of technology exhibits a strikingly uneven structure. Naur (1980) has shown that the old colonial patterns have reappeared in the structure of technology-transfer flows as erstwhile colonial relationships can readily be reconstructed from current paths of technology transfer, in general. A kind of asymmetry is oberved where technology trade among technology producers represents a kind of division of labor, whereas for the receivers of technology a new kind of dependency has emerged. As Naur so cogently points out, the typical receiver of technology among the LDCs "has changed in accordance with the requirements of international capital. The blacksmith has disappeared and so has autonomy" (1980, p. 255).

These results are strikingly consistent with the internalization postulate stated earlier and therefore suggest the working of quite deep-seated forces shaping the character of the relationship between the transmitters and the importers of technology. It is quite unlikely that the typical LDC's technological capability will be strongly affected in the positive direction if training possibilities are not provided by opportunities for local personnel to adapt and to modify technology to local purposes. Restrictions on the use and deployment of technology have implications for the secular growth of broad technical capability by current borrowers of technology and the existence of these argues for a more-aggressive and self-conscious concern by LDC authorities for insuring the existence of appropriate training possibilities in the face of rapid rates of technology transfer. Failing this, it is likely that education and training institutions in LDCs will become increasingly marginalized as imported technologies supercede local technologies and succeed in severing links that would normally exist between local needs, R&D, and the commercialization of the results of that R&D.

These results can be expected to be particularly pernicious to the extent that these imported technologies reflect the consumption patterns of small high-income groups in the population.

Technical Change and Institutional Change

Technical change affects the demand for, and supply of, institutional change, and it would be fortunate indeed if the patterns of technical change introduced by the multinational corporation would lead to appropriate institutional changes, not the least of which is a series of changes in the education and training sectors to more positively affect levels of external educational efficiency. A major concern of this chapter, however, is that the contrary is more likely to be the case, largely due to the way multinational firms function given the internalization thesis. This is tantamount to a kind of built-in institutional inertia that will significantly affect the external efficiency of schooling in the face of rapid technological changes. It should also be observed that this is so even without consideration of social factors such as, for example, the difficulty of upsetting powerful class interests that see the preservation of earlier schooling arrangements and possibilities as functional to their class-position preservation. Thus, despite the microeconomic argument that, given the demand for institutional change (a function of the new income streams generated by technical change), shifts to the right of the supply of institutional change will reflect advances in knowledge in the sciences and the law (Ruttan 1978), it is likely that the necessary responses in the field of education will not be forthcoming in the absence of strong public policy that recognizes the broad societal need for such responses. Increase in the price of labor, itself a function of technical change, could very well lead to increased capital intensity, whereas a more-appropriate long-term response would be a change in the content and quality of schooling to make schooling outputs more compatible with demands coming from industry.

Rate of change of technology is only one aspect of technical change to be dealt with. It is equally important to be concerned with the kind of technology transferred. Much has been written about the concept of appropriate technology, and there is very little consensus on its intrinsic meaning. However, one can invoke some low-level meaning that would allow convergence of views. Assuming that technology is inappropriate where such technology is inconsistent with factor availabilities and with long-term developmental objectives (not simply growth), then the foregoing argument suggests that much of today's technology imports must be to some extent inappropriate and lopsided.[3] Such is likely to lead to the adoption of equally lopsided and inappropriate education either in funding or in content. A central fact of modern schooling is its pervasive provision by the state. Under such conditions it is likely that educational reform, whenever it comes, will be consistent with, and pointed in the direction of, satisfying the social demand of the powerful class interests of international capital and therefore will address the concerns only of a small but articulate and powerful local-interest group.

Conclusion

An inference of the need for withdrawal by multinational corporations from LDCs would be quite wide of the mark of the real thrust of this chapter. The objective here is really to draw attention to the normal tendencies of multinational corporations in two areas—factor utilization and technology transfer—and the implied effect on educational external efficiency, or what I refer to as relevance. If in fact multinational-corporation activity tends to marginalize education and training and R&D systems in LDCs, then host countries will likely experience increased difficulty in mapping out and accomplishing the creation of self-sustaining technological capacity appropriate to their factor intensity and growth needs. Therefore, the analysis really argues for a stronger formal linkage between technology-policy bodies seeking to encourage the widest diffusion of modern technology consistent with broad macrogoals and education and R&D planners and bodies, whose job it is to plan the supply of appropriate local skills consistent with those goals.

Notes

1. The treatment here is of necessity somewhat selective. Mention should be made at least of the contributions of Aliber (1970) on a currency-premium theory; Magee's (1977) work on an appropriability theory of direct foreign investment; and the work of Dunning (1977), where several theories are considered in an integrated fashion under the internalization model. See also the recent work of Rugman (1979), who utilizes portfolio theory to explain international diversification. Hood and Young (1979) provide a patient textbook treatment.

2. I have been helped greatly in this section by the excellent study of White (1979) and the more-recent survey by Balasubramanyam (1980).

3. See Findlay (1978) for a very interesting way of structuring the microeconomics of technology transfer and grounding the concept of appropriate technology.

References

Aliber, R.Z. "A Theory of Direct Foreign Investment." In *The International Corporation,* edited by C.P. Kindleberger. Cambridge, Mass.: MIT Press, 1970.

Aroaz, A. *The Present Situation of Science and Technology in the STPI Countries: Science and Technology for Development.* Ottowa, Canada: International Development Research Center, 1980.

Bagchi, A.K. "On the Political Economy of Technological Choice and Development." *Cambridge Journal of Economics* 2 (1978):215–232.

Balasubramanyam, V.N. "Multinational Corporation, Choice of Technology and Employment in Less Developed Countries." Paper presented at the Sixth World Congress International Economics Association, Mexico, 1980.

Baranson, J. "Transfer of Technology and the Developing World: Conflict and Accommodation." Paper presented at the International Conference on Asia and the Western Pacific, Canberra, Australia, April 1973.

Biersteker, T.J. *Distortion or Development Contending Perspectives on the Multinational Corporation.* Cambridge, Mass.: MIT Press, 1978.

Biersteker, T.J. "The Illusion of State Power: Transnational Corporations and the Neutralization of Host-Country Legislation," *Journal of Peace Research,* 17 (1980), pp. 217–221.

Bornschier, Volker. "Multinational Corporation, Economic Policy and National Development in World System." *International Social Science Journal* 32 (1980):158–172.

Bruton, Henry J. "The Elasticity of Substitution in Developing Countries." Research Memorandum X 1045, Center for Development
Economics, Williams College, 1972.

Buchanan, N.S. *International Investment and Domestic Welfare.* New
York, 1945.

Buckley, Peter J., and Casson, Mark, *The Future of the Multinational
Enterprise.* London: Macmillan, 1976.

Cartapanis, Andre; Experton, William; and Fuguet, Jean-Luc. "Transnational Corp and Educational Systems in Developing Countries: An
Annotated Critical Bibliography." Mimeographed. Paris: UNESCO,
1977.

Caves, R.E. "International Corporations: The Industrial Economics of
Foreign Investment." *Economica* 38 (1971):1–27.

Chenery, H.B. "The Application of Investment Criteria." *Quarterly
Journal of Economics,* February 1953).

Coase, R.H. "The Nature of the Firm." *Economica* 4 (1937).

Creamer, Daniel B. *Overseas Research and Development by United States
Multinationals, 1966–1975: Estimates of Expenditures and a Statistical Profile.* New York: The Conference Board, 1976.

Daniels, M. "Differences in Efficiency among Industries in Developing
Countries." *American Economic Review* 59 (March 1969).

Dobb, M. *On Economic Theory and Socialism.* London: Routledge &
Kegan Paul, 1955.

———. "Second Thoughts on Capital Intensity." *Review of Economic
Studies* 24 (1956).

———. *An Essay on Economic Growth and Planning.* London: Routledge & Kegan Paul, 1960.

Dunning, J.H. "Trade, Location of Economic Activity and the Multinational Enterprise: A Search for an Eclectic Approach." In *The
International Allocation of Economic Activity,* edited by Ohlin. London: Macmillan, 1977.

Evenson, Robert, and Binswanger, Hans P. "Technology Transfer and
Research Resource Allocation." In *Induced Innovation,* edited by
Hans P. Binswanger and Vern Ruttan. Baltimore: Johns Hopkins
University Press, 1978.

Findlay, Ronald. "Some Aspects of Technology Transfer and Direct
Foreign Investment." Papers and Proceedings, *American Economic
Review.* May 1978, pp. 275–279.

Frank, Isaiah. *Foreign Enterprise in Developing Countries.* Baltimore:
Johns Hopkins University Press, 1980.

Fröbel, Heinrich, Kreye. "Export-Oriented Industrialization of Underdeveloped Countries." *Monthly Review.* November 1978.

Fröbel, Folker, Heinrich: Jurgen, and Krey, Otto. *The New International*

Division of Labour. Cambridge: Cambridge University Press and Les Editions de la Maison des Sciences de L'Homme, 1980.

Galenson, W., and Leibenstein, H. "Investment Criteria, Productivity and Economic Development." *Quarterly Journal of Economics,* August 1955.

Gershenberg, I., and Ryan, T.C.L. "Does Parentage Matter? An Analysis of Transnational and Other Firms: An East Africa Case." *Journal of Developing Areas* 13 (October 1978):3–10.

Girvan, Norman. "The Approach to Technology Policy Studies." *Social and Economic Studies* 28 (March 1979):1–53.

Hirsch, S. *Location of Industry and International Competitiveness*. London: Oxford University Press, 1967.

Hirsch, S. "An International Trade and Investment Theory of the Firm," *Discussion Papers in International Investment and Business Studies.* University of Reading 17 (1974).

Hood, Neil, and Young, Stephen. *The Economics of Multinational Enterprise*. London and New York: Longman, 1979.

Hymer, S. "The International Operation of National Firms: A Study of Direct Investment." Ph.D. dissertation, Massachusetts Institute of Technology, 1960.

Johnson, H.G. "The Efficiency and Welfare Implications of the International Corporation." In *The International Corporation,* edited by C.P. Kindleberger. Cambridge, Mass.: MIT Press, 1970.

Kahn, A.E. "Investment Criteria in Development Programs." *Quarterly Journal of Economics,* February 1951.

Kaplinsky, R. *Appropriate Technology in Developing Countries: The Bread Industry and Kenya*. Nairobi, 1977.

Magee, S.P. "Information and the Multinational Corporation: An Appropriability Theory of Direct Foreign Investment." In *The New International Economic Order,* edited by J.N. Bhagwati. Cambridge, Mass.: MIT Press, 1977, pp. 317–340.

Meyer, John W., and Hannon, Michael. *National Development and the World System*. Chicago: University of Chicago Press, 1979.

Naur, Maja. "Transfer of Technology—A Structural Analysis." *Journal of Peace Research* 17 (1980): 247–259.

Pack, Howard. "Substitutions of Labor for Capital in Kenyan Manufacturing." *Economic Journal* 86 (March 1976).

Polak, J.J. "Balance of Payments Problems of Countries Reconstructing with the help of Foreign Loans." *Quarterly Journal of Economics,* February 1943.

Reedy, Amalya, Kumar. "Problems in the Generation of Appropriate

Technologies." In *Appropriate Technologies for Third World Development*, edited by Austin Robinson. New York: St. Martin's Press, 1979, pp. 173–189.

Reuber, G. *Private Foreign Investment in Development*. London: Oxford University Press, 1973.

Rubinstein, A.H. "Organization and Research and Development Decision-Making within the Decentralized Firm." In *The Rate and Direction of Inventive Activity*. Princeton, N.J.: Princeton University Press, 1962.

Rugman, Alan M. *International Diversification and the Multinational Enterprise*. Lexington, Mass.: Lexington Books, D.C. Heath and Company, 1979.

Ruttan, Vernon. "Induced Institutional Change." In *Induced Innovation*, edited by Hans P. Binswanger and Ruttan. Baltimore: Johns Hopkins University Press, 1978.

Sen, A.K. "Some Notes on the Choice of Capital Intensity in Development Planning." *Quarterly Journal of Economics*, November 1957.

———. *Choice of Techniques*. Oxford: University Press, 1968.

Sercovich, F. "Technology Behaviour of Industrial Enterprises. STPI Module 11, International Development Research Center Paper. Ottawa, Ontario: 1980.

Södersten, Bo. *International Economics*. New York: Harper & Row, 1970.

Stewart, F. *Technology and Underdevelopment*. New York: Macmillan, 1977.

Tyler, William. "Labor Absorption with Import-Substituting Industrialization: An Examination of Elasticities of Substitution in the Brazilian Manufacturing Sector." *Oxford Economic Papers* 26 (March 1974).

Vaupel, J.W., and Curhan, J.P. *The World's Multinational Enterprises*. Geneva: 1974.

Vernon, Raymond. "International Investment and International Trade in the Product Cycle." *Quarterly Journal of Economics* 80 (May 1966):107–207.

———. *Sovereignty at Bay*. New York: Basic Books 1971.

———. *Storm over the Multinational*. Cambridge: Harvard University Press, 1979.

———. "The Product Cycle Hypothesis in a New International Environment." *Oxford Bulletin of Economics and Statistics* 41 (November 1979):255–267.

White, L.J. "Appropriate Factor Proportions for Manfacturing in Less

Developed Countries: A Survey of the Evidence.'' In *Appropriate Technologies for Third World Development,* edited by Austin Robinson. New York: St. Martins Press, 1979, pp. 300–341.

Wionczek, Miguel. ''Notes of Technology-Transfer through Multinational Enterprises in Latin America.'' *Development and Change* 7 (1976):135–155.

Witte, Anne D. ''Employment in the Manufacturing Sector of Developing Economies: A Study of Mexico and Peru.'' *Journal of Development Studies* 10 (October 1973).

5 Education and Labor Markets in LDCs

Carmel Ullman Chiswick

The literature on labor markets in LDCs, and especially on the relationships between education and the functioning of labor markets, has followed very closely on methodological developments associated with the analysis of human capital. The human-capital model is a behavioral model of labor supply that recognizes that labor as a factor of production is neither homogeneous nor exogenous to the economic system. Techniques for empirical analysis of this model are fairly well developed, and it has generated an enormous, and successful, literature that is still displaying much intellectual energy.

Yet this model actually deals with only one aspect of the relationship between education and development—namely, the incentive effect of the wage structure on the educational attainment (and labor-force participation) of the work force. A full analysis of the relationship between education and labor markets must consider demand as well as supply and the market for skill formation as well as skill utilization. These two markets are clearly interrelated. The supply of skills to the labor force is closely related (if not identical) to the demand for education providing those skills. Moreover, in many LDCs, the government is actively involved in the planning of development on the one hand and education on the other—that is, the government planner is a major factor in determining both the demand for skills in the labor market and the supply of educational places in the market for skill formation. This latter relationship is the primary focus of this chapter.

For simplicity of analysis, we assume that the goal of the education planner, as agent for the government in general, is to maximize aggregate income by judicious allocation of resources, education being one of the competing uses of those resources. We assume also that the labor market itself is competitive and unencumbered by either restrictive legislation or limited information. The educational planner must determine the number of places and quality of instruction at each level of formal schooling. He or she must also make analogous decisions about the size and content of nonformal and (at least implicitly) informal education and allocate resources among these various educational programs.

Although planners of this sort may be fully committed to a sound analysis of costs and benefits as the basis for decision making, there are frequently reasons why they do not wish to rely on current market prices and wages as good indicators of those costs and benefits. Thus the education planners' perceptions as to the purpose of education on the one hand and the nature of skill acquisition (hence costs) on the other is of crucial importance in determining the skill level and composition of the labor force.

Three different points of view are presented in this chapter for purposes of illustrating the principles involved. The perceptions of today's (postcolonial) planners as to the ability of ordinary workers to absorb skills through educational programs differ for the most part from the perceptions of their predecessors under colonial regimes. Among the latter, a distinction may be made between the French and the British perceptions as to the function of their Third World colonial education systems. These distinctions are analyzed in the next section, first with respect to education for the traditional sector and then with respect to the development of modern skills.

We then consider implications of the differences in planners' perceptions of the purpose of education. The third section is concerned with the structure of the LDC labor force, especially with regard to the distribution of workers between the modern and traditional sectors of the economy. The proposition is developed that the greater the emphasis on general entrepreneurial skills, as distinct from more narrowly defined production skills, the more rapid will be the growth of modern-sector employment. Within this context, we argue that the postcolonial educational philosophies tend to support the development goals for the economy as a whole. The fourth section discusses human-capital accumulation under different educational regimes and the consequent differences in development patterns.

The Purpose of Schooling

We assume from the outset that the educational planner is concerned primarily with education in the sense of skill formation; for the sake of this analysis, all other functions of the institutional structure called education in a particular country are irrelevant and hence ignored. Education is being used here in its broadest sense. It is not limited to (and does not necessarily include formal schooling, and it would certainly include) any nonformal or informal arrangement that constitutes a cost-effective means of acquiring skills.

It is also helpful to limit the discussion in this section to the case involving only two different skills. Since a formal analysis can be generalized readily from the two-skill case to the multiskill case, no loss of generality is entailed by this limitation. The two skills may correspond to the traditional and modern sectors respectively; alternatively, they may correspond to a dichotomy between rural and urban, between informal and formal sectors, between primary- and higher-schooling levels, or between blue-collar- and white-collar-skill types. Since each of these dichotomies appears in the literature on education and human capital in LDCs, any of them will do for the sake of analysis.

Education for the Traditional Sector

Considering the predominance of the rural family farm and the economic importance of the labor force employed in the traditional sector, it is no wonder that the educational planners' perceptions of that sector are of great importance. For example, if a planner perceives traditional farmers as being basically unskilled and incapable of either absorbing or applying modern skills, obviously little in the way of educational resources will be devoted to rural schooling. It would be optimal in such a situation to perceive the primary function of rural schools as the means of enabling the next generation to leave the farms for the modern sector. In contrast, if the traditional farmer is perceived as being ignorant rather than uneducable, it would make much more sense to allocate resources heavily to schools for children entering the traditional sector. The existence of a body of knowledge just waiting to be used to raise agricultural productivity could provide an enormous payoff that would then be spread widely through a large segment of the labor force.

Although there has been some experience with both of these extreme characterizations of the traditional farmer, neither is widely accepted in the literature today. The traditional-sector worker is certainly not thought to be uneducable, although he or she may well be resistant to being told what to do by someone whose experience is viewed as being deficient. At the same time, the notion of a preexisting body of knowledge just waiting to be applied by an educated farmer has proved to be overly optimistic, and today's rural educators have acquired a humility about the transferability of knowledge that their predecessors a generation ago clearly lacked.

An extremely useful approach to the question of traditional-sector skills is the distinction between *worker*, or *production*, efficiency on the one hand and *allocative* efficiency on the other.[1] Worker efficiency refers to how well a person can perform various tasks. It is the concept most often referred to as labor productivity, corresponding to the technical skill that is relevant for obtaining a particular quantity of output for a given amount of time spent working. Allocative efficiency refers to decision-making abilities. This is especially relevant for persons working as entrepreneurs or managers and is a major determinant of the economic profit of a firm. In the case of the traditional sector in which most farmers are also entrepreneurs and worker skills are cheap, allocative skills may be the primary determinant of farm incomes and a very important aspect of human-capital services available to the economy.

In a truly traditional environment in which all prices for products and factors of production are known and constant, allocative efficiency has no economic value—that is, once a particular production skill has been acquired, either in school or through some sort of apprenticeship arrangement, a new entrant to the occupation may copy the practices of previous workers and still maximize expected earnings. Nothing is to be gained from knowing about alternative ways of combining factors of production to obtain the same output since the old ways are still optimal given constant factor and product prices.

Once the economic environment begins to change, however, in the sense that relative prices are changing systematically (apart from the usual annual or cyclical variations), firms that continue to allocate factors in the old way are no longer maximizing profits. An entrepreneur who correctly perceives the change and who is able to determine the optimal allocation of inputs (and outputs) for the current set of market prices is maximizing profits; in the language of microeconomic theory, that person is running a more-efficient firm and earning economic profits that are a return to entrepreneurial capacity. Schultz argues that, especially in the context of traditional rural agriculture where worker productivity is low and commands a low market price, allocative skill is very important for rural incomes in an economy experiencing rapid change in economic structure.

The distinction between worker and allocative efficiency provides a number of useful insights into the role of education for the traditional sector. For example, the need for basic literacy and numeracy has frequently been assumed, and literacy rates frequently show up in aggregate cross-country analyses as an indicator of aggregate skill levels in the traditional sector. Yet careful studies as well as common sense indicate that, while it does tend to be associated with more productive farmers, literacy is neither necessary nor sufficient for high labor productivity in farming. Ironically, economists have tended to focus on raising rural-labor productivity through improvements in nonlabor factors, either physical capital (for example, improved seeds, fertilizers, machinery) or land (for example, land reform, irrigation, or other types of reclamation projects), adding almost as an afterthought that of course any such improvement must be accompanied by the knowledge needed for implementation.

The role of basic literacy and numeracy as tools for improving a farmer's allocative efficiency is more direct. These skills are important not because they contribute directly to a farmer's ability to cultivate and hence produce output but rather because they provide the tools for keeping abreast of new circumstances and opportunities and learning about different ways of responding to change. Similarly, while agriculture-related sciences may be helpful to enchance a rural worker's ability to produce farm output, they are primarily the means of providing farmers with the capacity to analyze new problems and situations and to respond optimally to change.

We may suppose that an important difference between the colonial and postcolonial regimes in many LDCs is the government's perception of the role of primary education for persons entering the labor force in the traditional sector. While colonial planners may have perceived the main function of rural primary schools to be the transmission of production-related skills for agriculture, the postcolonial planners often place more importance on the kinds of knowledge that help people deal with decisions in a changing world—that is, on allocative skills. Whether this difference arises from different evaluations of the demand for labor or of the abilities of students to learn is not really relevant to this analysis. What is relevant is that differences in the cost of producing the two different types of skill would result in different implications for the optimal level of schooling in the traditional sector.

Worker skills are normally cheaper to produce than allocative skills, especially if learning is to be limited to a few years of schooling, but diminishing marginal productivity of education sets in at an earlier stage for worker skills than for allocative skills. Figure 5–1 superimposes two sets of cost curves on the same demand curve for skills, one corresponding to the worker-skill (colonial) perception and the other to the allocative-skill (postcolonial) perception. The quantity axis in this figure gives the skill units embodied in an average worker, and the price axis gives the unit price of those skills. The average cost curve for the production of allocative skills (AC^a in figure 5–1) reflects increasing returns (that is, decreasing costs) per unit of skill over a longer range than the average cost curve for worker skills (AC^w) and a lower rate of diminishing returns for higher levels of education. The corresponding marginal cost curves, MC^a and MC^w, also reflect these conditions.

The downward-sloping demand curve in figure 5–1 expresses the

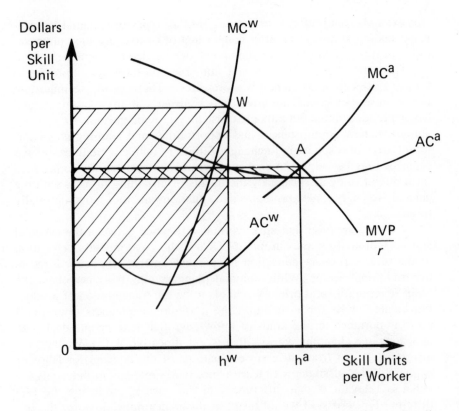

Figure 5–1. Optimal Levels of Worker and Allocative Skills in Traditional Sector

diminishing marginal productivity of skills of either type in the traditional sector; for simplicity, it is assumed that the two types of traditional-sector skill are sufficiently close substitutes in production that their demand can be combined. (Note that the marginal value product of skills, which determines their demand price, must be expressed as the present value of an earnings stream in order to be compared with the once-and-for-all cost of schooling, which is the supply price. This is approximated by dividing the marginal value product of each skill unit by the rate of interest, r.) The optimal level of each skill is determined by the intersection of the relevant MC curve with the demand curve, and the earnings of a worker with that skill level is the area of the rectangle determined by the origin and that intersection. The cost of schooling is the area of the rectangle determined by the origin and the height of the AC curve at the optimal skill level. The shaded area, which is the difference between these two rectangles, is the net present value of the investment in schooling in each case.

The two cost curves in figure 5–1 strongly suggest some of the differences in colonial and postcolonial education policy for the traditional sector. Colonial planners inferred a lower optimal level of schooling because of their perception of the function of schools as producing worker skills. In contrast, concern with allocative skills leads many postcolonial planners to infer a higher optimal level of schooling. A comparison of earnings under the two regimes would depend on the elasticity of demand for skills; in the event, it would seem that demand has been elastic and wages therefore higher in the postcolonial era, although this has hardly been demonstrated generally as a rigorous finding.

More important, perhaps, is the change (if any) in the net present value of schooling. Although it is not possible to infer a priori the direction of such a change, it would seem from figure 5–1 that the net value of skills constitutes a higher proportion of earnings for the coloial than for the postcolonial regime. If so, the cost of skill acquisition has become a higher proportion of earnings in the traditional sector than it used to be. One implication of this is that an increase in the traditional-sector labor force, which would have the effect of shifting the demand curve in figure 5–1 downward, has a greater depressing effect on the net present value of traditional skills in the postcolonial era. Thus, even though the labor force embodies more skills and earns higher wages than in the colonial era, population pressure would have a greater tendency to increase the incentive for people to leave the traditional sector to find jobs elsewhere.

Education and Modern Skills

Discussion of educational functions with respect to the formation of modern-sector skills is rarely couched in terms of worker versus allocative efficiency, but an analogous and analytically equivalent distinction appears. The manpower-development approach to educational planning tends to focus on production-related skills that are either currently in short supply or that are projected to be in the medium-run future. These tend to be for occupations classified as medium- or high-level blue collar, although in some cases managerial and administrative occupations are also of concern. In contrast, many educators resist the idea that schools should provide vocational training, favoring the notion that a broader focus on more-general knowledge will enhance a person's ability to choose the occupation best suited to his or her needs. These two approaches undoubtedly reflect differences in perceptions as to the relative importance of worker and allocative efficiency respectively.

Part of the difficulty with the case for developing modern-sector allocative efficiency in the schools is that decision making in that sector often requires substantial technical knowledge that may be closely related to production processes. A liberal-arts graduate with no production skills and little or no production-related experience may simply not have any relevant allocative skills either. Thus, a highly skilled technical worker trained for a specific production task may have to be used for essentially managerial functions simply because he or she has the best grasp of how the production process ought to work.

Difficulties of this sort arise when the distinction between worker and allocative skills is confused with the distinction between science and other subjects in the school's curriculum. This confusion is not peculiar to LDCs. Yet the problem is less severe in the developed countries because there are other avenues of acquiring information on which to base occupational choices. In fact, it is well known that most new entrants to the labor force will choose an occupation related to that of their parents and that this phenomenon may be understood to reflect the relative ease of acquiring accurate information about those occupations. In LDCs where modern-sector jobs are expanding rapidly, many of the new entrants to those jobs must come from families with limited modern-sector experience. An important function of education in LDCs must be to help new entrants to the modern sector labor force to become qualified for occupations that at the beginning of their education they may not even know exist.

Thus primary schools, even in rural areas, have a double educational function: In addition to raising skill levels for the traditional sector, they must provide enough knowledge of relevance for the modern sector to enable mobility between the sectors. From the point of view of the primary-school curriculum, this is most easily achieved if allocative efficiency is the basic skill type being taught for both sectors. If traditional-sector schooling were to emphasize the development of allocative skills, with nonformal and informal education taking much of the burden for the accumulation of production skills, and if modern-sector education were to include a sound knowledge of production skills as the basis for the exercise of allocative skills, then students whose futures lie in either sector may be educated in the same classrooms.

We may remark at this point that such a view of the nature of education and the economy has been historically rather more characteristic of U.S. educational philosophy than of either the British or the French, the two educational systems with the greatest influence on colonial structures in LDCs. The French colonial educational philosophy has tended to emphasize workers' production skills in the traditional and modern sectors alike, it being assumed that any allocative skills that might be needed in the economy could be imported from France. (Since most professional and technical occupations are characterized by the need for allocative skills, people in these occupations would also have to be imported.) The British colonial educational philosophy placed somewhat more emphasis on decision-making skills, not so much for their economic implications perhaps as for their political function of educating the electorate. Regardless of the intention, however, British colonial education appears to have been characterized not only by broader access (as compared to the French) but also by a built-in conflict between the acquisition of allocative skills on the one hand and the relegation of indigenous labor to essentially nonallocative jobs on the other.

Education and Labor-Force Structure

Differences between colonial and postcolonial educational planners in the perception of the nature and purpose of schooling have important implications for the structure of the labor force and, ultimately, for the economy's ability to modernize and develop. Education implies the accumulation of human capital, and like any capital stock, the more human-capital formation that takes place, the higher the productivity of workers. In addition, there is the balance between the modern and traditional sectors. It is best to think of human capital as being of two types, one corresponding to each sector. Thus, the educational planners affect not only the amount of human-capital formation that takes place within each sector but also the between-sector allocation of educational-investment resources.

The incentive for traditional-sector workers to acquire the education needed to work in the modern sector depends on a comparison of the net present values of investment in the two sectors. The earnings differential alone is not sufficient whenever costs differ as well, and educational planners must be concerned with the full direct costs of schooling. For a given wage differential between the two sectors, the larger the difference in costs (with the modern skills being more costly to produce), the smaller the incentive to train more modern-sector workers.

This relationship is illustrated in figures 5–2 and 5–3. Figure 5–2 pertains to the traditional sector and is similar to figure 5–1; figure 5–3 pertains to the modern sector and is analogous to figure 5–2. In each figure, the area of the rectangle defined by the origin and the intersection of the marginal cost curve with the demand curve is the earnings of a worker; the area of the rectangle defined by the origin and the height of

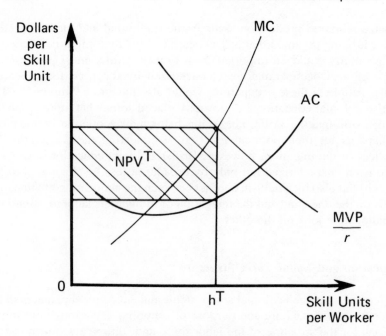

Figure 5–2. Traditional Sector

the average cost is the total cost of acquiring a given level of skill; and the difference between these two areas (shaded in the figures) is the net present value of the skills.

The allocation of workers between the two sectors is optimal if and only if the net present value of the skills is the same for both sectors, as illustrated. If costs were higher in the modern sector (for example, if the modern-skill AC curve were to shift upward), the net present value of modern skills would be less than for traditional skills, implying overinvestment, or too many workers, in the modern sector. In contrast, if the modern-sector AC curve were to shift downward, the net present value of an investment in modern skills would exceed the value of an investment in traditional skills. It would be profitable to educate more workers for the modern sector. Doing this would increase the number of modern-sector workers, thus causing the marginal value product of skills to decline in that sector; this decline would be reflected in figure 5–3 by a shift downward in the demand for skills. At the same time, a corresponding reduction would occur in the number of workers in the traditional sector that would be reflected by a shift upward in the demand for those skills. The initial reduction in educational costs for the modern sector thus not only provides an incentive for increasing the proportion of the labor force in that sector but also results in raising the optimal skill level of the

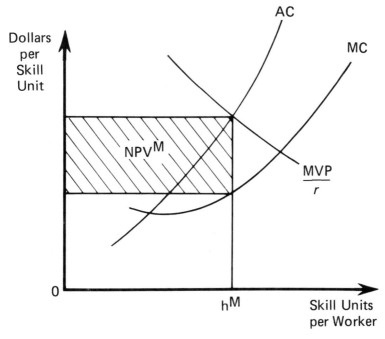

Figure 5–1. Modern Sector

traditional worker and reducing the optimal skill level of the modern worker.

Suppose, for purposes of illustration, that colonial planners viewed traditional skills as being fairly simple, easily learned in a short amount of time after which diminishing marginal productivity of education sets in quickly and the MC curve becomes fairly inelastic. As discussed earlier, it would be optimal to educate traditional-sector workers only to a fairly low level. The inelastic marginal cost curve for that sector also implies that increases in demand (which might be caused by, say, increased value of the product produced) would raise earnings but would have little effect on the optimum level of skill for traditional workers. At the same time, the low cost of traditional-sector education as compared to modern would suggest a relatively low payoff to educating people for the modern sector and, hence, a small proportion of the labor force with modern skills.

Now suppose, by way of contrast, that postcolonial planners view the differences in educational costs between the two sectors as being considerably smaller. This might be the case, for example, if allocative skills, which tend to be the same for all enterprises, were viewed as being important for everyone. It might also be the case if the modern sector were viewed as being dispersed throughout the countryside, less concentrated with respect to industrial branch or geographical area than during the colonial regime. If costs were similar for acquiring the two types of skill, wage differentials would more accurately reflect differences in the net present value of an investment in skills. A large wage differential between sectors would give a greater incentive to acquire modern-sector skills if the cost of that investment were only slightly higher than the cost of acquiring traditional-sector skills, in contrast with the situation discussed previously in which the cost of modern skills was much higher than that for traditional skills.

This suggests that the postcolonial view of the nature of skill formation and the purpose of education should lead to a larger proportion of the labor force in the modern sector than in colonial times as well as a more highly educated traditional labor force. It also suggests a decline in the average skill level of workers in the modern sector as that sector loses its elite status. The extent of this decline depends, of course, on the elasticity of the modern-skill marginal cost curve, being greater the more elastic the curve. Thus, if modern skills are viewed as being primarily production skills, with an inelastic marginal cost curve, as in the French colonial regimes, the observed decline in modern-skill levels will be much less important than the reduction in the modern-sector wage as a labor-market response to the change in educational structure. In contrast, if modern skills were viewed as primarily allocative with a more-elastic marginal cost curve, the value of skills would not change very much but there may be a substantial reduction in the amount of skill embodied in each worker. To some extent this difference in response is reflected by differences in ex-French and ex-British colonies—that is, while for both sets of countries the postcolonial regime tends to view the traditional sector similarly, differences in the French and British perceptions of the modern-sector labor force tend to persist into the postcolonial era.

Implications for Economic Development

Although the analysis in this chapter has focused on the relationship between the optimal allocation of investment and educational policy, a consideration of the implications of this relationship for economic development is of some interest. Two aspects of development must be distinguished here: (1) capital accumulation and (2) modernization. This section deals briefly with each of these topics within the context of the analysis in the preceding sections.

Clearly, capital accumulation as a source of wealth must be considered to include human capital. An important difference exists, however, in that the quantity and quality dimensions must be distinguished in the case of human capital. While, from the efficiency point of view, only the total number of skill units available matters, from a development-policy perspective, the human capital/labor ratios, or the average skill levels, are also important. Thus, a given increase in skill units obtained from an increase in the labor force, ceteris paribus, is less of a step toward economic development than the same increase obtained through improvements in skill levels.

Implicit in this statement is the notion that development implies an upgrading of the labor force with respect to skill levels. This attitude is made even more explicit in the literature on modernization where economic development is associated with a shift in the composition of the labor force away from traditional and toward modern types of skill. This requires an a priori knowledge as to which skills are which, a knowledge that is often not available or premised largely upon unsupported assumptions about the nature of production processes. Nevertheless, it may be said that skills corresponding to levels of education beyond the primary level are typically considered to be modern and that their dissemination is associated with this aspect of economic development. Economic development may be said to have taken place unambiguously if the occupational composition of the labor force has shifted in their favor and if, at the same time, the skill levels of people in the nonmodern occupations have been increasing.

In most cases, increases in the level of aggregate demand will cause substitution in favor of modern (more costly) skills. The extent to which this occurs requires knowledge not only about the education-cost functions but also about the labor-demand function—that is, the elasticity of substitution in production between the different types of skill. Much evidence exists to support an optimistic view for a highly elastic relative-demand curve for modern labor. Although there are some countries in which institutional barriers to mobility are quite strong, in most places people with modern technical and allocative skills can find satisfactory employment (other than in the government bureaucracy) without excessive delay.

The question remains as to whether a particular change in educational policy will have the effect of increasing development in this sense. The illustrative examples in the preceding sections have been suggestive that development is more apt to take place in planning regimes that place a greater emphasis on the formation of allocative rather than productive skills. However, this outcome clearly depends crucially on assumptions made about the relative elasticities and positions of the various education-cost curves as well as of the demand for factors of production. Overall, the more elastic the education-cost curves, the greater will any increase in demand stimulate the accumulation of human capital per worker.

Note

1. This distinction was initiated and developed by T.W. Schultz. For a recent and elegant statement, see "The Value of the Ability to Deal with Disequilibria," *Journal of Economic Literature* (1980), pp. 827–846.

6

Education and Emigration from Developing Countries

Ransford W. Palmer

Up until the 1950s, the economic-development literature emphasized the role of physical capital as the principal agent in the process of economic development. By the late 1960s, disappointment with the impact of physical-capital formation on development had set in, and the emphasis switched to the role of human capital, primarily education and training. As developing countries increased their outlays on education, their populations became more literate and their labor forces acquired more skills. These developments in turn raised the expectations of the younger entrants into the labor force, who regarded traditional low-wage jobs as unacceptable. The result in many countries has been a surplus of better-educated workers in search of the elusive high-status job that society and the market gave to a smaller number of their immediate predecessors.[1] In their search for income and status, many workers have emigrated to developed countries where economic opportunities are perceived to be greater. Thus, one side effect of accelerated public expenditures on education in developing countries may be described as the leakage of human capital to advanced countries.

While people have been migrating from developing countries to the developed countries of Europe, as well as to some of the more advanced among the developing countries, for a long time, the phenomenon of migration from developing countries to the United States over the past two decades has been particularly striking. The purpose of this chapter is therefore to examine at a macrolevel the relationship between the level of education and development in LDCs and the occupational composition of emigration from these countries to the United States. In other words, the basic question is: Given a certain U.S. demand for the services of immigrants from developing countries, to what extent is the nature of the supply of immigrants from a particular country affected by its level of development relative to the United States, as well as by its level of education?

The Growth of Public Expenditure on Education

While public expenditures do not reflect the total educational effort in
countries where education is also privately financed, in most developing
countries the preponderant share of expenditures on primary and secondary education is financed by the public sector. Between 1965 and 1976,
UNESCO data show that public expenditure on education in developing
countries rose from 3 percent to 4.1 percent of GNP, compared to an
increase from 5.1 percent to 6 percent for the developed countries. On
a per capita basis, this meant an increase from $5 to $21 for the developing
countries, compared to an increase from $87 to $289 for the developed
countries. Despite the gaping disparity, these figures do suggest a slight
narrowing of the public-expenditure-on-education gap.

The growth of public expenditures on education in developing countries has been to a significant extent influenced by the increasing urbanization of the population and by policies designed to provide universal
education up to the secondary level. For poor countries, the growth of
the cost of education beyond the primary level accelerates much faster
than it does for developed countries. Zymelman has shown (see table
6–1) that while the unit cost per student at the secondary level was 1.3
times that for the primary level for Organisation for Economic Co-op-
eration and Development (OECD) countries, it was almost 3.5 times for
developing countries. At the level of higher education, the disparity is
even sharper: roughly 3.4 times the primary level for OECD countries
and 24 times for developing countries.

The acceleration of the unit cost of education beyond the primary

Table 6–1
**Percentage Distribution of Educational Budgets and Unit Costs, by
Level of Education, circa 1973**

	Educational Level		
Item	Primary	Secondary	Higher
OECD	38.1	40.7	16.2
Developing countries	48.1	30.2	16.7
Unit cost per student in relation to GNP (developing countries/OECD countries)	0.94	2.48	6.58
Unit cost per student by educational level (primary = 1)			
OECD	1	1.31	3.44
Developing countries	1	3.47	24.13

Source: Manuel Zymelman, "Patterns of Educational Expenditures," Working Paper No.
246 (Washington, D.C.: World Bank, November 1976), p. 81. Cited in Albert Berry,
"Education, Income, Productivity, and Urban Poverty," in *Education and Income,*
Working Paper No. 402 (Washington, D.C.: World Bank 1980).

level underscores the high price of education in developing countries. Table 6–1 shows that a relatively larger share of a poor country's GNP is required to educate each student beyond the primary level. In this regard, Lewis has observed that "all production or provision of services which depends on using educated people is much more expensive, in relation to national income, in poor than in rich countries." Thus, Lewis argued that "the main limitation on the absorption of the educated in poor countries is their high price, relatively, to average national output per head."[2]

That the economy is unable to absorb the relatively high-priced pri-mary-and-secondary-school graduates at current wage rates is not to be considered a justification for cutting back on the production of educated people, however, since the long-run adjustment process will lower both expectations and relative wage rates.[3] The phenomenon of the long-run-adjustment process involves not only the lowering of worker expectation regarding his personal status but also the effort of the employer to increase the status of the job. As Albeda puts it:

> Although we know that the higher the stage of development of a country, the more important is its demand for qualified and highly qualified labor, we can never tell exactly how far the high qualification is a necessity, and how far it is a result of a combination of availability of qualified people and arguments of status on the part of employers.
>
> When higher education is demanded not because the job requires it but because the employers (in trade unions) are trying to increase the status of a job, a certain overqualification is the result.[4]

To the extent that the adjustment process at home leads to lower expectations for new entrants into the labor force and to a slower growth in wage rates for employed workers, it may encourage some workers to exploit perceived economic opportunities abroad. Within this sequence of development, the large urban centers in many developing countries become staging areas where potential emigrants prepare for emigration. Preparation, of course, may not be limited to formal education; it may also include on-the-job training as well as a period of psychological orientation to the life-style of the metropolitan destination. Because the influence of the metropole on developing countries is typically channeled through their large urban centers, these centers provide the ideal staging areas for psychological conditioning.[5] Thus, in the larger view of pop-ulation movement, the city in developing countries is both a terminal point for internal migration and a crucial way station for those who later emigrate.[6]

Not all the internal migrants to the city will necessarily benefit from whatever upgrading the city provides. Benefits will depend, among other things, upon their age, their level of education upon migration to the city, and the amount of resources that public policy can reasonably allocate to education and training. Indeed, the benefits of any upgrading may take a generation to materialize, so that the people who emigrate a generation later are likely to be better educated than those who migrated to the city a generation earlier.

Education and Emigration Patterns

The United States, over the last two decades, has tapped the increasing supply of educated people in several developing countries to fill vacancies within its own labor market. The high share of professional and technical immigrants to the United States since the revision of the immigration laws in 1965 is prima facie evidence of the growth in the number of these workers in the labor force of the major supplying developing countries.[7] Table 6–2 shows substantial gains in the share of those receiving education at the primary, secondary, and higher levels in selected developing countries between 1960 and 1977. In the Philippines, the share enrolled in secondary education has more than doubled, while in South Korea it has grown more than threefold. In table 6–3, the share of skilled workers

Table 6–2
Growth of Adult Literacy and Enrollment in Primary, Secondary, and Higher Education for Selected Developing Countries, 1960–1977

Country	Number Enrolled in Primary School as Percentage of Age Group		Number Enrolled in Secondary School as Percentage of Age Group		Number Enrolled in Higher Education as Percentage of Population Aged 20–24		Percentage Adult-Literacy Rate	
	1960	1977	1960	1977	1960	1976	1960	1975
Honduras	67	89	8	13	1	6	45	57
Philippines	95	105	26	56	13	24	72	87
Colombia	77	103	12	39	2	9	63	81
Ecuador	83	101	12	44	3	28	68	74
Dominican Republic	98	102	7	27	1	9	65	67
Jamaica	92	97	45	58	2	7	82	86
South Korea	94	111	27	88	5	11	71	93
Mexico	80	116	11	39	3	10	65	76
Panama	96	86	29	115	5	22	73	78
Taiwan	95	100	33	76	4	12	54	82
Trinidad and Tobago	88	81	24	38	1	5	93	95
Venezuela	100	104	21	38	4	21	63	82

Source: World Bank, *World Development Report* (Washington, D.C., 1980).

Table 6–3
Education, Emigration, and per Capita GNP Ratios for Selected Countries

Country	Public Expenditure on Education as Percentage of GNP (average for 1965–1976) E	Share of Age Group Enrolled in Secondary Schools (average for 1960 and 1976) s	Ratio of per Capita GNP in Sending country (Y_s) to that of United States (Y_{US}), 1977 $\dfrac{Y_s}{Y_{US}}$	Share of Professional, Technical, and Kindred Workers in Total Emigration to United States (average for 1969–1976) M
India	2.7	24	0.017	42.6
Iran	3.4	30	0.253	27.3
Iraq	4.7	29	0.181	11.5
Jordan	3.5	34	0.083	9.3
Korea	2.8	45	0.096	14.6
Pakistan	1.9	14	0.022	37.6
Philippines	1.9	41	0.052	26.7
Thailand	3.2	19	0.049	19.2
Egypt	5.2	29	0.037	35.8
Mexico	3.2	24	0.131	1
Dominican Republic	2.5	26	0.098	2.3
Jamaica	5.2	51	0.135	5.2
El Salvador	3.2	16	0.064	4.9
Honduras	3.4	11	0.048	4.9
Panama	5.2	41	0.143	6
Argentina	2.9	44	0.203	7.5
Brazil	2.5	15	0.159	9.6
Chile	3.9	36	0.136	13.6
Colombia	2.2	24	0.084	6
Peru	4.1	32	0.098	11.3
Venezuela	4.7	30	0.312	8.9

Sources: World Bank, *World Development Report 1979*, (New York: Oxford University Press, 1979). UNESCO, *Statistical Yearbook 1978–1979.* (Paris: UNESCO, 1980). U.S. Immigration and Naturalization Service. Unpublished data.

among the emigrants from these two countries to the United States averaged 27 percent and 15 percent respectively between 1969 and 1976.

Table 6–3 also shows that, in addition to the level of development indicated by the ratio of each country's per capital GNP to that of the United States, distance plays an important role. The countries that have had the highest share of professional and technical workers in their total emigration to the United States have not only had a low per capita GNP ratio but also are farthest geographically from the United States.[8] Since distance indicates the cost of travel, it is safe to assume that the better educated are better able to meet these costs, hence their greater share among the emigrants to the United States. In contrast, only 1 percent of the vast Mexican emigration into the United States was classified as professional and technical workers, which underscores the pattern that the nearer the developing country is to the United States, the smaller the share of professional, technical, and kindred workers among its emigrants to the United States.

While it cannot be argued that all the highly skilled immigrants received their postsecondary training in their home countries, it is indisputable that the skills they bring to the job market in the United States were made possible by public investment in their education at the primary and secondary levels in their country of origin.

Emigration and the Returns to Education

In strict cost-benefit analysis, the public sector can recover its investment in education if the discounted value of the future flow of tax revenues generated by the employment of each worker is equal to the public cost of the investment in his education. If he is not employed, this cost cannot be recovered; if the number of years he works is substantially reduced by unemployment, the discounted value of the tax revenues from his employment will be lowered. Even if he emigrates and sends back remittances, these remittances are likely to be used entirely for consumption purposes and may generate little in the way of tax revenues. From this perspective, the best of all possible worlds appears to be one in which a lifetime of tax-revenue-generating employment is provided at home.

Clearly, no amount of investment in education and job creation can stem completely the willingness to emigrate. In fact, this would not be desirable since emigration is a time-honored way for many individuals to improve themselves. What is desirable, however, is that some equilibrium point be reached at which the value of human-capital outflow is financed by the excess of the discounted tax revenues from those who are gainfully employed.

Traditional cost-benefit analysis can be at best only an extremely rough guide to decisions affecting public investment in education in developing countries because the investment itself will generate changes that are impossible to predict and therefore to measure. Furthermore, a number of social and cultural factors ignored by this analysis tend to weaken its relevance in poor countries. For example, the World Bank has observed that traditional cost-benefit analysis may overstate the social costs implied by the unemployment of those with secondary education in developing countries:

Since the unemployed are young, with few dependents and often supported by their families, and since most of them eventually find jobs, neither the social nor the private costs associated with this unemployment are as serious as might appear.

Some governments have virtually guaranteed public-sector jobs for postsecondary leavers whether or not there has been socially productive work for them to do. This can result in a major drain on government revenues and impede the diffusion of educated manpower into more productive uses as well.[9]

However, the very practice of guaranteeing public-sector jobs for postsecondary leavers also artificially inflates the marginal social rate of return on investment in education. If we argue, as Fields does, that the marginal social rate of return is the appropriate guide for assessing the costs and benefits of educational investment, then the additional output of the employed educated worker over the output he would have produced were he not educated would be the marginal social benefit.[10] When the public sector hires a high-school graduate and pays him more than he would have earned had he not gone to high school, there is an automatic increase in marginal social benefit because public-sector output is measured by cost. No matter if this additional government worker contributes nothing to the total output of real goods and services. Thus this positive social benefit from investment in his education provides the justification for further public investment in that kind of education. The problem is aggravated, as Fields points out, when cost-benefit analysts use the average rather than the marginal rate of return. The resulting overstatement of the rates of return on investment in education provides misleading signals to policymakers who determine educational priorities. Psacharopoulos, for example, has found that the social rate of return to investment in developing countries ranges from 27 percent for primary to 13 percent for higher education, a range substantially larger than that for developed countries.[11] The logical implication is that more public investment in education should be undertaken yet the encouragement of more private investment in education at certain levels would probably improve the allocation of scarce investment resources nationally.

In spite of the higher social rates of return on education in developing countries, the great international migratory flow of educated people is from developing to developed countries with market economies. The major factor stimulating this flow is the gap between domestic and foreign private rates of return to investment in education in developing countries. For the worker who emigrates for economic reasons (the type of emigrant with which we are primarily concerned), his action is prima facie evidence that the domestic private rate of return on his investment in education cannot support the level of living he expects to enjoy. He emigrates to

realize a higher private rate of return. We call this the foreign private
rate of return on domestic investment in education. Therefore, the gap
between the domestic and foreign private rate of return is the critical
determinant of emigration.[12] Thus it can be argued that investment in
education in developing countries leads to emigration to the extent that
emigration is perceived to provide a higher rate of return on that investment. The size of the perceived gap is limited by the difference in the
level of development between the sending and the receiving countries;
this difference is illustrated in figure 6-1.

As a country develops, the rate of return on investment in education
declines. Emigration shifts the rate-of-return curve E to E^1. At a low
level of development, L_1, emigration increases the rate of return sub-

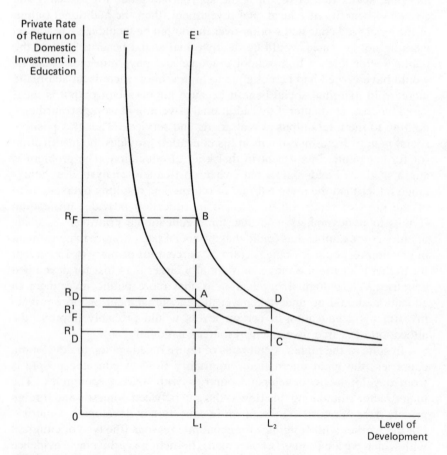

Figure 6-1. Rates of Return to Education in Relation to Level of Development

stantially from OR_D to OR_F. As the economy reaches a higher level of development at L_2, the extent to which emigration can increase the rate of return is substantially smaller. The implication is that development reduces the willingness to emigrate by reducing the gap between the two rates of return on domestic investment in education.

The Hypothesis

If, at a lower level of development, people with more education perceive a wide gap in the foreign and domestic private rates of return on their domestic investment in education, they will act to close that gap by emigrating. Thus, at a given level of development, education creates the perception that is acted upon by those who have the ability to do so.

Although in figure 6–1 emigration is treated as an exogenous factor that shifts the rate-of-return curve to the right, it can be treated as a variable influenced by both education and the level of development.[13] The fact is that the difference in private rates of return on education is rooted in the difference in the levels of development between the sending and the receiving countries. Education allows people to better perceive these differences. When they act on their perception, the result is emigration. Thus, both the perception and the action are determined by a combination of the level of development and education.

However, education does more than merely illuminate the rate-of-return gap; in the passage of time it also helps to narrow it. As it illuminates the gap it helps to narrow, the propensity of educated workers to emigrate will decline. Our purpose here is not to examine the extent to which education reduces international income disparity. It suffices to mention World Bank studies by Psacharopoulos, Berry, and Fields appearing in *Education and Income* edited by Timothy King.[14]

The basic question we wish to address empirically is the following: Given a sample of developing countries at different stages of development, to what extent does the combination of the level of education and the level of development in each country help to explain the willingness of its educated workers to emigrate to a developed country—namely, the United States?

Empirical Analysis

For the purpose of this study, the level of education is measured in two ways: (1) public expenditures in education as a percentage of GNP and (2) the percentage of persons of high-school age enrolled in high school.

The level of development is measured as the ratio of per capita GNP in the sending country to per capita GNP in the receiving developed country—the United States. The willingness of educated workers to emigrate to the United States is measured as the share of skilled emigrants in the total number of emigrants from each sending country. The definition of an immigrant to the United States is that used by the U.S. Immigration and Naturalization Service—that is, someone who has been issued a visa for permanent residence in the United States.

If the education variable is E and the migration variable M, our hypothesis may be restated algebraically as

$$M = m\left[\frac{E}{\left(\frac{Y_s}{Y_{US}}\right)}\right]$$

where Y_s and Y_{US} are the per capita GNP for the sending country and the United States, respectively. Two implications flow from this formulation. One is that if the numerical value of the education variable is the same for all countries, the level of development as measured by Y_s/Y_{US} will be the sole determinant of migration. The other implication is that in countries in which the level of development is lowest, the greater the likely impact of increases in the level of education on emigration.

Our sample includes twenty-one developing countries that have been the major suppliers of immigrants to the United States since the revision of the U.S. Immigration Act in 1965. The empirical analysis uses data published by the World Bank, the United Nations, and the U.S. Immigration and Naturalization Service.

Ordinary least-squares-regression technique is used to estimate the following equation:

$$M = aE^{*b},$$

where

$$E^* = \left[\frac{E}{\left(\frac{Y_s}{Y_{US}}\right)}\right]$$

The choice of this equation form is based on the assumption that as we move up the development scale (that is, as the value of E^* declines), the propensity to emigrate will fall at a declining rate. E^* then becomes the proxy measure for the gap between the domestic and foreign private rates of return on domestic education.

The logarithmic transformation of $M = aE^{*b}$ is

$$\text{Log } M = \log a + b \log E^*.$$

The estimated value of b is the elasticity of M with respect to E^*.

The data for the regression analysis are provided in table 6–4. Two regressions were run using two definitions of the independent variable, E_L^* and E_s^*. E_L^* is the share of public expenditures on education in GNP divided by the ratio of per capita GNP in the sending and receiving countries, and E_s^* is the share of the high-school-age population enrolled in high school divided by the ratio of per capita GNP. The ratio of per capita GNP is our index for the level of development; the higher the ratio, the higher the level of development.

The following are the results:

$$\text{Log } M = 0.059305 + 0.605894 \log E_L^*$$
$$(21.27) \ R^2 = .95$$
$$\text{Log } M = 0.770546 + 0.093753 \log E_s^*$$
$$(20.71) \ R^2 = .95$$

The t statistics are in parentheses.

Table 6–4
Data for Empirical Analysis

Country	Log M	Log E$_L^*$	Log $_s^*$
India	1.62941	2.20085	3.14953
Iran	1.43616	1.12710	2.07372
Iraq	1.06070	1.41330	2.20466
Jordan	0.96848	1.62428	2.61236
Korea	1.16435	1.46389	2.67089
Pakistan	1.57519	1.93601	2.80366
Philippines	1.42651	1.56229	2.89675
Thailand	1.28330	1.81491	2.58850
Egypt	1.55388	2.14768	2.89415
Mexico	0	1.38739	2.26293
Dominican Republic	0.36173	1.40654	2.42374
Jamaica	0.71600	1.58546	2.57715
El Salvador	0.69020	1.69897	2.39794
Honduras	0.69020	1.85003	2.36003
Panama	0.77815	1.55991	2.45743
Argentina	0.87506	1.15229	2.33586
Brazil	0.98227	1.19590	1.97451
Chile	1.13354	1.45637	2.42275
Columbia	0.77815	1.41664	2.45591
Peru	1.05308	1.62118	2.51388
Venezuela	0.94939	0.67210	1.98272

Source: Calculated from data in table 6–3.

From these results, the R^2 indicates that both E_t^* and E_s^* explain 95 percent of the variation in M, which is the share of professional, technical, and kindred workers in total emigration. Both regression coefficients are highly statistically significant, and their signs are as we expected them. It is clear that an increase in the value of the E^* variable tends to increase the share of skilled workers in total emigration. However, the regression coefficient of the E_t^* variable (0.605894) is quite a bit larger than that of the E_s^* variable (0.093753) suggesting that E^* has a greater impact on M when public expenditure on education as a percentage of GNP is used as a measure of the level of education. In our analysis, the two factors affecting the size of E^* are the level of education and the level of development. On the one hand, given a certain level of development, an increase in the level of education will increase the value of E^*, causing M to grow. On the other hand, given a certain level of education, an increase in the level of development (an increase in the ratio of sending- to receiving-country per capita GNP) will reduce the value E^*, causing M to decline.

Conclusions

Although the policy significance of the results of the preceding analysis is restricted by the quality of the data used and the level of aggregation of the analysis, the results do underscore the phenomenon that rich countries benefit from the effort of poor countries to improve their stock of human capital. The policy context of this phenomenon, however, is complicated by the fact that some developing countries are known to encourage the emigration of skilled workers in order to augment the inflow of foreign exchange through worker repatriation of earnings or to rid themselves of highly educated workers who represent a potential threat to domestic stability.

The overarching reality is that as developing countries accelerate their investment in education, they can expect to lose a portion of their enlarged human-capital stock to developed countries because there is usually a lag between investment in education and the growth of economic opportunities. Such leakage of human capital may even be destabilizing in the sense that it may extend the lag between investment in education and the growth of job opportunities. Thus, if the rich countries that benefit from the inflow of the capital from poor countries are seriously interested in accelerating the economic development of the poor countries, they cannot rely on the long-term equilibrating process to equalize economic opportunities, for this process itself may be destabilizing. The rich countries must forgo a compensatory mechanism through which they can accelerate the reduction in the fundamental international economic imbalances that pull human capital away from poor countries.

Notes

1. W. Arthur Lewis, "Education and Economic Development," *Social and Economic Studies* 10 (June 1961):116.
2. Ibid., pp. 114–115.
3. Ibid., pp. 115–116.
4. W. Albeda, "Manpower Problems in a Full Employment Economy," in *Employment Stabilization in a Growth Economy,* (Paris: OECD, 1968), p. 85.
5. This argument may be regarded as an extension of either the stepwise process of internal migration or the aggregate-level replacement process [for a recent discussion of these issues, see Dennis Conway, "Step-wise Migration: Toward a Clarification of the Mechanism," *International Migration Review* 14 (Spring 1980):3–14].
6. This hypothesis of the city as a staging area for international migration may not necessarily be valid for a country like Mexico that has an extensive border with the United States. In response to the question as to why those seeking employment outside the rural community in Mexico shun cities in their own country as potential destinations, Wayne Cornelius writes that "the usual response given by the migrants is two-fold: (1) jobs are too hard to find in most Mexican cities, and (2) even if one does find work there, it pays too little to meet one's needs" [Mexican Migration to the United States: Causes, Consequences, and U.S. Responses" (Prepared for the Brookings Institution–El Colegio de Mexico Symposium on Structural Factors Contributing to Current Patterns of Migration in Mexico and the Carribbean Basin, Washington, D.C., 28–30 June 1978)].
7. However, it is important to emphasize that the occupational composition of immigrant workers to the United States is also influenced by the U.S. demand for certain types of skills. The migration data, therefore, reflects not only the forces at work in the origin countries but also those in the destination country.
8. The more developed a country is, the greater its demand for professional and technical workers. Hence emigration from countries with a high per capita GNP ratio is expected to have a smaller share of professional and technical workers.
9. World Bank, *World Development Report 1980* (Washington, D.C., 1980), p. 51.
10. Gary S. Fields, "Education and Income Distribution in Devel-

oping Countries: A Review of the Literature," in *Education and Income: World Bank Staff Working Paper No. 402*, ed. Timothy King (Washington, D.C., 1980), pp. 231–315.

11. George Psacharopoulos, "Returns to Education: An Updated International Comparison," in *Education and Income: World Bank Staff, Working Paper No. 402*, ed. Timothy King (Washington, D.C., 1980), pp. 73–109.

12. This is analogous to the expected income differential in the Todaro model of internal migration. See Michael P. Todaro, "A Model of Labor Migration and Urban Unemployment in Less Developed Countries," *American Economic Review* 59 (March 1969):138–148.

13. It is fully recognized that emigration is not possible unless a demand for immigrants exists that expresses itself through the institutional process of issuing visas. The extent to which migrants respond to this demand will depend upon how they perceive the differential in the private rate of return on their education. Both the level of their education and the level of development of the sending country will influence this perception.

14. Timothy King, ed., "Education and Income," Working Paper No. 402 (Washington, D.C.: World Bank, 1980).

Bibliography

Albeda, W. "Manpower Problems in a Full Employment Economy." In *Employment Stabilization in a Growth Economy*. Paris: OECD, 1968.

Berry, Albert. "Education, Income, Productivity, and Urban Poverty." In *Education and Income: World Bank Staff Working Paper No. 402*. Washington, D.C.: World Bank, 1980.

Conway, Dennis. "Step-wise Migration: Toward a Clarification of the Mechanism." *International Migration Review* 14 (Spring 1980): 3–14.

Cornelius, Wayne A. "Mexican Migration to the United States: Causes, Consequences, and U.S. Responses." Prepared for the Brookings Institution–El Colegio de Mexico Symposium on Structural Factors Contributing to Current Patterns of Migration in Mexico and the Caribbean Basin, Washington, D.C., 28–30 June 1978.

Fields, Gary S. "Education and Income Distribution in Developing Countries: A Review of the Literature." In *Education and Income: World Bank Staff Working Paper No. 402*, edited by Timothy King. Washington, D.C.: World Bank, 1980.

King, Timothy, ed. *Education and Income: World Bank Staff Working Paper No. 402.* Washington, D.C.: World Bank, 1980.

Lewis, W. Arthur. "Education and Economic Development." *Social and Economic Studies* 10 (June 1961):113–127.

Psacharopoulos, George. "Returns to Education: An Updated International Comparison." In *Education and Income: World Bank Staff, Working Paper No. 402,* edited by Timothy King. Washington, D.C.: World Bank, 1980.

Todaro, Michael P. "A Model of Labor Migration and Urban Unemployment in Less Developed Countries." *American Economic Review* 59 (March 1969):138–148.

World Bank. *World Development Report 1980.* Washington, D.C., 1980.

7

Resource Availability, Equality, and Educational Opportunity among Nations

Stephen P. Heyneman

Equal Opportunity in Theory

The concept of equal educational opportunity is both radical and ancient. Contrary to the practice of deciding opportunity on the basis of one's family, Plato first proposed that occupational preparation be renewed with each generation and based upon what each individual was able to achieve for himself.

Implementation of this footrace remained relatively dormant until the Industrial Revolution. Before then, families were the primary economic unit, and the appropriate function of education was to maintain the productivity of the family. Skills were passed from father to son. Until the time when children were not expected to remain within the family economic unit, educational opportunity, much less the equality of opportunity, was hardly relevant. Today occupational choice is less determined by the family than at any time in human history. Only in the most isolated areas—among desert and mountain tribes, for example—is father-to-son occupational transfer automatically conducted with no intervening influence from the economy (for example, urban migration) or the state (for example, education). This world change in the nature of occupational selection makes the equality of educational opportunity a universal issue.

An equal-opportunity strategy accepts that as long as human beings differ, some will utilize resources more efficiently and more quickly. The purpose of all equal-opportunity strategies is to assure that, as nearly as possible, all chances to utilize resources are equal. Key to the concept is the notion of equal exposure to something. Equal exposure assumes the equal distribution of that something. This something we call resources. Whether resources are equally utilized does not determine whether equal opportunity has been achieved. The philosophy of equal opportunity acknowledges that inequalities in utilization will not disappear.

The views and interpretations expressed in this chapter are solely those of the author and, in particular, do not necessarily reflect those of the World Bank.

Whether some inequality is morally acceptable in a just society is the subject of a current dialogue between the fields of sociology and moral philosophy (Rawls 1958, 1971; Coleman 1973, 1974; Nozick 1975; Bane 1975). In effect, the arguments, pro and con, can be reduced to the following: If one is to accept an equal-opportunity strategy, it means that one must accept the existence of appropriate, or proper, differences among people. Society must agree that these differences are just and have been achieved fairly—for example, differences in sports, chess, or physics.

When faced with a demand for equalizing opportunity between regions within countries, several definitional criteria must first be met. As a practical matter, a policy can only succeed if the resources to be distributed meet four checks proposed by Bell and Robinson (1978): (1) that it be based upon something that can, in fact, be distributed; (2) that a unit of analysis (neighborhood, region, and so on) be specified; (3) that the degree of distribution be measurable; and (4) that the consumers agree that the item should be fairly distributed.

Equal Opportunity among Nations

Classroom Availability

Out of the United Nations agreements signed at the end of World War II emerged a new international definition of what we are now calling basic human needs.[1] There were guarantees of freedom of many kinds—from hunger; from persecution; from prejudice based upon race, sex, religion, or national origin—as well as a guarantee of education. Now three decades have passed, and it might be worthy to begin reviewing what the world has accomplished in the meantime. One could hardly argue that the world is freer from prejudice or persecution. Also, hunger today is a catastrophe that, if anything, appears to be more serious than ever. The only area in which the world can demonstrate advancement, in a universal sense, is in the field of education. This advancement has been made in spite of all the obvious handicaps so frequently cited in the popular press, such as population growth, civil war, political and economic inexperience, and poverty and competitive economic priorities.

The explanation for such advancement is not difficult to discern. Education may be the only human right that is in the interest as much of the geographic periphery as the center and that is to the economic benefit of both producer and the consumer. Parents think of schools as instruments for occupational life chances, and in low-income countries, the recent examples of upward mobility through education have been dramatic indeed. Parental demand for educational opportunity, coupled with the economic and political obligation of the authorities to supply it, account for the recent expansion of formal schooling at levels unprecedented in human history. Universal primary-school enrollment has now been achieved in thirty-five middle- and upper-middle-income countries since World War II, including Argentina, Trinidad, Gabon, Malaysia, and thirty-one others (table 7–1). In the thirty-six poorest countries (GNP = U.S. $265/year or less), first-level education has increased from an average of 48 percent of the school-age population in 1960 to 58 percent in 1965, to 64 percent in 1975, and to 70 percent in 1977.

As important as this 70 percent figure is, even more indicative of the degree of social change in the last few decades is a disaggregation of that figure by grade level. On the average, about twice as many children are enrolled in grade one than in grade four. This 70 percent enrollment figure therefore is a significant understatement of the proportion of children who begin school. The fact is that by the end of this century, every child born will probably be able to enter a grade one of some kind (see Meyer and Hannan 1979).

Classroom Quality

Although significant advances have been made in the availability of a place in a primary-school classroon, gross differences remain between poor and rich countries in what pupils can expect to find in those classrooms when they enter. Primary schools in the developing world are typically of poor quality in both inputs and outcomes. The education of teachers and the availability of furniture, equipment, and materials are normally well below the standards considered as minimal for schools in the industrialized societies. In 1977, for example, there were ten pupils

Table 7–1
Primary-School-Enrollment Ratios in Low- and High-Income Countries, 1960–1975

National GNP	Number of Countries	Percentage of Gross Enrollment			
		1960	*1965*	*1970*	*1975*
Low (GNP): less than $265	36	48	58	61	64
Lower (middle): $265–520	21	59	65	69	73
Intermediate: $520–1,075	21	71	84	95	102
Upper-middle: $1,075–2,500	14	85	93	96	102
Total					
Low and middle income	92	57	66	71	75
High income	—	114	118	120	120

Source: Education Sector Policy Paper, World Bank, 1980.

for each available primary-school textbook in the Philippines (Jamison and Montenegro 1980). In 1978, the monetary value invested in furniture and materials in the average fourth-grade classroom in Bolivia was approximately U.S.$0.80/pupil. This is one-sixtieth of what was invested per pupil in the state of Maryland during the same year (table 7–2). In a survey conducted in four of the eight educational regions in Bolivia, not a single primary school was found to contain a film projector, a slide projector, a card index, a duplicating machine, or a calculator. In rural areas, only one in ten had a typewriter, only one in two had a bookshelf, and only one in three children even had a chair (Heyneman 1979).

Even recently constructed primary-school buildings are without safety standards. Walls frequently collapse; roofs have large holes; wind and rain disrupt classroom activity as a matter of course. Classrooms are dark and stuffy. Students are forced to squat on the ground and write by balancing an exercise book or slate on their knees. Teachers have no office. Student desks, if available, wobble on three legs; chairs have no backs; stools have but half a seat (Heyneman 1980). Similar situations

Table 7–2
The Cost of Primary-School Teachers and School Supplies in Four Countries
(U.S. dollars)

Country	Cost of Supplies per Pupil	Cost of Salaries per Pupil	Ratio of Supplies, LDC/United States	National per Capita Income (1977)
El Salvador[a]	1.15	25.80	1:44	570
Bolivia[b]	0.80	78	1:63	315
Malawi[c]	1.24	14.60	1:40	140
United States (Maryland)[d]	50	1,354	—	7,950

[a]Average for urban/rural, cycle I and cycle II schools. Source: W. Loxley and S. Heyneman, "The Influence of School Resources on Learning Outcomes in El Salvador," Education Department, World Bank, September 1980.

[b]$B 470 million was allocated for recurrent expenditures in FY1973; divided by the enrollment of 296,649 = unit cost of $B 1,584, an equivalent of U.S.$79/pupil, of which less than one percent was spent on nonpersonnel services, materials, supplies, and equipment. Source: UNESCO, *Education in Bolivia: An Essential Output for Socio-Economic Balance*, Annex II-36 (Paris, 1975).

[c]Source: Malawi Education Sector Survey, 1978; and S. Heyneman, *The Evaluation of Human Capital in Malawi*, Working Paper No. 420 (Washington, D.C.: World Bank, 1980). It should be borne in mind that the entire cost for educational supplies in Malawi (up to 1978) was shouldered by the parents of school children, not by the state.

[d]1981 figures for Montgomery County, Maryland: cost/pupil of elementary classroom teachers = $1,017; nonclassroom salaries = $337; supplies, books, and equipment = $46; furniture, building repairs = $4. Source: Montgomery County Public Schools, private communication with the author.

have been found in El Salvador where the average annual investment in supplies, books, and equipment is approximately U.S.$1.15/pupil (Loxley and Heyneman, 1980).

The gap in educational quality between low- and high-income countries is large; it is also widening. As more and more pupils enter school, less material is available with which to teach them. In 1960, the average OECD country invested 14 times more per pupil than any of the thirty-six countries with per capita incomes of below U.S.$265 per year. By 1965 the difference had grown to 16:1; by 1970, to 22:1; by 1975, to 31:1; and by 1977, to 50:1 (World Bank 1980a).

Effects of Low Educational Quality on Economic Productivity

Perhaps the most serious oversight of educational planners in the 1960s was to ignore the issue of educational achievement. They can no longer ignore this issue. The fact is that schools are being asked to transfer an increasing number of cognitive skills and amounts of factual knowledge. Areas of mathematics and science are being taught to primary-school students that, ten years ago, were taught to secondary-school students; and secondary-school students are being taught areas that before were taught only in university (or, in some cases, not discovered).[2] The amount of science, mathematics, and reading capability has a significant bearing on, among other things, the degree of economic productivity to be expected from the general population. The case of irrigation farming is illustrated in table 7–3.

We know that there are approximately four different levels of technology involved in irrigation agriculture (Harma 1979). The most basic level is the one that is passed from father to son. For that level, little or no schooling is required. The second level of technology is the one that utilizes a fertilizer. However, to successfully apply fertilizer requires rudimentary literacy and a knowledge of addition, subtraction, and division. If a farmer has none of these skills, then he will have to depend upon the one-to-one advice of an extension agent, and he will have to follow it by rote. This is expensive and frequently unproductive because small errors in interpretation can lead to significant losses. The third level of irrigation farming utilizes high-yielding varieties of seed and careful allocations of pest controls and fertilizer. For this a farmer needs to understand the principles of long division, multiplication, and other more-complex mathematical procedures; he must also possess an ability to read and write and have at least a rudimentary knowledge of chemistry and biology. The fourth level involves all of the aforementioned inputs but

Table 7–3
Four Basic Stages of Agricultural Productivity and Their Requirements

Farmer-Entrepreneurs[a]	Agricultural Inputs	Minimum Cognitive Requirements
Technology A: Traditional farming (techniques passed from father to son)	Local varieties	Addition, subtraction—not necessarily acquired through formal education
Technology B: Intermediate technology	Small quantities of fertilizer	Addition, subtraction, division rudimentary literacy
Technology C: Fully improved technology	High-yielding varieties, proven seeds, seed rates/acre, fertilizer rates/acre, pest-control rates/acre	Multiplication, long division, and other more-complex mathematical procedures; reading and writing facility; rudimentary knowledge of chemistry and biology
Technology D: Full irrigation farming	All aforementioned inputs; tubewell access during the off-season and water rates/acre	Mathematics; independence of written communication; high reading comprehension; ability to research unfamiliar words and concepts; elementary chemistry, biology, physics; and a regular access to information from print as well as electronic sources

[a]Direction from agricultural extension agents is helpful at any stage, but the essence of a farmer-entrepreneur is his ability to calculate his own production function.

also includes tubewell access during the off-season. For a farmer to operate efficiently at this level he needs to be able to communicate in writing, to research unfamiliar words and concepts himself, to understand the basic concepts of chemistry and biology and some physics, and he needs to have dependable access to new information from print as well as electronic sources. The lesson we have learned is very simple: To move farmers from one level of technology to another requires that the farmer possess certain minimal cognitive skills. The result of not understanding the principles on which the expected technology is based—with pesticides, for example—can be catastrophic to agricultural yields. Moreover, the cognitive requisites for insuring the efficiency of irrigation farming are no less than the manufacturing and service industries.

Levels of Learning in Postcolonial Countries

The available evidence from which one can compare the amount of science and other knowledge acquired after, for example, six years of schooling is scarce. The results of the International Association for the Evaluation of Educational Achievement (IEA) studies conducted between 1973 and 1975 in eighteen countries, including four low-income countries (Iran, Thailand, India, and Chile), are the world's best source of achievement data. Though any comparison—whether between pupils, schools, districts, or countries—should be approached cautiously, international comparisons of this kind are proving to be a sobering experience. There are differences among high-income countries, of course, in the amount of science knowledge and reading comprehension acquired, but these differences are, by comparison, trivial. The most compelling distinctions are those between pupils in high- and low-income countries. A typical finding shows the average score of students in the four low-income countries to be in the bottom 5–10 percent of students from the fourteen high-income countries (World Bank 1980b).

Determinants of Learning in Postcolonial Countries

Since the 1960s, sociologists have been trying to discover the magic formula for determining classroom achievement. The typical approach has been to survey a nationally representative sample of schools, to quantify each of the goods and services available in those schools that is likely to determine achievement, and then, after holding sex, socioeconomic status, and age constant, to attempt to measure the effect of school-quality characteristics in the aggregate as well as item by item. Most of us are aware of the results. So much of the variance in school achievement is accounted for by preschool characteristics (socioeconomic status for the most part) that the portion attributable to school quality has been at best unimpressive. This has worried educators as well as producers of school equipment and textbooks, and rightly so. The basic conclusion from these studies is, simply put, that better books or equipment are not the primary determinant of the acquisition of knowledge in classrooms, and as an investment on the part of taxpayers, new physical facilities, equipment, and textbooks appear to be ineffective. This debate is still continuing, but however ambiguous the efficacy of school physical quality in high-income countries may be, no such ambiguity exists in low-income countries. The evidence we have to date would suggest that school quality in low-income countries can explain twice and even three times the level of achievement variance that it can in high-income countries, and the

poorer the country in economic terms, the greater the impact on achievement school quality seems to have ($r = -.67$, $p < .001$) (Heyneman
1976, 1980a, 1980b; Heyneman and Loxley 1981, 1982).[3]

Which inputs can be expected to raise student achievement in the
developing world? The evidence is relatively scarce. A strenuous search
of the available literature from the last two-and-a-half decades could
locate only 30 studies in Africa, Asia, Latin America, and the Middle
East that used statistical techniques to assess the cognitive impact of
teacher training. By comparison, almost 400 of such studies were published in the United States in a single year.[4] Similar imbalances exist with
respect to the evidence on textbooks, duplicating machines, audiovisual
aids, educational radio, and television—in fact, with respect to all school
resources. Furthermore, results from available studies are not unambig-
uous. Smaller class size and longer teacher-training programs are not
always associated with higher achievement levels.

One of the most consistent indicators of higher achievement is the
availability of textbooks and other printed materials (Heyneman, Farrell,
and Sepulveda-Stuarto 1978; Heyneman and Jamison 1980). Table 7–4
lists fifteen studies that report twenty assessments of the relationship
between the availability of printed material and student outcomes. Although different methodologies were used and the quality of the data is
far from uniform, the positive relationship between input and outcome
in seventeen of the twenty cases suggests that, of any characteristic on
which we have data, textbooks are the single most important and consistent contributor to improved learning in schools.

The Response of the International Community

The demand for educational investment is slowly experiencing a shift in
emphasis, away from the requirements for universal primary education
and toward the requirements for higher levels of learning. This shift in
investment need is reflected to some degree in the lending program of
international organizations such as the World Bank. As far as one can
predict, the bulk of the bank group's capital investment in education will
continue to assist the expansion of specific educational institutions—96
percent of the resources dispersed between fiscal years 1970 and 1974
and 93 percent between fiscal years 1975 and 1978—but this proportion
is expected to decrease. By fiscal year 1983, it is expected to decline to
less than 85 percent. The remainder is accounted for by increases in
lending, not to specific institutions but for curriculum development, radio,
television, educational administration, and particularly, increases in the
development, production, and distribution of learning materials. By fiscal

Table 7–4

Availability of Reading Material and Student Outcomes in Low-Income Countries: Synopsis of the Literature

Author	Country	School Level	Outcome Measures	Relationships	Comments
Beebout (1972)	Malaysia	Grades 10, 11	Achievement gains in secondary school; used national examinations	+	Random sample of 89 schools; $n = 7,674$.
Comber and Keeves (1973)	Chile, India, Iran	Primary ten-year olds	Science achievement	+, +, −	International Evaluation of Educational Achievement
Farrell and Schiefelbeim (1974)	Chile	Primary grades 6–8	Math, language achievement	+[a]	National sample of primary schools
			Educational aspirations	+	
		Same cohort, four years later	Type of secondary school entered	+[a]	
			Survival to end of secondary school	+	
Fuller and Chantavanish (1977)	Thailand	Primary grade 3	Language and math achievement	+[a]	
Haron (1977)	Malaysia	Twelve-to-thirteen year olds	Bahasa Malaysia, English, math, science, history, geography	+[a]	National probability census sample; $n = 6,000$.
Heyneman and Jamison (1980)	Uganda	Grade 7	National tests in English, math, general knowledge; Ravens Progressive Matrices used as ability control	+	Results stronger for English than math or general knowledge; random sample of primary schools in eight districts
Jamison and Montenegro (1980); Heyneman and Montenegro (1980)	Philippines	Grades 1, 2	Filipino, math, science achievement	+[a]	National reduction of pupils to textbooks ratio from 10:1 to 2:1; gains over a year ranged from .18 to .51 standard deviations; national sample of primary schools

Table 7–4 continued

Author	Country	School Level	Outcome Measures	Relationships	Comments
Jamison, Searle, Galda, and Heyneman (1980)	Nicaragua	Primary grade 4	Mathematics	+[a]	Pre- and posttest scores over one year in 88 randomly selected classrooms
Lynch (1974)	Ecuador	Grade 1	Reading, math, science achievement	0	88 purposively sampled classrooms; assessed new texts
ODEPOR (1976)	El Salvador	Grades 2, 3, 5, 6, 8, and 9	Spanish, math, social and natural science	+	National probability sample of schools; household data
Simmons and Askoy (1972)	Tunisia	Individual students, grades 4–8	Arabic, French, arithmetic achievement	+	44 village students; 80 students from an urban suburb
Smart (1978)	Ghana	Grades 8, 9	Reading comprehension	+	40 rural experimental and control schools; used pre- and posttests over two years; treatment was access to a school newspaper
Thorndike (1973)	Chile Iran	Primary ten-year olds	Reading comprehension	+ –	International Evaluation of Educational Achievement
Wolff (1970)	Brazil Rio Grande do Sul	Primary grade 1	Promotion to grade 2 based on teacher assessment	+[a]	Random selection of 5 percent of schools; $n = 20,000$

[a]Stronger with low socioeconomic status and/or rural students.

year 1983, the bank group's education sector is expected to be investing U.S.$50 million/year in classroom software alone—up from U.S.$1.6 million/year a decade earlier. For example, 5 percent of the education projects contained a textbook component in fiscal year 1975; 10 percent in 1976; 25 percent in 1977. By fiscal year 1978 this figure had risen to 40 percent. In conjunction with bank group investments, every student, or a very large proportion of students, has, or will now have, textbooks in the following countries: Malawi, Brazil, Lesotho, Swaziland, Jamaica, El Salvador, the Philippines, Benin, and Indonesia.[5]

Future Developments

Anyone living in North America, Japan, or Europe—Western or Eastern—who is eighty years old will remember a time when basic education was not universal. One can easily forget how recent universal schooling is, even in areas of the world characterized by high per capita incomes. The fact is that universal schooling of a minimum standard—and other basic necessities such as freedom from starvation, innoculation against infectious disease, and the like—is the norm. Regardless of political structure, whether socialist or capitalist, these standards are the product of a universal willingness for populations to tax themselves and to distribute the benefits of that taxation with sufficient equality within their countries so as to lay a standard foundation of social health. Though considerable debate ensues over the manner in which income, land, and capital are distributed, the same debate, even in capitalist countries, does not occur over educational opportunity.[6]

This phenomenon of a universal willingness to be taxed for a universally accepted purpose is relevant internationally. For the last two generations (thirty-five years), all high-income countries have taxed themselves to assist people in countries other than their own. To be sure, the amount and purpose have differed from one country to the next and over time. However, even in periods of inflation, high unemployment, and negative balance of payments, no country has ceased to tax itself for the purpose of international assistance.

The issue for the 1980s is very simple. All high-income nations have come to accept the principle of self-taxation to establish a basic foundation for their own populations and in some fashion to assist those in countries other than their own. The question is when high-income nations will come to accept the principle of self-taxation to assist those in countries other than their own to acquire something that is regarded as the norm in high-income countries.

All countries now accept that every person should have access to

education. However, within wealthy countries—both socialist and capitalist—access has been defined in more-precise terms. Today the industrialized world commonly finds that the nature of educational
opportunity also includes the quality of that opportunity and that, unless
students have a reasonable level of resources to which they are exposed,
the requirements for equal education have not been met. What has
emerged—though by no coordinated effort—is, in fact, a standard for
educational opportunity that today varies in only slight degrees from one
high-income country to the next. This standard includes both a place in
school and a reasonable level of quality of that place.

Where postcolonial countries are concerned, in the past the standard
definition for the equality of educational opportunity has included only
a place in school. Now this is changing. When a grade-four school child
in Bolivia or India or Malawi has access to only one-sixtieth the level
of resources as the child in Europe or North America (even were there
to be universal schooling), no equality of educational opportunity exists.
To be sure, the world has something to be proud of in the field of
education. It will be possible—for the first time in human history—for
every individual at a given age to have an opportunity to begin schooling.
This may in fact come to pass in our own lifetime. However, this is not
a sign that an equality of opportunity has been accomplished between
nations. The fact is that a substantial level of new resources will now
have to be generated by, and directed toward, postcolonial countries if
pupils in those countries are to find anything approaching an equality of
opportunity after entry into school has been obtained.

Notes

1. It might be helpful to remind ourselves of what was agreed to
when the United Nations adopted the Universal Declaration of Human
Rights in December 1946, Article 26: "Everyone has the right to education. Education shall be free, at least in the elementary and fundamental
stages . . . and higher education shall be equally accessible to all on the
basis of merit."

2. In the 1850s, third-year students in one of North America's highest
rated universities (Columbia) could not compute an interest rate, say how
much three-fourths of five-fifths came to, or prove the Pythagorean theo-
rem (Nevins and Thomas 1952).

3. Contrary to what Jencks et al. (1972, 1979) conclude is true for
the United States, some evidence suggests that the quality of a primary
or secondary school is a robust predictor of a person's success in the
labor market, substantially more powerful, for example, than a person's

family background (Schiefelbein and Farrell 1980; Heyneman and Currie 1979; Fry 1980; Heyneman 1980b).

4. Educational Resources Information Center lists 388 titles published on this subject in the United States in 1977. A recent review of the evidence from low-income countries could locate only 23 studies between 1963 and 1977 (Husen, Saha, and Noonan 1978). A subsequent review, which made a specific effort to locate studies published in non-European languages, found a slightly higher number (Avalos and Haddad 1979).

5. Indonesia alone is estimated to have as many students in primary school as North America.

6. The subject of the debate is the degree to which equal educational opportunity is present, not whether to have it.

References

Avalos, B., and Haddad, W. *A Review of Teacher Effectiveness Research in Africa, India, Latin America, Middle East, Malaysia, Philippines, and Thailand: Synthesis of Results.* Ottawa: International Development Research Center, 1979.

Bane, Mary Jo. "Economic Justice: Controversies and Policies." In *The Inequality Controversy: Schooling and Distribution Justice,* edited by Arnold M. Levine and Mary Jo Bane. New York: Basic Books, 1975, pp. 304–326.

Beebout, H.S. "The Production Surface for Academic Achievement: An Economic Study of Malaysian Secondary Education." Ph.D. dissertation, University of Wisconsin at Madison, 1972.

Bell, W., and Robinson, R.V. "Equality, Success, and Social Justice in England the United States." *American Sociological Review* 43 (April 1978):125–148.

Coleman, J.S., et al. *Equality of Educational Opportunity.* Washington, D.C.: U.S. Government Printing Office, 1966.

Coleman, J.S. "The Equality of Opportunity and the Equality of Results." *Harvard Educational Review* 43 (1973):124–37.

———. "Inequality, Sociology and Moral Philosophy." *American Journal of Sociology,* November 1974, pp. 739–764.

Comber, L.C., and Keeves, J.P. *Science Education in Nineteen Countries.* New York: John Wiley & Sons, 1973.

Fry, G.W. "Education and Success: A Case Study of the Thai Public Service." *Comparative Education Review* 24 (1980):21–34.

Fuller, W.P., and Chantavanish, A. *A Study of Primary Schooling in Thailand: Factors Affecting Scholastic Achievement of Primary*

School Pupils. Bangkok: Office of the National Education Commission, 1977.

Harma, Risto. *The Farmer-Entrepreneur and His Prerequisite Prior Education in Agricultural Development*. Washington, D.C.: World Bank, 1979.

Haron, I. "Social Class and Educational Achievement in a Plural Society: Peninsular Malaysia." Ph.D. dissertation, University of Chicago, 1977.

Heyneman, S.P. "Influences on Academic Achievement: A Comparison of Results from Uganda and More Industrialized Societies." *Sociology of Education* 49 (1976):200–211.

Heyneman, S.P. "Primary Education in Bolivia: What's Wrong?" Mimeographed. Washington, D.C.: Education Department, World Bank, December 1979.

Heyneman, S.P. "Differences between Developed and Developing Countries: Comment on Simmons and Alexander's Determinants of School Achievement." *Economic Development and Cultural Change* 28 (1980a):403–406.

Heyneman, S.P. "The Evaluation of Human Capital in Malawi," Working Paper No. 420. Washington, D.C.: World Bank, 1980b.

Heyneman, S.P., and Currie, J.K. *Schooling, Academic Performance, and Occupational Attainment in a Non-Industrialized Society*. Washington, D.C.: University Press of America, 1979.

Heyneman, S.P., Farrell, J.P., and Sepulveda-Stuarto, M. "Textbooks and Achievement: What We Know," Working Paper No. 298. Washington, D.C.: World Bank, 1978.

Heyneman, S.P., and Jamison, D.T. "Student Learning in Uganda: Textbook Availability and Other Factors." *Comparative Education Review* 24 (1980):206–220.

Heyneman, S.P., and Loxley, W. "The Effects of Primary School Quality on Academic Achievement across 29 High and Low Income Countries." Paper presented to the Annual Meeting of the American Sociological Association, Toronto, August 1981.

Heyneman, S.P. and Loxley, W. "Influences on Academic Achievement across High and Low Income Countries: A Re-Analysis of IEA Data." *Sociology of Education*, January 1982.

Heyneman, S.P., and Montenegro, S.P. "Social Environmental Factors which Influence Student Learning in the Philippines." In *Improving School Quality in the Philippines: Evaluation, Research, and Educational Policy*, edited by D.T. Jamison and G. Feliciano. Manila: University of the Philippines Press, 1980.

Husen, T., Saha, L.J.; and Noonan, R. "Teacher Training and Student Achievement in Less Developed Countries," Working Paper No. 310. Washington, D.C.: World Bank, 1978.

Jamison, D.T., and Montenegro, S.P. "Evaluation of the Philippines Textbook Project: Multivariate Analysis of Data From Grades 1 and 2." In *Improving School Quality in the Philippines: Evaluation, Research, and Educational Policy,* edited by D.T. Jamison and G. Feliciano. Manila: University of the Philippines Press, 1980.

Jamison, D.T.; Searle, B.; Galda, K.; and Heyneman, S.P. "Improving Elementary Mathematics Education in Nicaragua: An Experimental Study of the Impact of Textbooks and Radio on Achievement." *Journal of Educational Psychology* (forthcoming).

Jencks, C.; Bartlett, S.; Corcoran, M.; Crouse, J.; Eaglesfield, P.; Jackson, G.; McClelland, K.; Mueser, P.; Olneck, M.; Schwartz, J.; Ward, S.; and Williams, J. *Who Gets Ahead? The Determinants of Economic Success in America.* New York: Basic Books, 1979.

Jencks, C.; Smith, M.; Acland, H.; Bane, M.J.; Cohen, D.; Gintis, H.; Heyns, B.; and Michelson, S. *Inequality: A Reassessment of the Effect of Family and Schooling in America.* New York: Basic Books, 1972.

Loxley, W., and Heyneman, S.P. "The Influences of School Resources on Learning Outcomes in El Salvador." Unpublished manuscript, Education Department, World Bank, Washington, D.C., 1980.

Lynch, P.D. "A National Textbook Program: Promise and Frustration." Paper presented to the Annual Meeting of the American Educational Research Association, Chicago, April 1974.

Meyer, J.W., and Hannan, M.T., eds. *National Development and the World System: Educational, Economic, and Political Change, 1950–1970.* Chicago: University of Chicago Press, 1979.

Neumann, P.H. *Publishing for Schools: Textbooks and the Less Developed Countries,* Working Paper No. 398. Washington, D.C.: World Bank, 1980.

Nevins, A., and Thomas, M., eds. *The Diary of George Templeton Strong.* New York: Macmillan, 1952.

Nozik, R. "Distributive Justice." In *The Inequality Controversy: Schooling and Distributive Justice,* edited by Arnold M. Levine and Mary Jo Bane. New York: Basic Books, 1975, pp. 252–276.

Oficina de Planeamiento y Organizacion (ODEPOR). *The Relations of Social, Economic, and Cultural Factors and National Achievement Exam Results.* El Salvador: Ministry of Education, 1977.

Rawls, John. "Justice as Fairness." *Philosophical Review* 67 (April 1958):164–194.

———. *A Theory of Justice.* Cambridge: Harvard University Press, 1971.

Schiefelbein, E., and Farrell, J.P. "Education and Occupational Attainment in Chile: The Effects of Educational Quality, Attainment, and Achievement." Unpublished manuscript, World Bank, Education Department, Washington, D.C., 1980.

Simmons, J., and Askoy, S. "Schooling for Development? Students and Workers in Tunisia." Unpublished manuscript, Harvard University, Department of Economics, Cambridge, 1972.

Smart, M.N. "The Densu Times—Self-made Literacy," *Development Communication Report* 21(January 1978).

Thorndike, Robert L. *Reading Comprehension in 15 Countries: An Empirical Study*. Stockholm: Almquist and Wiksell, 1973.

Wolff, L. *Why Children Fail First Grade in Rio Grande do Sol: Implications for Policy and Research*. Rio de Janiero: U.S. Agency for International Development, 1970.

World Bank. *Education Sector Policy Paper*. Washington, D.C., 1980a.

World Bank. *World Development Report, 1980*. Washington, D.C., 1980b.

8

Assessing the Impact of Nonformal Education on National Development Goals

Nat J. Colletta and
Donald B. Holsinger

Very few people agree on the role that nonformal education should play in developing nations. A small but articulate minority of people—the deschoolers—have for years proposed that nonformal programs relevant to the real needs of developing societies should replace schools. It is also claimed that schools can never be made over to serve basic development goals. A far larger number of people see nonformal programs as permanent parallels to, but not replacements for, a nation's formal schools. Still others view nonformal efforts as exclusively transition or stopgap programs, assigned to care for a nation's excess of unschooled children only until such time as sufficient schools exist to accommodate everyone of school age. Whether this balance comes about through decreasing the size of the school-age cohort or crash school building construction is unimportant—nonformal programs serve the interim need.

The question of which alternative planners have decided to pursue is of considerable importance because the decision has determined the way in which they have invested in curriculum development, facilities, and the preparation of personnel. Often in arriving at the decision there has been insufficient recognition of differences between what nonformal programs should do and what they can do. An expensive error is to claim that nonformal education should play a particular role if, in fact, there are good reasons why it cannot.

Over the past several years, the term *Nonformal education* has not only gained popular currency but also has accumulated a relatively thick mantle of general bibliographies, case studies, and readers, as well as a number of more-specific writings on alternative forms of educational delivery, on the development of appropriate materials and the design of training programs, on planning and coordination, and on political, economic, and sociocultural implications.

Nonformal education is not a new concept. Variants of this approach have appeared before under terms such as *out-of-school education*, the *shadow-school system*, the *educational complex, learning networks*, and *nonconventional education*. In most instances these formulations have reflected concern for the inability of a school-based educational system adequately to meet the needs of a society in change. Nonformal education, in its most recent formulation, grew out of the realization that universal compulsory schooling, with its high costs and labor-intensive character-istics, is not always the most effective technology for meeting the diverse learning needs of postcolonial societies. Nonformal-education theory questions the adequacy of a system of learning organized rigidly within limited time periods and circumscribed space, the dogmatism of en-trenched subject matter, and status inequality perpetuated by social-mo-bility patterns tied to academic achievement and the alienation and wastage of youth reflected in high dropout rates.

The recognition of these limitations fostered a new direction in ed-ucational thought, originally questioning the adequacy of ordinary formal schooling: Can a system found on Western models, confined narrowly in space and to a single phase of human development, with fixed resources and inflexible patterns of human interaction, be capable of meeting the rapidly proliferating, multifaceted needs of the new nations in the early years following independence? From the beginning, the problem of de-fining nonformal education by drawing attention to supposed limitations in its well-established sibling has given rise to suspicions that it is a metaphenomenon incapable of a separate existence.

Toward a Definition of Nonformal Education

After Philip Coombs coined the term *nonformal education* in his incisive delineation of an impending world educational crisis published in 1968, a vast amount of time, energy, and resources was expended simply in trying to define the term. It was described by some as all systematic communication of skill, knowledge, and attitude provided outside the limits of the formal school or as all education outside the conventional academic stream. Others attempted to define it more positively by specific context. Amidst this barrage of definition, usually by negation, of dis-tinctions between education, schooling, and training, and the sociological contradiction of a nonsystematized system, a useful distinction did emerge between three basic modes of education transmission: formal, nonformal, and informal. These approaches can be loosely connected to the broad educational objectives of knowledge, skill, and attitude generation. A further theoretical step was taken when these modes of transmission, each related to an aspect of human development, were placed together to show the ways in which nonformal and informal education complement, extend, or function as alternatives to the formal mode. In the process of mod-ernization, the formal mode is usually more effective in meeting the

cognitive needs for literacy and numeracy, while the nonformal and informal modes respond more appropriately to the need for motor skills
and the formation of appropriate attitudes respectively. Thus knowledge,
skill, and attitude generation were seen to be closely aligned with formal,
nonformal, and informal modes of transmission in a structural-functional
paradigm along the order of a Weberian ideal typology, though it should
be noted that each mode can be charged with a varying mix of such
generative functions; the fit is not rigid.

At this point, definitions of these three forms of education would
help to clarify the issue. By formal education, we mean the deliberate
and systematic transmission of knowledge, skills, and attitudes (with the
stress on knowledge) within an explicit, defined, and structured format
for space, time, and material, with set qualifications for teacher and
learner, such as are typified in the technology of schooling. Informal
education is the incidental transmission of attitudes, knowledge, and skills
(with the stress on attitudes) within highly diverse and culturally relative
patterns for the organization of time, space, and material, and also for
personal roles and relationships such as are implicit in varying configu-
rations of the family, household, community, and of course, the school.
Nonformal education is like formal in the deliberate and systematic transmission of knowledge, attitudes, and skills, except the stress is on skills.
In terms of process, it avoids the technology of formal schooling, per-
mitting a more-diverse and -flexibile deployment of space, time, and
material, and accepting a relaxation of personal qualifications in response
to the structure of the work place. Thus, the subsidiary distinguishing
definitions of these three modes of educational transmission pertain to
three areas: (1) the degree of deliberation; (2) the varied deployment of
the structural elements of space, time, material, and people; (3) the relative emphasis on the functional principles of knowledge, skill, and attitude generation.

Early work toward a clearer definition of nonformal education merged
with a broader concept of transmission and an enlarged panorama for
educational inquiry. At this point the direction changed from the academic
pursuit of definition to a field search for examples and case studies that
would permit an elaboration of the concept. This search for defining
characteristics revealed that nonformal education was a process with
which anthropologists and educational romanticists had been working for
decades. Notions such as cultural transmission, indigenous education,
human ecology, progressive education, and natural education took on
renewed meaning. Unfortunately, an integrated and multidisciplinary effort at clarification was hampered by rigid lines of academic separation,
fortified by specialized jargon. Only more recently have the concepts of
socialization, conditioning, communication, enculturation, and learning
begun to fuse into an integrated concept of nonformal education.

One prominent notion that nonformal education draws from earlier transmission theory is the view that the process of interchange between teacher and student is dynamic, real, experience based, and oriented to meeting basic human needs in a specific sociocultural context. In effect, the transmission is immediate, and it is the critical link between man and the environment in the struggle for survival. Learning and productivity become one, as the waste of scarce natural resources or human energies in the storing of competencies as abstract symbols for unguaranteed use at some later time is minimized. Literacy and numeracy, in the Western sense of these terms, are neither prerequisites for participation nor equated or confused with the concept of intelligence. The transmission is highly task oriented, and competence is measured by functional ability to meet basic needs for survival rather than certification of abstracted achievement. Moreover, the space and time dimensions of the process are relatively open ended.

Learning, or transmission, adjusts itself to accord with the changing demands of the life cycle and the environment. Each transaction can be viewed as a complete unit, not necessarily as a step toward a second- or third-level transaction. Learning needs (as survival skills) are met wherever and whenever they arise by the most immediately appropriate methods. The human dynamics of this process are multidirectional. Peer learning plays as significant a role as intergenerational transmission. Frequently work, learning, and play blend into the same activity. Lines of transmission often run along natural networks of exchange, distribution, and consumption, both social such as extended family structures and physical such as natural waterways. This structural-functional fit between man, education, and environment could be described as an "educological" system, the very fiber of which is the process of transmission.

Thus, the contemporary characterization of education in terms such as modular instruction, open education, competency-based education, field-centered learning, lifelong education, and total-learning systems and the analytical breakdown of nonformal education in terms of structure, content, methods, sponsorship, and so on have a theoretical basis in the history of man's attempts to come to terms with his environment.

Implementation: The Politics of Nonformal Education

When nonformal education moves from the academic realm to the field, theory is confronted by the realities of political struggle among development agents over control of territory and resources. Endemic issues of policy control and resource allocation continually weaken efforts to synchronize and coordinate diverse educational efforts in the interests of an integrated and total, "educological" human-resource-development program. Like their academic counterparts, competing development agents wrap their purposes in insulating terminology (that is, in agriculture it is extension; in manpower, training; in health, service; in education, community education) in order to legitimize their organizational activities and to protect both territory and resources from others who seek to expand their own power through a redefinition of activity and function.

Ironically, however, most development agents work in strikingly similar contexts. Cooperation is possible because a mutual desire exists to increase productivity and services in order to raise levels of basic human sufficiency. The normative or policy conditions under which the agents operate are often similar, and they frequently share client populations and, indeed, facilities. Consequently, there is usually a possibility for effective coordination, providing the mutual fears of exploitation and absorption could be reduced. We have observed that what is required in order to take advantage of theoretical and technical exchange is an intervention strategy capable of eliciting this latent coordination, thus maximizing cooperation between development agents. It is true that the centripetal tendencies of total coordination could result in a decrease in innovation and an increase in bureaucracy, a disposition certainly to be checked, but an optimum degree of coordination could minimize redundancies and foster creative programming. Indeed, the very issue that inhibits coordination—the allocation of scarce resources—is the condition that makes cooperation necessary in order to ensure that these same resources are not dissipated or constricted by constraints and inequities of a splintered system.

Besides the problems of competing development agencies, each with its own interests and concepts of priorities to protect, nonformal education faces another kind of political problem. Development is not solely a matter of quantitative growth, but it is also a qualitative enterprise with concern for objectives such as an equitable distribution of resources. If egalitarianism is viewed by development agents as an essential part of the enterprise, nonformal education could be used as a mechanism for increasing opportunity to the poor and the dispossessed, thus challenging elitism inherent in a socioeconomic inheritance supported by a narrowly defined formal school-based system. Nonformal education has been proposed as an outflanking maneuver in support of social reconstruction. Others have held that such education might have the reverse effect of buffering school-established elite-mass separation by serving as a pacifier, diverting the energy of the masses toward lower-status occupation. Guyot has maintained that while nonformal education could broaden the spread of educational opportunity, it would also probably have the effect of streamlining rather than eliminating the current elite pattern.[1]

Criticisms such as these lead us again to stress the crucial importance of respect for the relationships among its parts. There is otherwise a high risk of creating a multidimensional-transmission pattern (that is, urban industrial-based system, rural agricultural-based system, coastal agricultural-based system, and so on), leading to differentiated rewards, both economically and socially.

A further aspect of nonformal education that is often overlooked is its potential use for the political socialization outside, beyond, or supplementary to the school. In particular, where schooling cannot reach large sections of the school-age population and effectively co-opt the students' energies for the state, nonformal schooling in the form of youth-service programs may be used to meet this ideological objective. National scouting movements, young pioneers, volunteer schemes, and other such service-oriented programs, as Paulston states, "have frequently been used to 'cool down' aspirations for formal schooling, to remove youth from the labor market, and to co-opt peer groups and enable adult-making agencies to influence the youth culture."[2] It is both unwarranted and naive for nonformal-education theorists to think of such programs only in terms of their knowledge- and skill-generating capacities. Conversely, sufficient evidence exists to state that these programs, while serving political ends, also help to ease the break with traditional environments, do offer certain material advantages, and open up opportunities for occupational advancement.

The Economics of Nonformal Education

Political motivations blend into economic concerns as the central issue becomes how to use learning networks to link people's needs to systems of production in the most efficient and effective manner. The problem is to bridge the gap between training and employment, learning and production (contribution), so that wastage of human energies and natural resources is minimized while the equitable distribution of goods and services is maximized. In short, the challenge becomes one of how to make capital-intensive educational activities more productive and labor-intensive productive activities more educational—that is, how to match human-resource development with a changing opportunity structure, to market demands, through a transmission network that links production with training. This has been a fundamental concern of development organizations since they have recognized the need to absorb trained persons into a fluctuating labor market in a harmonious fashion, thus providing technical skills to support a growing economy while at the same time

providing political stability through the generation of employment opportunities.

While it is true that the universal extension of formal education is
still a remote aspiration, Hunter's reminder that "school-based education
has extended far beyond the present opportunity to use it in most countries" is also valid.[3] There is little need to call further attention to Foster's
point that emphasizing vocational schooling is a shortsighted solution.[4]
J.S. Furnivall put this succinctly when he wrote, "The encouragement
of technical qualifications implies that it is possible to create industries
by training men to practice them."[5] Clearly, learning has to move as
closely as possible to the point of utilization and productivity. Callaway's
stress on apprenticeship is one firm step in this direction.[6] Owen's and
Shaw's suggestion of a "knowledge-communication-production-sys-
tem," emphasizing horizontal rather than vertical relationships as central
to reconsidering development, is another step in meeting the problem.[7]
Further information can be gained from examination of the experience
of Tanzania, Cuba, and China in the modification of schools into production units and of farms and factories into education units. Governments
could consider the subsidization of educational components in the private
sector as one strategy for moving learning closer to the point of productivity. Here the division of nonformal-education financing into public and
private sectors becomes an additional issue. In terms of cost-effectiveness
analysis, much work is still to be done on such experimental linkages
between learning and productive activities.

Turning to a discussion of cost-effectiveness as compared with cost
efficiency, the overlap between the politics and the economics of nonformal education becomes increasingly evident. Cost-effectiveness, as
Hilliard shows, is not a matter of dollars and cents, a quantitative assessment of the human values expressed in ideological tenets and political
structures.[8] We cannot be concerned only with the image of an affluent
society, but we must recognize the needs of a human society as well.
What is at issue goes beyond the traditional emphasis on economic growth
to its concomitant political relationship with distribution. One cannot
separate the economic and political issues of production from the intervening forces of educational transmission.

One further question is whether or not nonformal education is a new
answer to the problem of providing adequate employment for the presently
schooled unemployed, thus displacing the earlier manifest objective of
providing training and employment opportunities for the nonschooled.
Thus, formal and nonformal educational strategies might join to form a
huge welfare bureaucracy for the more-effective placement of the politically volatile schooled but unemployed elites, while perpetuating a con-

venient system of mass exploitation, with increasing inefficiency and ineffectiveness. To decipher the political economy of nonformal education, transmission and opportunity structure must be examined as a symbiotic whole in the process of development.

The Sociocultural Dimensions of Nonformal Education

Concentration on problems of transmission in relation to political and economic structures cannot exclude consideration of, and respect for, the existing cultural environment. The entire theme of institution building in development theory often implicitly assumes that viable institutions exist within the user context. This attitude ignores reality, is ethnocentric and discriminatory, and thus in consequence, limits impact over time. Externally induced opportunities are most fruitful when they are presented within the context of the receiver's capacity for comprehension, for then it is possible to effect a smoother transition to a new cultural world view.

Human-resource-development agents cannot, therefore, expect success founded upon the false premise that external forces operate in a vacuum. They should neither assume that natural networks of leadership, organization, and transmission are lacking nor that the projected needs for change imposed by external agents will have greater legitimacy and acceptance in the community than the logic of needs as established by indigenous processes. Peasants may be more rational than many development agents are capable of seeing or willing to admit because their perceptions are based on the communal accumulation of experience. Development agents can greatly improve their relationship with user communities, and thus enhance their contribution, by taking better account of formal and informal processes of indigenous decision making and by recognizing the validity of indigenous sanctioning and transmission channels as practical educational networks for novel messages. This requires understanding and respect for indigenous values, reward systems, learning styles, mental processes, human-interaction patterns, and other culturally specific variables as both constraints on, and inputs to, a successful human-resource-development program. The fact that development agents and local communities may be operating under different definitions of reality rooted in variant world views must be recognized and worked with in the process of maintaining cultural continuity in the face of adaptive change. Indeed, this is the core of the problem, from which can come the greatest release of energy. This is the point at which an "educological" strategy, stressing cultural ecology, holds the greatest potential from a development perspective. Between formal schooling, the agent usually of a wider universe of knowledge but often transmitted as an alien imposition, and informal education, as the bearer of cultural continuity and community values, nonformal education can play a harmonizing and adaptable role. The application of this principle could possibly be one of the greatest strengths, and challenges, of the nonformal-education movement.

Considerable work has been done in establishing the ties between formal schooling and value acquisition, and it now appears almost axiomatic that the longer a child has been exposed to the organizational milieu of schooling, the more modern are his attitudes and values. Other researchers have invested their energies toward the end of understanding the relationship between nonformal education and the production in children, and more commonly, in adult learners, of attitudes considered to be modern. *Modern* is normally understood in this context to mean a set of personal dispositions that is thought to render an individual competent to deal with the requirements of urban industrial life. Of course, social and economic development cannot be understood to occur exclusively within the urban industrial sector. Consequently, if education is to assist harmoniously in the development of rural areas, it would follow that what is needed is not that people be modern so much as that they have the disposition and the skill to find local solutions to real and pressing problems.

From Nonformal-Education Theory to Research and Evaluation

We began this inquiry into the maze of nonformal education by looking at its origin and the reasons for its popularity in postcolonial societies. We proceeded to explore its definition and character. We then turned to a discussion of some key operational issues in this area as viewed from several disciplinary perspectives. While setting out a paradigm for nonformal education by which we might eventually hope to assess its effectiveness, along the way we distilled from the whole a small number of propositions. These propositions restate in summary form the beliefs of nonformal-education theorists and developers concerning the conditions for its effective deployment, provide essential distinctions between it and other modes of educational transmission, and define the its relationship to other social forms and functions. We do not claim that these propositions are testable as stated, and they do not exhaust all possible derivations from the literature on this topic. We see them as a convenient summary useful to a future empirically based evaluation and possibly stimulating to our colleagues in the ongoing discussion of whither nonformal education.

1. Formal, informal, and nonformal education are structurally unique. The components of each may be distinguished in terms of content, medium, and methodology. While they share the critical structural elements of space, time, material, and people, they are uniquely differentiated by their techniques (methodology) for organizing these elements.

2. The unique structural arrangements in a given methodology integrate the components of content and medium into the gestalt of a distinctive mode of education. This gestalt enables a particular mode to perform certain educational functions better than others.

3. Formal education is more effective when the educational function is cognitive, abstract, and evaluative, as best represented in technology of schooling. Informal education is more effective when the educational function is affective, related to values and beliefs, as best illustrated in the sociocultural techniques of family, peer group, and community. Nonformal education is more effective when the educational function is psychomotor, concrete, and skill oriented, as best exemplified in the technologies of the work place.

4. Formal education is best at storing knowledge in the form of thought; informal education is best at storing emotion in the form of sentiment; and nonformal education is capable of wedding thought and sentiment into useful action (praxis).

Nonformal methods are best at meeting real needs arising from concrete objectives of physical survival, while formal and informal methods are better equipped to attend to felt needs and abstract goals in relation to sociopsychological adaptation.

5. Nonformal and informal education modes are more conducive to the promotion of smooth cultural transmission and graduated behavioral change because they operate in a context of sociocultural reality that is directly meaningful and manageable for the user because these modes are open and thus more flexible in space and time and because they frequently make less distinction between work, learning, and recreation. Formal education abstracts the user from sociocultural reality; defers activity, participation, and immediate meaning and practice of what is transmitted; functions in a closed time and space frame; and can result over time in cultural alienation that can only be justified in the learner by a process analogous to conversion.

6. The closer the fit between educational mode and culturally specific variables—namely, the learning styles, reward systems, cognitive style, human-interaction patterns, value orientations, and so on—the higher the perceived legitimacy of the educational agent, the more acceptable the message, the greater the success of transmission.

7. Although different in structure and priority of educational function, the formal, informal, and nonformal modes are not found in isolation or

as serving only a single educational function. If transmission is recognized as a life process, then formal, informal, and nonformal may weave in and out of one another, taking priority according to changing individual- and social-development strategies of the life cycle: for example, informal, childhood, family; formal, adolescence, school; nonformal, adulthood, work. Thus, formal, informal, and nonformal education interface in a way such that each can support the other.

8. Philosophical assumptions about man and nature condition the style of relationship between the human-resource-development agent and the user population in either a pedagogical strategy, an androgogical strategy, or a mixture of the two. These strategies relate closely to formal, informal, and nonformal education respectively.

9. The varying modalities of transmission can be perceived as critical linkages in a larger human-resource-development strategy connecting environmental factors, user demands and needs, and development policies and objectives. Educational planning can be scientific, total, and "edu-cological" to the degree that it seeks an empirical match between structural arrangements (transmission modes) and behavioral objectives (development goals in terms of knowledge, skill and attitude generation) in an environmentally specific manner (cultural and physical), in order to meet human learning needs (cognitive, affective, psychomotor) as related to a changing opportunity structure, both efficiently and effectively (humane, material, cost-benefit).

10. All three transmission modes are capable of being exploited for political purposes in terms of both resource allocation and political socialization. All three can narrow or broaden the gap between class, ethnic, and geographical divisions as a function of the manipulation of differential payoff attached to each. Nonformal education, however, has the potential of greater cost efficiency due to its ability to move the cost, along with the transmission process, closer to the point of use and productivity. This ability can be strategically linked to progressive egalitarianism and integration.

We believe that a critical need exists to reassess the impact of investment in nonformal education on national development goals over the past two decades. Because nonformal education is a conceptually untidy social form, it is unfair to pass judgment on all projects going under this label from evidence restricted to a single case or category of cases. There are several comprehensive and recent reviews of nonformal-education projects around the world. These are descriptive and analytical only insofar as they locate projects within types. What is needed is a more empirically based review of evaluation data taken from a representative sample of projects. The sample should be stratified along several dimensions:

Geographic location,

Program type (extended primary schools, skill centers, mobile training units, and so on),

Development goal (test scores, job acquisition, proportion literate,
five-year plans, and so on).

The necessary research objectives are, first, to define the several
forms or structures that nonformal-education projects have assumed. We
will examine a sample of major externally assisted projects and attempt
to classify them into a small number of groups according to their salient
features. Once grouped in this fashion, it will be possible to examine the
social, political, geographical, economic, and demographic context pre-
dominately associated with nonformal-education projects of a certain
type. By working backward from the principal dependent variables that
worked (for example, skill attainment, level of literacy reached, employment gained, and so forth), one can then determine the salient features
of those projects that have been most successful. These features will
become the independent variables that will be used to test major hy-
potheses in data separately derived. The purpose is to gain insight into
the circumstances under which such schooling succeeds and fails in reach-
ing its goals.

Second, elucidate the social goals that planners have sought to achieve
through nonformal education. Project objectives cover a broad range of
social concerns. Some are closely coupled to traditional educational and
schooling goals such as, for example, student achievement, upgrading
teachers, and curriculum reform. Other goals are more remote from educational processes and causal connections more difficult to establish.
Among these are enhanced employability, greater earnings, and access
to institutions of higher learning. Research should examine the arguments
advanced for such linkages and discuss in turn their theoretical adequacy,
empirical validity, and policy relevance.

The third research objective is to determine the relationship between
program costs and benefits. Research should investigate the kinds of data
that have been collected and suggest strategies for analysis that will yield
instructive insights into total and unit costs and social and private benefits.

Fourth, assess the history of project success in terms of local funding
after donor assistance has expired. To what extent have nonformal-education projects proven so worthwhile that they have continued once
external loan or grant assistance is withdrawn? The fundamental question
is the extent to which nonformal education is merely a donor phenomenon.

Last, understand the relationship between consumer demand for nonformal education and the needs perceived by social planners. It is nec-

essary to know the extent to which nonformal-education projects have been built on a foundation of firm evidence of consumer demand for it. Obviously, it is fundamental to investigate the contention that nonformal schooling does not work because it is regarded as inferior to conventional schooling by the very people it seeks to serve. Under what circumstances are the educational deficiencies seen by planners as real needs effectively translated into high consumer demand for a nonformal-education project designed to address those same deficiencies?

Future research will draw heavily upon published and unpublished evaluation documents, program-monitoring data, and project descriptions. Researchers will try to distill from the massive amount of information available the outline of the major dimensions of the nonformal-education movement, its reported successes and failures. Finally, they must identify those areas that represent unanswered questions for which reanalysis of available evaluation data is insufficient. In these areas, additional evidence will be required for a comprehensive review.

Nonformal education was originally discovered by donor agencies without an empirical basis for judging its effectiveness. Now, apparently, many of these same agencies are ready to discard it—again, without empirical basis. We hope this summary and the future work we have outlined will contribute to the data required for sound policy decisions to be taken.

References

Callaway, Archibald. "Nigeria's Indigenous Education: The Apprentice System." *Journal of African Studies* 1 (1964):62–69.

Foster, Philip. "The Vocational School Fallacy in Development Planning." In *Readings in the Economics of Education,* edited by Mary Jean Bowman et al. Paris: UNESCO, 1968, pp. 614–629.

Furnivall, J.S. *Colonial Policy and Practice in the Netherlands Indies.* New York: New York University Press, 1956, p. 386.

Guyot, James F. "Who Gets What When Education Is Deformalized?" In *New Strategies for Educational Development,* edited by C.S. Brembeck and T.J. Thompson, Lexington, Mass., Lexington Books, D.C. Heath and Company, 1973, pp. 129–137.

Hilliard, John F. *The Economic Value of Nonformal Education.* Unpublished paper presented at the International Conference in Nonformal Educaton, Michigan State University, East Lansing, Mich. (April 27, 1974), p. 3.

Hunter, Guy. *The Best of Both Worlds?: A Challenge on Development Policies in Africa.* London: Oxford University Press, 1967, pp. 96–113.

Owen, Edgar, and Shaw, Robert. *Development Reconsidered: Bridging the Gap between Government and People*. Lexington, Mass.: Lexington Books, D.C. Heath and Company, 1972.

Paulston, Rolland G. "Nonformal Educational Alternatives." In *New Strategies for Educational Development*, edited by C.S. Brembeck and T.J. Thompson. Lexington, Mass.: Lexington Books, D.C. Health and Company, 1973, p. 79.

9

The Dilemma of Educational Planning

Douglas M. Windham

In the last three decades, educational planners in postcolonial societies have seen the perception of their role by scholars and political decision makers deteriorate from one of critical importance to one of only practical necessity. The accumulation of educational failures—again, as perceived by the external observers of the process—has led to a devaluation of the planners' credibility and an increasing malaise toward the whole process of educational management. Specific areas of manpower demand, and the ongoing social pressure for, generalized educational access (and, often, the political importance of teacher and student groups) have retained education's position in most national budgets. However, fewer politicians or senior bureaucrats now pronounce education to be the major vehicle for social change, and fewer still actually believe it can play this role.

The decline of education's credibility is directly linked with the decline in the status of the educational planner. However, education is not alone in this critical reexamination of its determinant effects. Other social-investment areas also have undergone eclipse in recent years as the inflated promises of the 1960s have failed to be realized in population control, rural health, and community development. In contrast to these other social-investment activities, unfortunately, education is seen as the area of greatest shortfall between performance and promise.

Yet education—with the frequent exception of national defense—absorbs more societal resources than any other publicly financed activity. Also, regardless of the perceptions of failure, no society appears prepared to either yield its control over education or to abandon the basic postcolonial commitment to educational expansion. The central quandary for the educational planner is, then, the need to design a scheme for cost-effective management within an enterprise of increasingly diverse forms

This chapter is based upon the author's long-standing interest in the issues of individual choice and educational planning. The earlier work upon which this version is based was supported by the International Institute of Educational Planning, the Harvard University Analysis and Methods of Educational Planning Project, and the Stanford University Institute for the Study of Educational Finance and Governance. The conclusions and opinions are the author's sole responsibility.

159

that continues to engender often unrealistic and uncertain benefits but that produces all-too-certain and immediate costs.

The Macroeducational-Planning Dilemma

In providing financial and advisory assistance to the educational systems of developing nations, the international-support agencies have behaved as if a clear understanding existed of the educational-planning process. This approach has created one of the central dilemmas faced by the educational-planning specialist. For example, the contemporary research and policy emphasis on how education is planned presupposes affirmative answers to the questions of whether education can be planned and, if so, whether it should be planned. Of course, the last question is more appropriately stated as: In what circumstances should a particular form and level of education be planned, and what type of planning is appropriate for a given social objective? This restatement of the planning problem emphasizes the futility of any discussion of education that assumes that it is an inter- or intranationally homogeneous social institution.

Social scientists and policymakers alike use *education* as a shorthand phrase even though they realize that it exists in a variety of forms. However, language has a power of its own, and as a result, one can read a variety of statements—by scholars and policymakers alike—about what education is, what it can do, and how it should be planned. Admittedly, the macroeducational models of planning appear to be more concerned with aggregate flows of students or resources into, through, and out of the educational system. Even in the least developed postcolonial nations, education already exists in such myriad forms that level, type, location, and a number of other characteristics must be known before student or resource flows can be interpreted relative to social or economic goals. The greatest need in the study of educational planning is for policymakers, practitioners, and scholars of education to at all times specify the exact educational experience under study. Even the critics of educational planning often have fallen into this semantic trap; in suggesting alternatives to traditional planning models they must also be concerned about the education that cannot be planned under new forms of direction.

For example, it is quite simple to expand the quantitative outcomes of schooling. The period of 1945–1975 has seen successes of this sort throughout the postcolonial states, rich and poor. What is much more difficult to plan is an expansion of education that maintains the previous level of educational quality, whether measured by cognitive scores, rates of employment, or expected lifetime earnings. The current macroeducational techniques of social demand, rate of return, and manpower planning will never be able to be used in planning a system that is simultaneously responsive to individual student motivations and general economic incentives. When combined with systems of general rather than specific educational subsidization, the macroeducational methodologies are restricted even further in their social utility.

In discussing planning, one must always differentiate between the structural planning that takes place at the center of the educational system and the individual planning occurring with each student and family unit. Here, the latter form of planning will be termed *decision making* so that this important distinction is maintained. The central educational planner deals largely with the same quantitative artifices found in the macroeducational methodologies, such as expenditures per pupil, average student-teacher ratios, mean teacher qualifications, textbooks per child, and so on. The individual student and his family are faced with a quantitative reality of a specific school, a specific teacher, and a specific number and quality of materials. This quantitative divergence between the artifices of the central planner and the realities of the individual student/family is the basis for the advocacy here for a much more-microeducational bias in the study of planning education of all levels and forms.

The response to this may be that this argument carried to an extreme would require educational planning that would apply to only a single student—exactly so. The most important educational decisions will always be those that are made at the student-specific, microeducational level. The complex interactions of the student with his parents and siblings, his peers, the teacher and headmaster, and other proximate individuals will determine the success or failure of the educational exercise. Summed over all the students at all levels, such interactions will determine the success or failure of a particular form of education, and summed over all forms, these interactions will create the outcome of that mythical entity, education.

The interaction described here is quite distant from the activity normally dealt with by central educational planners. A second misconception, equally as limiting as the one of education homogeneity, is that the primary-education planners are the bureaucrats who sit in state, regional, or national educational ministries. In fact, these bureaucrats, no matter how powerful, are never the most important actors in the planning of education. All educational outcomes, no matter how successfully structured within the educational system, are ultimately determined by the individual decisions made by the individual administrators, teachers, students, and families throughout the system. The students are more influenced by the actions of parents and teachers than by local administrators and more by the actions of local administrators than by those of the central planning bureaucracy.

The central planning apparatus obviously has a very important role because the structures they create place limits on how much freedom will exist for individual decision making. The most useful conception of the central planning role is that it creates the conditions for potential outcomes. Local administrators, through their successes or failures of implementation, extend or further limit this potential; parents and teachers create the proximate environment for educational achievement; and individual students determine the actual outcomes. To the extent that the planning bureaucracy depends on a macroeducational technique that is insensitive or antithetical to the individual decision-making criteria of students, a serious dislocation will result between planned goals and realized outcomes.

The centralized educational-planning system can also create patterns of incentives to which the educational participants can react. Some incentives are nearly mandatory—for example, compulsory school-attendance laws for children of a certain age. Parents and children can avoid such incentives only at the risk of legal action. Some incentives are quite subtle—for example, different levels of subsidization for various programs of study at the university level. Many participants may be ignorant of the fact that if they major in a postsecondary physical-science curriculum, the government will spend more on their education than if they specialize in the humanities or social sciences. Even if aware of differential subsidization, the educational participant is usually free to choose a less-subsidized course of study—that is, to ignore the government's incentive. An additional complexity is suggested by the preceding example: The government planner may generate incentives that are unintended or may even run counter to basic social policy.

What is gained by the emphasis on the heterogeneity of educational experience and the nonexclusivity of governmental educational planning? First, one is allowed to appreciate why the use of education as a solution to a wide variety of societal problems has led to failures that have, in turn, reduced government confidence in education. Second, macroeducational planning can be seen to be limited to the crudest forms of educational direction and to be sharply restricted in its ability to deal with the diversity of educational needs existing in most postcolonial nations. Third, the agnostic approach to macroeducational planning proposed here allows one to understand more clearly why governmental educational planning requires an improved understanding of the calculus of individual decision making concerning education as well as integration of educational-planning activities with the general economic and social planning engaged in by the government. Educational planning at the central- or regional-government level rarely operates with an information base that a private entrepreneur would consider to be adequate for decision making.

The entrepreneur, unless an inveterate gambler or able to avoid account-ability for his actions, would never make a decision touching the number of human lives or involving the sums of money with which the educational planner is routinely involved without much more information. Centralized educational planning in the last three decades has often seemed to be maximizing action, rather than achievement, of specific goals. Too often, building schools and producing teachers with certain degree levels be-comes a substitute for dealing with the real qualitative issues of educa-tional outcomes and fiscal accountability.

The educational planner, under pressure from his own government's political leadership and often under the tutelage of so-called international-education experts, will often initiate dramatic educational changes that are unjustified by the state of knowledge of educational research. Such reform is easier and politically more palatable than the discovery of the actual determinants of educational failures. Trial and error is a legitimate scientific process, but one can make a strong case for more-modest and -marginal changes in education while awaiting a better understanding of education and its social role.

The lack of integration of governmental educational planning and general economic and social planning stands in sharp counterpoint to the educational-planning decisions made within individual homes. In the home, the parents and/or students must relate their educational decisions to a variety of other socioeconomic pressures. The need for children's work, in the home or outside; the effect of education on future employment and pay probabilities; and the changing role of women or minorities are all factors that will impact upon the family as it attempts to rationalize its plans.

A final major advantage of the alternative view of educational plan-ning in reducing the planner's dilemma is the opportunity it allows to envision an educational system wherein educational experiences would remain varied but could become more complementary to the perceived needs of the individual decision makers. The centralized planner has no monopoly on wisdom and may not even have an advantage in terms of relevant information. Why, then, should governmental educational-plan-ning systems not be designed so as to exploit the decision-making ability of the populace? Only the socialist nations have had the courage to be honest in regard to this question; they assert that the citizen is simply not to be trusted to make the decision in the best interest of society. However, even in the most totalitarian systems, it is impossible to legislate or to regulate all behavior, and thus the government is still forced into the frequent use of incentives rather than direct control.

To summarize, the complexity of educational experience and the multiplicity of educational decision makers reduces the common conception of the powerful centralized educational planner to an absurdity. Even in nondemocratic societies, a majority of educational-planning activities involves the creation of incentives rather than the issuance of mandatory regulations. If one accepts this view of education and educational planning, the dilemma of whether educational planning can be done and to what extent it should be centrally, rather than individually, governed becomes more susceptible to productive debate. It has already been noted that the importance of education as a behavioral, political, social, and financial entity is such that one cannot imagine a government that would not feel some obligation toward planning, even if such activity were restricted to the most limited provision of information for individual decision making.

The succeeding section of this chapter discusses the manner in which macroeducational policy might become more synergistic with individual choice. The effect of bureaucratic forms of governance on the demand for information and the specificity of program design is stressed. The purpose of this next section is not only to sensitize the reader to the false premises of contemporary planning techniques but also to increase an appreciation of the planning alternatives potentially available.

The Role of Individual Decision Making

While recognizing the obvious truth that the educational system of a nation is intertwined with larger social and economic systems, educational research and planning, based upon a more-detailed understanding of the mechanisms of individual decision making within education, can make a contribution to the rationalization of the educational system. Once any part of the social system is improved, the government policymaker and researcher can understand more easily the causes and effects of continuing inefficiencies and inequalities in the remainder of the system.

It is important to emphasize that no incentive, planned or not, can have a predictable effect unless it is perceived and understood by the individual decision maker and is consonant with the determinants of the individual's decision-making behavior. The racial integration of schools in the United States has been delayed largely because the incentives for integration have failed to anticipate the basis of individual decisions made by students and families of both major racial groups. Vocational emphases in secondary schools and ruralization of the curriculum have both been extremely difficult in most postcolonial nations because of opposition by individual students and families. Planning of education, to have any success in producing predictable outcomes, must be grounded in a better understanding of individual decision-making criteria. Thus, information flows and policy incentives must be seen as major forces determining planning success. This success is only in terms of the planners' achieving the desired incentive message; constant auditing of effects will be necessary to assure planners that responses are in line with their expectations as well as being those they desire.

Personal accountability is at the core of any effective system of incentives. However, one must recognize that increased individual assumption of the costs of a decision implies a prerequisite need for equitable social structuring of decision making. Individual decision making is capable not only of maintaining existing social distortions, but also, without proper safeguards, it can become a conduit through which extant injustices are exacerbated. The product of individual accountability systems will be in line with the individual's perception of the established incentives; whether the motives for establishing these incentives and the effects of decisions based upon them will be good is a decision each individual will be left to make. If one accepts the assertion that improved rationality and explicitness in education can lead to marginal improvements in resource allocation and distributional equity, then incentive-based programs deserve serious consideration—especially when one recognizes that these programs will serve to highlight continuing inefficiencies and inequities in both education and other social systems.

The two research areas upon which this new perception of educational planning is based should be explored. The first of these is the area of public choice and especially public choice as applied to education.[1] The emphasis in this chapter on the use of private-incentive signals to affect individual behavior is itself a natural evolution from the behaviorist assumptions that lie at the heart of neoclassical economic theory. The major contribution of the public-choice literature has been to clarify the previously implicit assumptions of the centrist rationale for public activity. Even where democratic forces are at work, one of the major insights provided by public-choice analysis has been to show the degree to which such political processes can deviate from the market optimums or even equilibriums.[2] Such deviation is not itself evidence of policy error, but it does require that some justificaton exist for what are apparently actions reducing individual welfare or at least the welfare of one group for the benefit of another.

While public-choice theory has set the stage, so to speak, the theory of bureaucracy has provided a conceptual vehicle to which specific analysis of behavior in higher education may be joined. One of the most valuable of these models is found in the work of Wintrobe, but the early contribution of Leibenstein is especially significant.[3] The concept of X-efficiency, which originates with Leibenstein, suggests that measures of effort rather than traditional measures of productive efficiency determine the individual success within most organizations. The purpose of the economic analysis of bureaucracies is to specify more directly the forces within an organization that lead to the type of behavior observed by Leibenstein and others.

From this literature one can create a model of individual decision making within an organization in which each individual's response in a decision context is predicated upon formal guidelines:

How closely are the decisions of the individual audited by those superior to him in the organization?

What penalties attach to wrong decisions?

What rewards attach to correct decisions?

What rewards attach to the absence of individual decision making— for example, a straightforward following of existing rules and regulations?

The recent literature on bureaucracies suggests that under a "pure-authority" system (Wintrobe's terminology) the superiors within an organization will attempt to discourage innovation among their subordinates in decision-making matters. Such discouragement could be achieved by increasing the probability of the subordinate being discovered (through increasing the auditing of individual decision making), by increasing the sanctions applied against decision making on the basis of individual discretion rather than organizational regulations, or by reducing the potential rewards for a correct decision that is at variance with the decision at which the superiors would have arrived through use of the regulations. Because of the unequal distribution of power inherent in the bureaucracy's hierarchical order, subordinates face a high probability of receiving the blame for bad discretionary decisions and a low probability of receiving credit for any positive innovative decision.

In the pure-authority system, most workers will adhere to the rules and regulations very carefully since only such adherence protects them from probabilities that are, on the net, negative. Only an employee with a great taste for risk will engage in discretionary behavior in such a context. In such a system, the institutionalization of academic criteria for reasons of tradition or convenience is a very likely result; this is true both for the purposes of initial employment and placement and promotions.

The pure-authority system can involve serious inefficiencies in cases in which decisions must be made concerning nonroutine processes. The greater the variance from routine processes, the greater will be the inefficiencies inherent in the pure-authority system. Because such inefficiencies can be destructive of the organization if it operates in a competitive environment, pure-authority systems are more characteristic of public- and monopoly-capitalist enterprises. In these cases, the inherent inefficiencies of the authoritarian decision system can be accepted by those at the top of the authority hierarchy because the costs can be externalized to consumers, taxpayers, or users of the public programs. The inefficiencies may be considered by the staff to be an acceptable cost for the stability of the organization.

An additional factor affecting the public propensity for authoritative bureaucratic organization of education is the uncertain nature of the output of the education enterprise. In education, at whatever level, systems of accountability have been difficult to design precisely because of the vagueness and the multiplicity of the outputs of education. Without a system of accountability, it is impossible to differentiate between good and bad decisions, and therefore, employment, pay, and promotion must all be based upon some artificial criteria. At the extreme, initial employment becomes a situation synonymous with a life-tenure agreement because superiors have no basis to remove an employee who follows the rules (whatever the result of such obedience). Superiors will be reluctant to introduce subjective evaluations because these same standards could then be applied by their own superiors. As a result, the bureaucracy rapidly creates its own raison d'être, emphasizing the benefits of the staff members, separate from whatever was the original mission for which society had chartered it.

In systems in which accountability is possible, the administrator has a variety of devices with which he can encourage his subordinates to make better discretionary decisions—namely, a more-systematic auditing of the results of decisions, stronger rewards and penalties, and an adjustment of basic payment systems away from a large fixed amount to one involving larger payments (commissions, bonuses, and so on) for specific achievements. It is interesting to note the convergence of interests between the demands of unionized workers and the bureaucratic form of organization. For whatever reason the early prohibitions in Western societies that barred the unionization of public employees were instituted at the time, these restrictions can now be seen to have a strong justification in the convergence of the anti-efficiency biases inherent in both union and bureaucratic behavior. Similarly, antimonopolist legislation can be seen as a vital necessity in preventing the evolution of capitalist bureaucracies. The native Galbraithian notions of the countervailing effects of union and company monopolism are invalidated in the recognition that unions, whether negotiating with capitalist, bureaucrat, or commisar, can externalize the costs for both themselves and their employers onto the general society.

This discussion of bureaucracies is relevant to the area of education in two main ways. First, it helps one understand some of the internal operations of the educational system and why the educational establishment itself is rarely a source for productive change, dramatic or otherwise. Second, the bureaucratic model is valuable in understanding how administrators of educational systems establish incentives for decisions individual families must make about alternatives in education.

Within this process, the role of information to decision makers may be seen as crucial. Information, as any other factor of production, must be cost-effective—that is, it must be the least cost means of achieving a desired end. In almost all contents, decisions should be made without full information because the marginal cost of the increment in information will not be justified by its cost. It is proper to suggest here that many of the manpower-planning activities and investment-return estimates made by planners and researchers violate this criterion themselves. The marginal policy value they have does not justify their cost. When one imputes the additional cost of probable misinterpretation or misuses of the results of such research (for political or other purposes), the present education-research-information process becomes subject to accountability questions itself. The issue here is not whether research can be valuable but whether researchers and planners have been realistic and careful in their assessment of the research needs for their systems.

The role of information in this discussion of incentive-based planning relates to this problem. The planner is seen to have three main operational alternatives:

1. Improving the flow of information to educational consumers/decision makers concerning the noncontrolled results of education (for example, wage scales or employment probabilities by course of study);
2. Improving the flow of information about, or altering the impact of, government-controlled incentive effects (subsidization; prerequisites for, and length of, degree programs; or public employment, pay, and promotion policies);
3. Creating totally new incentive patterns by altering existing educational policies.

The relative importance of alternative one to alternatives two and three varies, depending upon the importance of the public role in the society's economy. In developed economies with a relatively articulated labor-market infrastructure and a predominance of nonpublic employment, the public educational planner can achieve great advances simply by improving the flow of information to the individual decision makers. To the extent that the public sector dominates in either the provision of education or the employment of graduates, the planner has the opportunity to affect both the incentives themselves and the information flow about the incentives to the potential users of the system.

To illustrate the three ways in which bureaucratic theory may be useful in educational planning, one may begin by studying the internal organization of education in a competitive-market as opposed to a bureaucratic context. In a market system of education, two effects would predominate given the exclusion of monopolistic forces. First, the forms of education would be more varied and the units or organization relatively small to reflect the variety of consumption and investment outputs desired by purchasers of the education product. Within adequate consumer safeguards, the pressures of competition will force educational firms to be more responsive to the demands of individual students both in provision of instructional methods and courses of study. A pure-authority-bureaucratic educational organization could evolve only if some institution were able to create a degree of monopolistic control over a level of education or a specific curricular field such as law or medicine. One of the regrettable characteristics of the provision of education within the Western democracies is that they presently represent the worst effects from both market- and centrist-control systems. Rather than the attractive atomism described here, the U.S. and Western European models, and their copies in the postcolonial world, combine state subsidization with highly variable amounts of direct supervision, with the result that the taxpayers who finance the system find it an increasingly hard one either to understand or to control. Graduates of the system are subsequently faced with either a relatively competitive or monopsonistic labor market, with the result that planning errors in educational decision making accrue to the unemployed or underemployed graduate as well as to the taxpayer.

In the nonmarket model of education common to Eastern Europe and other socialist areas, the public sector both provides education and controls the major employment activities of society. This system is, in fact, a more rationally consistent approach to the educational system than the mixed public-subsidization/private-employment model. Chuprunov and Tul'chunskii note quite clearly that, in the USSR, "the planning of higher education . . . is an essential part of national economic planning" and express the rather optimistic view that "a planned socialist system makes it objectively possible to guide progress on a reliable scientific basis."[4] Education can be truly controlled or planned completely only within a social context of general economic control. Educational failures, which are most visible in economies in which publicly financed graduates are faced with a relatively open market for their abilities, are less obvious in centrist economies. The bureaucratic inefficiencies already noted in authority systems, pure or otherwise, assure that planning in such centrist economies will be less objective and less scientific than their planners may wish to admit. The cost of the inefficiencies may not be as visible but will exist as underemployment and production inefficiencies. The primary argument for such centrally based planning is the distributive advantage that the expense of educational failure is absorbed by a large group of consumers/taxpayers rather than by the individual graduates. The contention of this chapter is that the improved use of individual responsibility in educational decision making would reduce the present inefficiencies of such a system without necessarily foregoing the existing distributive advantages.

It has been suggested that the participants in the educational hierarchy are rarely the motivators for dramatic change. It should now be recognized that in the cases of monopolistic private systems or public provision of education, the innovational stagnation is but a special case of the normal inertia of bureaucratic organization. The primary danger is that systems of education, even if originally organized in a manner appropriate to the perceived needs of the time, will be slow to adapt to the changing demands upon education over time.

Given the importance of the flow of information from education, the labor market, and research and planning activities to the individual decision maker (student, parent, or administrator), an important research question is how much information is received and to what degree does it enter into the individual decision-making process? Many educational decisions appear to be made with little calculation of the eventual use to which educational attributes are to be put after graduation. Within such a context, rewards and sanctions can be instituted to improve either the convergence of private with public preferences or, less coercively, the private assumption of the costs of decisions that are not consonant with public goals. If educational costs were heavily subsidized and students were free to choose educational institutions and courses of study, then a divergence would be created between the individual criteria for investment and the public criteria. The result normally will be that more individuals consume more education than is socially optimal at any point in time and that they will probably engage in courses of study that do not reflect the economic requirements of their national economy. The subsidy underwrites not only the cost of free choices but also of erroneous and even careless ones.

The educational incentives faced by an individual are further clouded if public-employment policies are sending out a signal that educational specialization at advanced levels is meaningless in terms of employment and economic success. The work in the United States by Freeman has indicated that students, even within highly but not totally subsidized higher-education systems, do adjust to the signals of a relatively free labor market and change specializations to meet changes in demand.[5] In this process, they are limited by the amount and accuracy of information, its costs, their own aspirations and preferences, their time discount, and the opportunity for making discretionary judgments.

The government planner, who must make decisions affecting the educational order of society, will face the same decision calculus. However, the more distant the planner/administrator is from the actual event to be decided, the less exact and relevant will be the data base upon which decisions are made. In educational planning, the defect in a centrally administered system of any appreciable size works in both directions. Not only is the administrator not fully informed but also his instructions to subordinates and participants will become less clear the more distant (in time and space) they are from him. The parents and students who are making higher-educational decisions (even if they are only residual decisions about acceptance of an offer of admission to college or how much effort to put into studies) may fail to receive or may misinterpret the planner/administrator's actions. While these problems can be alleviated to a degree by decentralization, many governments may feel that they do not have an adequate supply of qualified personnel to allow such a devolution of command. It is paradoxical that governments fail to take advantage of the individual's decision-making ability at the personal level where decision making is easiest and that they then are forced to centralize the decision making more and more because the very nature of aggregation makes the decision process more complex.

From the traditional discussion of the proper role of the public sector in any economic activity, one can formulate the educational programs that government can legitimately undertake even within an otherwise competitive free-enterprise system. It may be necessary to protect students from possible educational fraud by proprietary institutions; the government may need, in an emergent economy, to create the infrastructure for efficient allocation within the labor market; and it may be necessary to sponsor research on both educational effects and on the results from the implmentation of previous governmental policy. Finally, there is one area in all economies where a crucial role remains to be played and where government may well have to be the catalyzing agent—namely, the generation and distribution of information.

Much of the information concerning education and the labor market will be casually generated and distributed and therefore subject to error in fact as well as inequality in incidence. A major source of casual information upon which individuals will be basing their decisions about education will be the working of the labor market and the resulting structure of occupational rewards and status. The factors in a decision may be viewed as dichotomous: cost effects and benefits effects. The benefits effect in education decisions will include the immediate-consumption aspects of education as well as the long-run benefits to the educated person as a consumer and family member. However, one may expect the benefits calculation for most persons to be dominated by the perceived monetary and nonmonetary returns from employment.

The biases that exist in the casual labor-market-information system are likely to be in the direction of overstating possible employment and pay. The student in the rural village is more likely to hear of the urban success than of the urban failure. Even if the employment and pay probabilities are correct, one must also consider the tendency of individuals to overestimate their own chances for success.

Educational decision making can lead to especially unfortunate results when the second part of the equation—personal costs—is quite low. In theory, the citizen should realize that he will pay taxes in the future to finance education for others, but this is rarely considered in the citizen's support for subsidized education and is quite correctly considered irrelevant at the margin in the personal decision to pursue additional education. With very low costs attached to the educational-attendance decision, the normal response of students will be to attend even if probable benefits are small. Thus, the subsidization allows the student to externalize the costs of bad educational decisions to the public taxpayer. If the society also provides substantial employment guarantees for upper-level graduates, even if their training is not actually needed or if unemployment-insurance programs exist, the student is allowed to externalize the results of his poor educational choice even further.

Poor information and excessive educational subsidization also explain another phenomenon common to education—that is, overproduction of graduates and yet continuing shortages in terms of quality and in certain specializations. If the labor-market information received by students fails to articulate the difference in demand for school graduates by quality and specialization, and if subsidies are generalized rather than specific to the areas of high demand, it is hardly surprising that the graduates produced are not the graduates society requires. Bureaucratization of employment policies, in the public sector or in large private companies, will also aggravate this problem because the pay and promotion system may not provide differential rewards in terms of quality or specialization. In this instance, the labor market is transmitting clear information; the employment policy itself is counterproductive.

Toward Resolution of the Planning Dilemma

We express here a twofold hope that researchers and planners will concentrate more on education's variety rather than its seeming unity and that the use of the tremendous resource of individual decision making will be directly exploited. Most postcolonial nations face serious shortages of resources for education. Why, then, should one create planning systems that fail to take advantage of the skills and abilities of local communities and individual families and students?

Sources of optimism do exist. Diverse postcolonial societies such as Cameroon, Bangladesh, and Indonesia presently have, as part of their educational-planning structure, explicit programs designed to support the national educational goals through local and individual efforts. Almost all programs of universal primary education and nonformal literacy have been forced to recognize and to utilize the assets inherent in their local citizenry. What is needed is a greater effort to provide a methodological framework within which such efforts can be better planned, implemented, evaluated, and revised.

Notes

1. See, for example, J.G. Head, "Public Goods and Public Policy," *Public Finance,* 1962, pp. 197–221; M. Friedman, "The Role of Government in Education," in *Capitalism and Freedom,* (Chicago: University of Chicago Press, 1962), pp. 85–107; S. Feltzman, "The Effect of Government Subsidies-in-Kind on Private Expenditures: The Case of Higher Education," *Journal of Political Economy,* 1973, pp. 1–22; K.W. Roskapm, "Public Goods, Merit Goods, Private Goods, Pareto Optimum, and Social Optimum," *Public Finance,* 1975, pp. 23–35; E.K. Browning, "Tax Reductions versus Transfers in a Public Choice Mode," *Public Finance Quarterly,* 1976, pp. 77–87; J.E. Coons and S.D. Sugarman, *Education by Choice: The Case for Family Control* (Berkeley: University of California Press, 1978); and J.S. Coleman, "Choice in Education," in *The Analysis of Educational Productivity,* vol. 2, ed. C. Bidwell and M. Windham (Cambridge, Mass.: Ballinger, 1980), pp. 233–255.

2. G.S. Fields, "The Allocation of Resources to Education in Less Developed Countries," *Journal of Public Economics,* 1974, pp. 133–143.

3. R. Wintrobe, "The Economics of Bureaucracy" Ph.D. diss., University of Toronto, 1976; and H. Leibenstein, *Beyond Economic Man: A New Foundation for Microeconomics* (Cambridge: Harvard University Press, 1976).

4. D. Chuprunov and L. Tul'chunskii, "USSR: Economic Planning and the Financing of Higher Education," in *Educational Cost Analysis in Action: Case Studies for Planners* (Paris: UNESCO, 1972).

5. R.B. Freeman, *The Market for College-Trained Manpower: A Study in the Economics of Career Choice* (Cambridge: Harvard University Press, 1971).

10 Education and Parental Decision Making: A Two-Generation Approach

Nancy Birdsall and
Susan Hill Cochrane

An understanding of the relationship between education and development requires that we understand the process whereby decisions are made to educate children in the first generation and that we examine the consequences of that education for the children's children—the second generation. An analysis of both the determinants and consequences of education requires that we examine the variables affecting household decision making. In this chapter, we structure the discussion of some of these issues around a simple model of household decision making.

Figure 10–1 captures in simple form the idea of the household-decision model and the two processes we examine. The individual characteristics of parents (generation one), including parents' education and the household's economic and social environment, are pictured as inputs that affect certain outcomes for children (generation two), including their education, their health, and their numbers. In the first part of this chapter, we focus on how the combination of inputs affects a particular outcome, the children's education (the dashed line). In the second part, we focus on how a specific input, parents' education, affects the set of outcomes for children (the dotted lines). Finally, we discuss briefly the interdependence of the three outcomes for children.

A Household Model of Children's Schooling

Our assumption is that the household (not the individual child) makes the decision regarding schooling, at least at the primary and secondary levels.[1] In this regard, the model is in the tradition of household models that deal with various family decisions—for example, labor supply, fertility, migration. The basic idea behind family decision making, or household models, is that the family or household, as an economic unit,

The views and interpretations in this chapter are those of the authors and should not be attributed to the World Bank, to its affiliated organizations, or to any individual acting in their behalf.

maximizes a single utility function that encompasses the preferences of all members. The arguments of the utility function are leisure for household members and consumption goods. A critical point is that the consumption goods can be produced at home as well as purchased in the market. Many goods are produced by combining purchased articles with household members' time, such as meals served at home. Constraints are thus total time available to all members (since time is necessarily divided between work for income, work at home, leisure, and in the case of children, school), the wage rates that members can command, and the flow of services from existing capital assets and land. Given these constraints, different members of the household allocate time to different activities. Since members are likely to have different wage rates, specialization is not surprising. A common example is specialization of a husband (who usually commands a higher wage than a wife) in work for income and specialization of a wife in so-called household production. Children often specialize in schooling.

The first premise of the schooling model is that parents derive utility from knowledge of the expected future income of their children; children's expected future income can be increased by sending them to school.[2] Parents also derive utility from consumption of goods and from leisure time in this period.

Income of children in the next period is a function of time children spend in school, expenditures on schooling, a set of child-specific characteristics that affect the returns to each unit of time a child spends in school, and an uncertain factor for parents—the good or bad luck of the child in the market as an adult. Returns to schooling can vary across individuals—for example, because of differences in their innate ability or because of imperfections or discrimination in the labor market.

Parents face a tradeoff, however, between present household consumption and children's future income. The tradeoff occurs because schooling is not free to the household. There are direct costs such as those for books, uniforms, transportation, and fees, and in developing countries, there are indirect costs such as the children's foregone labor. The time children spend in school and the money costs of school necessarily reduce total-family work time and total consumption of goods in the present. Put another way, the household faces a budget constraint, or what can be called a full-income constraint, where full income includes the time available to household members as well as cash. Total spending and money cannot exceed the sum of unearned income and earned income. Earned income depends on the wage rates of husband, wife, and children; the amount of time spent working by husband, wife, and each child; and the number of children. Time of children is divided between leisure, school, and work (at-home production and in the market), and time of adults is divided between leisure and work (at home and in the market).[3]

On the basis of this simple household-demand model, we can specify a set of equations representing the quantity demanded by households of various commodities including not only schooling of children but also leisure of household members and spending (of time and money) on health, nutrition, housing, and other consumption goods. The quantity demanded for each of these choice, or endogenous, variables is a function of a set of predetermined, or exogenous, variables including the prices of schooling, housing, and so on; the price of household members' time, or their wage; and an unearned-income variable and the variables that may affect expected returns to schooling, such as discrimination and children's ability.

It is possible to estimate any one of the quantity-demanded functions for health, fertility, and so on as well as for child schooling, independent of others, as long as there is information on all the exogenous variables in the model. Thus, for estimation purposes, it is necessary to observe all prices but unnecessary to observe values of endogenous variables other than the one under scrutiny. The quantity of schooling demanded can be estimated using the following equation:

$$D_{sj} = D_{sj}(P_s, P_x, W_h, W_w, W_c, V, T, C),$$

where D_{sj} represents the schooling demand of family j; P_s represents the price of school, which is discussed later; P_x is the price of other goods; Ws are the wage rates of husband, wife, and children; V is unearned income; T is the taste of the household for schooling, which may be captured by parents' schooling; and C is a vector of variables representing returns to schooling.

It is also possible to estimate household demand for health of members and for fertility; in those cases the price of health and of numbers of children would play a particularly important role, as does the price of schooling in the equation. The same set of household variables (wages, income, education of parents, and tastes, shown as inputs in figure 10—1 affects demand for each of the commodities shown in the figure as outcomes for children.

The demand for schooling in the jth household is thus a function of the wage rates of husband and wife as well as children and of prices of all goods. Changes in any one of these exogenous variables, holding constant the others, can entail some change in the time children spend

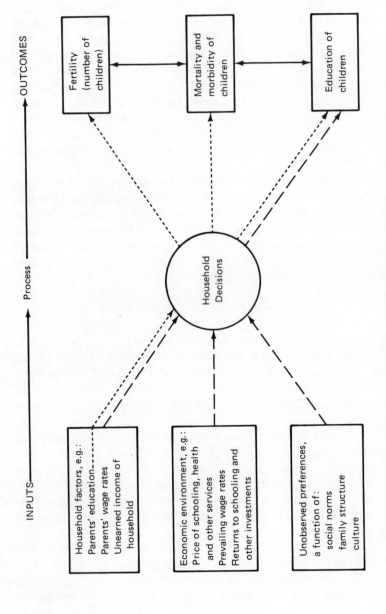

Dashed line discussed in the section on determinants of children's schooling
Dotted line discussed in the section on consequences of parents' education for children

Figure 10–1. Education as a Determinant and Consequence of Household Decision

in school and in spending on school. A change in schooling demand will be the result of a combination of both price effects, holding utility constant, and income effects, holding prices constant. For example, with income held constant, the effect of an increase in the child wage (W_c) on time children spend in school should be to reduce time in school (the own-price effect—that is, an increase in child wages, utility held constant, will increase the value of time of children at work and thus decrease time in school). If children work more hours, the household may also have more income; the increase in income will increase total household consumption and could increase time in school, offsetting the wage effect—whether by enough to have a net positive effect of time in school depends in part on how easily children can combine work and school schedules. The effect of a change in the price of school goods (P_s) is more straightforward; when school costs more, households will buy less of it, all other things the same.

Similarly, consider the effects of a change in the mother's wage on children's time in school. On the one hand, if children substitute for mothers in work at home, an increase in adult-female wage rates, income held constant, could increase the opportunity cost of children's time and reduce their time in school. On the other hand, of course, increases in wage rates for skilled women that are viewed as permanent by households would also increase the returns to schooling of girls and could encourage school attendance.

Figures 10–2, 10–3 and 10–4 illustrate how the model can be applied. The horizontal axis of figure 10–2 measures the endogenous variable of concern: quantity of schooling per child in a family measured, for example, as the number of grades completed at a given age. On the vertical axis are the exogenous price variables; for simplicity the vertical axis can be thought of as measuring the price that most directly affects schooling: P_s (which is not specific to households but to certain geographical areas). The demand curve, F_{11}, applies to family[1] living in a particular geographical area, area[1]. The demand curve can be thought of as a function of exogenous family-specific variables such as family unearned income; wage rates, actual or potential, of husband and wife; the opportunity cost to the family of sending a child to school and the factors that affect returns to schooling, especially innate ability of children, and sex, race, and other characteristics that might influence the parents' perception of expected returns.

A second family with a higher demand curve in the same area (F_{12}) purchases more schooling (S_{12}). A third family with a lower demand curve (F_{23}), but residing in area[2], purchases more schooling (S_{23}) than the first family because the price it faces is sufficiently lower.

In figure 10–4, a rationing situation is pictured. In area 3, local

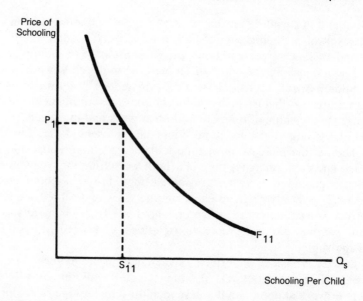

Figure 10-2. Demand for Schooling of Family 1 in Area 1

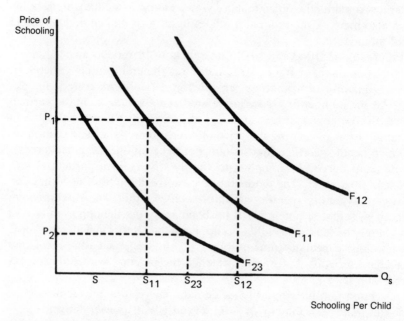

Figure 10-3. Demand for Schooling of Three Families in Two Areas with Different Schooling Prices

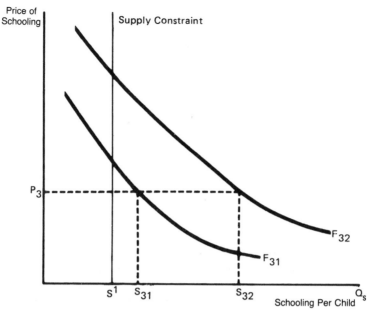

Figure 10–4. Demand for Schooling in an Area with Rationed Schooling

schooling has a low price, (P_3), but its supply is limited and some households cannot obtain the amount of schooling (S_{31}, S_{32}) they would want at the prevailing price. They are constrained to consume at the point S. The rationing can take several forms: overcrowded classrooms, so that in effect it is quality that is rationed; a limited number of grades, so that children cannot go beyond the top grade available; or rationing of available places, so that some children are excluded altogether. With rationing of available places, there is the possibility that rationing is not random, but is correlated with household characteristics. For example, the poor are less likely to obtain admittance even when they are prepared to pay the prevailing price piece-rate.

The actual shape of the demand curve for a particular household with a given set of characteristics (income, education of parents, and so forth) is not known. Only a point on the demand curve, as described by those characteristics, is observed. The object of analysis is to generate from observed Ss (for households for whom the supply constraint does not apply), Ps, and household points a set of typical demand curves. The shape of such curves indicates what the elasticity of demand with respect to exogenous changes in prices and household income is and, thus, how changes in those exogenous variables would affect change in the quantity of schooling per child demanded.

Empirical Findings

Studies of the demand for (or determinants of) child schooling are still relatively rare for developing countries. Table 10–1 is a partial list of such studies, most of which at least implicitly utilize some form of the household model. Most are based on analysis of data not collected for the explicit purpose of understanding household demand for schooling. Their chief difficulty is lack of detailed information on the availability and quality (what we have called price) of schools to households; a second difficulty is lack of information on the local labor market and thus on the prevailing child wage (opportunity cost of the child going to school) and on the private returns to schooling.

In the table, the characteristics of the sample used in each study and the type of price or rate-of-return variable, if any, are shown. Virtually all studies test the effects of parents' own characteristics on their children's education. As discussed in the next section, even when income and wage rates are not known (or used), parents' education is. However, only a few studies have included any proxy at all representing the economic environment households face—for example, the price of schooling in terms of availability and quality or the return to schooling as an investment. We now turn to a discussion of some of these studies. We will first look at the effect of access to schooling and then at the effect of the child wage and the rate of return. In the section on second-generation effects, we look more at the most critical of the parent characteristics for children's schooling and other outcomes—parents' own education.

Price of Schooling: School in the Village, Distance to School, and School Quality

The presence or lack of a school in the village is the simplest measure of availability for rural households. In a surprising number of studies, however, the presence of a school does not have a significant effect on enrollment or grade attained; this is the case for rural India (Makhija 1980; Rosenzweig 1979) and Nepal (Lockheed and Jamison 1981). In a study of one area of the Philippines, the presence of a particular type of complete six-year primary school did have a significant positive effect, in contrast to the presence of a regular primary four-year school or a secondary school. The complete six-year primary schools tend to be better equipped and often serve as centers or feeder schools for the four-year schools; their effect may be due more to quality than to presence per se. In another region of the Philippines, having a primary school did increase male enrollment (Paqueo 1981). Presence of a school may be too crude

Table 10-1
Data of Total Teacher Income to Number of School-Age Children by Region

Authors	Country	Date of Survey or of Other Data	Sample Characteristics	Exogenous Variables Reflecting Price or Rate of Return	Sign if Price Variable Significant
Birdsall (1982)	Brazil	1970	2,021 urban and 1,741 rural children aged 15, nationwide	Child-teacher ratio / Mean education of teachers by region	+ / +
Birdsall (1981)	Malaysia	1976–1977	Children aged 12–16 from sample of 1,262 households, nationwide	Distance to primary school / Distance to secondary school	N.S. / —
Birdsall (1980)	Colombia	1967–1968	1,433 households in 4 major cities	None	N.A.
Chernichovsky and Smith (1979)	Botswana	1974–1975	1,060 households in rural areas, nationwide	None	N.A.
Clark (n.d.)	Guatemala	1974–1975	800 households in 4 rural and 2 semi-urban areas in Guatemala	None	N.A.
Clavel and Schiefelbein	Chile	1969–1970	787 to 917 households, nationwide	None	N.A.
Cochrane, S., and Jamison, D. (1978)	Thailand	1981	955 individuals 5–25 in 22 rural villages	Distance of village to lower primary school / Distance of village to upper primary school	N.S. / (—) for males N.S. for females
Datta and Meerman (1980)	Malaysia	1964	782 households, peninsular Malaysia	None	N.A.
Evenson and Banskota (n.d.)	Philippines	1963–1968 then 1977	320 households in rural area of Laguna province	Wage of child (predicted)	+
Harrison (1980)	Malaysia	1976–1977	1,262 households, peninsular Malaysia	Distance to nearest public secondary school	N.S.
Knowles and Anker (1975)	Kenya	1974	1,074 households from 7 of 8 provinces	None	N.A.

Table 10–1 continued

Authors	Country	Date of Survey or of Other Data	Sample Characteristics	Exogenous Variables Reflecting Price or Rate of Return	Sign if Price Variable Significant
Lockheed and Jamison (1981)	Nepal	1977–1978	795 households in 6 panchayats in 2 districts: Bara and Rautahat	Distance to primary school	—
				Distance to secondary school	N.S.
				Availability of primary school in village (dummy)	N.S.
				Availability of secondary school in village (dummy)	N.S.
Lewis (1978)	Turkey	1973	3,461 men and 2,882 women, nationwide	None	N.A.
Makhija (1980)	India	1968–1971	4,118 households in rural areas, nationwide, restricted to self-employed farming families where eldest child was aged between 5 and 14.	Whether or not there is a school in village	N.S.
				Whether or not there is a cottage industry or a small-scale industry in village	+ for girls, N.S. for boys
				Net cropped area adjusted for irrigation	N.S.
				Percentage of gross cropped area under high-yield varieties	N.S.
Paqueo (1981)	Philippines	1978	1,903 households from 100 randomly selected Barangays in Bicol region	Availability of primary school	+ for boys, N.S. for girls
				Distance to primary school	– for boys, N.S. for girls
				Distance to secondary school	N.S. for boys N.S. for girls
Pearse (1979)	Indonesia	1971	595 households in 4 large cities, 5 towns, 6 small towns and their districts, in East Java	Distance of community from school	N.S.

Study	Location	Date	Sample	Variable	Result
Peek (1976)	San Salvador, Khartoum		2,600 urban households; 1,200 urban households	None	N.A.
Quizon (1981)	Philippines	1977	584 households in 40 villages in the province of Laguna	Availability of public primary school in village	N.S.
				Availability of public intermediate school in village	+
				Availability of public secondary school in village	N.S.
				Child wage	N.S.
Rosenzweig (1981)	India	1968–1971 (wage rates 1961 and 1971)		Expected wages of boys	+
				Expected wages of girls	+ for girls, N.S. for boys
				Expected wages of children	– for boys, N.S. for girls
				Presence of school in village	+ for boys, N.S. for girls
Rosenzweig (1978)	Philippines	1968	National Demographic Survey of 7,237 households	Province-level average child wage of working children	N.S.
Rosenzweig (1980)	India	1968–1971	979 households, rural India, nationwide (with mother aged less than 55 and having at least one child aged 5–15)	Child wage for district, in agriculture	N.S.
				Standardized employment rate for girls	–
				Standardized employment rate for boys	N.S.
				Availability of school in village	N.S.
				Land size (acres)	+ for girls, N.S. for boys

Table 10–1 continued

Authors	Country	Date of Survey or of Other Data	Sample Characteristics	Exogenous Variables Reflecting Price or Rate of Return	Sign if Price Variable Significant
Rosenzweig and Evenson (1977)	India	1961	189 districts (out of 232 districts) in 13 states, rural areas	Daily field wages of children	– for boys, N.S. for girls
				Rupees per net acre sown	N.S.
				Average land holdings per land-owned households, in acres	N.S.
				Number of factories and workshops in districts	
Sanguinetty (n.d.)	Paraguay		569 households (Asuncion)	None	N.A.
	Peru		1,357 households (Lima)		N.A.
	Venezuela		1,173 households (Maracaibo), all urban		
Wery (1977)	Philippines	1968	8,444 students in urban, 3,915 students in rural, from National Demographic Survey	Ratio of average provincial wage with secondary education to average wage of those with primary education	N.S.[a]
				Ratio of average provincial wage of those with tertiary education to average wage of those with secondary education	N.S.[a]

Notes: N.A. means not applicable because no price variable was used.

N.S. means the price variable used was not statistically significant (5 percent level).

[a]Except wrong sign in 3 of 10 equations for females (stratified by urban/rural end of level of education).

a proxy for overall availability, particularly in parts of India and Nepal where the walk to a nearby village that does have a school could be very short.[4]

Distance of the community from the school does show up as having a deterrent effect on hours spent in school (Birdsall 1981) and on grade attained in Malaysia (Harrison 1980). Distance of the community from a school does not matter in Java, Indonesia (Pearse 1979), where no households are very far from a school. [For a sample in northern Thailand, access to lower primary school (grades one to four, which is almost universal), had no effect on achievement nor enrollment, but for males five to thirteen, access to upper primary school had a significant effect on enrollment, and for males fourteen to twenty-five, access to upper primary school five years ago had a significant effect on attainment (Cochrane and Jamison 1981). This is similar to results in the Philippines.]

Distance of the household from school, a more-accurate measure than distance of the community as a whole, is a deterrent in Nepal (Lockheed and Jamison 1981). However, even distance of the household from school is a crude measure because the effect of distance itself must be combined with availability of transportation and roads since the real factor is probably travel time and cost. In some cases, moreover, distance of the household from a school might actually be endogenous, if, for example, parents choose their residence to facilitate their children's attendance at school.

Analysis of the effect of distance has also been done by geographers in the context of school mapping. There is evidence, for example, that very few primary-age students in developing countries travel more than five kilometers to school. In Algeria, 80 percent of students live within two kilometers; even in less-populated Uganda, almost 65 percent live within two kilometers.[5] Using school-mapping and student-residence data does not allow at all for study of differences among households in demand for schooling as governed by household-specific characteristics such as income and parents' education. Obviously, some households will send children farther than others. In short, we are still a long way from understanding how densely schools should be built in order to maximize enrollment.

The fact that results across a variety of samples are not particularly consistent, is due not only to the fact that presence of a school and distance need not reflect travel costs and time. A more-serious measurement issue is that it is probably not only access that affects enrollment but also the quality of available schools. The variables for presence of a school and distance cannot capture effects of crowding or differences in availability of books, paper and writing materials, and qualifications of teachers. On all such measures, there is evidence of considerable variation (at the least between rural and urban areas) within poor countries and that poor countries are much worse off than rich countries.[6] In Brazil in 1970, for example, the average education of primary and secondary-school teachers varied from as low as three years in parts of the rural Northeast to about twelve years in the urban south. Results from a study of the determinants of schooling in Brazil (Birdsall 1982) indicated that school quality, measured by mean teacher education and an indicator of expenditures per child in 169 different areas of the country, had a significant impact on children's attained years of schooling within both urban and rural regions. The elasticity of responsiveness of households to differences in these measures of quality was substantial.

Child Wage and Rate of Return

Parents who send their children to school do so at least in part because schooling is an investment; it yields a rate of return based on its immediate costs relative to its expected future benefits in terms of higher income for educated children. Immediate costs include direct costs, for example, of fees, school uniforms, books, and transportation. Direct costs may be a barrier [in Botswana direct costs were estimated to equal 5 percent of income of poor households (Chernichovsky 1981)], but for public schooling they probably do not vary much within countries and have not been studied as a determinant of differences among households in school-enrollment probabilities.

However, a few attempts have been made to test the effect on child schooling of the indirect cost of foregone labor. The district-level child wage had a negative effect on both districtwide enrollment rates in India (Rosenzweig and Evenson 1977) and on household-level enrollment (Rosenzweig 1981). Provincial child-wage rates had no effect on provincial enrollment in the Philippines (Rosenzweig 1978), possibly reflecting the higher income and much higher average school enrollment in the Philippines compared to India. Individual wage rates for children, predicted for all children using a wage equation for those reporting earnings, had a positive effect on enrollment in one area of the Philippines (Evenson and Banskota n.d.). This was undoubtedly due to the strong effect of education on the predicted child-wage rate (no other variables in the child-wage equation were significant), which produced a kind of circularity.

What is noteworthy, however, is that the wages of educated children were higher in this region than those of uneducated children. This effect of education on the child wage indicates a return to schooling even prior to entering the adult labor force and points out the tradeoff parents face in agricultural regions where more education for children increases not only the future income of children as adults but also the current income of households. Such a tradeoff is most likely to occur in regions where technological change is occurring, since education has a payoff in terms of improving adults' and even children's ability to make allocative decisions in rapidly changing conditions.[7] Thus, for rural India in the early 1970s, there is some evidence that though the child wage had a negative effect on schooling, living in a new-technology (Green Revolution) area had a positive effect, controlling for the higher adult wages in those areas (Rosenzweig 1979).

The fact that child wages capture both a cost effect (higher opportunity cost) and an incentive effect (the wage increases with education) makes it all the more difficult to unravel the underlying causes of school participation. The same is true even for adult-female wages. On the one hand, higher female wages attract women into the labor force, and in India they have been shown to reduce school enrollment, presumably because children substitute for mothers in child care and other work at home (Rosenzweig 1981); on the other hand, rising female wages, particularly for skilled women, increase the incentive to educate girls. The key in analysis may therefore be to distinguish between the effect of wage increases for the unskilled and the educated.

Empirical specification of the return to schooling is even more difficult. We found only one study, for the Philippines, in which an effort was made to relate current wage differences among those working to school enrollment. In that study, prevailing wage differences by level of education (university versus secondary, secondary versus primary, primary versus none) had no apparent effect on child schooling.[8]

We have reviewed the evidence available on the effect of the economic environment on the schooling of children. Household-specific characteristics affect the demand for schooling as well. Among the most important of such variables is the education of the parents. In the next section, we review the effect of parental education on children, including the investment in child schooling, the health and survival chances of children, and the number of children born—the second-generation effects of education.

The Second-Generation Effects: Parental Education's Impact on Children

The household is unique in that it combines economic production and reproduction and, therefore, is the nexus of decision making about family size, child health, and investments in education. Parental education should be expected to alter these decisions. The effects of education, however, cannot be expected to be simple and monotonic because education alters the preferences of household members, knowledge, decision-making ability, self-confidence, and control over economic resources. Education's effect through all these channels may not operate in the same direction in all cases.

The evidence available on how parental education affects children is basically of two kinds: (1) cross tabulations of fertility, child survival, or child schooling by parental education, controlling for mother's age or child age; and (2) multiple-regression studies in which parental education is used as an independent variable. These two kinds of studies differ in their availability on various topics and in what they can tell us about the relationship.

Fertility has frequently been cross tabulated by parental education in both census and survey reports. Cross classifications of child survival by parental education have only recently become available as questions allowing one to indirectly measure mortality have come to be included on censuses and surveys. The relationship between parental education and child schooling is not routinely published in censuses or surveys even though the data are usually available. Cross tabulations are valuable for showing the net effect of parental education in the second generation through all its various channels. Thus, data of this kind provide a valuable first step to understanding.

The multivariate studies provide us some insight into the channels through which parental education operates. Unfortunately, multivariate studies differ substantially in terms of the other explanatory variables included, and thus the coefficients of parental education have very different meanings in various studies. The model just discussed illustrates the complexities involved in identifying the appropriate specification.

In examining the evidence, we concentrate on the most widely available form of evidence on each relationship so that we can maximize the number of developing countries covered by our discussion.

Parental Education and Children's Education

The data available on the effect of parental education on child schooling differ from that on child survival and family size. Routine cross tabulations are not carried out on the relationship between the two variables.

Therefore, the ony data we have on the relationship are from multivariate studies. These were summarized in the studies in table 10–1.

There is an almost universal positive relationship between child schooling and parental education. Given the consistency of this finding, it is worthwhile to single out the few deviations from the normal pattern. Data from the Laguna study show father's education is not significantly related to the education of sons and daughters (Evenson and Banskota n.d.). Data from India show that mother's education is not significant but that father's is (Makhija 1980). Data from Botswana show that parental education is positively related to enrollment and years completed but negatively related to hours spent in school of those currently enrolled (Chernichovsky 1981). In addition to these clear cases, cases also exist in which parental education has the expected sign but in which the coefficient is not always significant.

The only study that has fairly consistent negative relationships is that reported by Peek (1976). His study uses discriminant analysis to divide the sample into those in school and those not in school. While most variables have the expected effect, wife's education never has a positive, significant effect and, in fact, has a negative, significant effect in three of four cases. In this survey, husband's education has the expected effect ony for sons in San Salvador and Khartoum. Father's education has a small, but negative effect on the school attendance of daughters in both cities. The results of this study are the most difficult to explain, and the author offers no hypothesis for the perverse coefficients of mother's education.

The lack of significance of mother's education in the Indian study may be due to the very low levels of female education. In the two samples used, female education averages less than one year, while male education averages over four years. An alternative explanation is that wives in the Indian sample have very little power in family decision making. Other analysis in the Makhija study tends to support this point. Female education has no effect on the enrollment of children aged five to nine in extended families or in the total sample that pools extended and nuclear families. In nuclear families, however, wife's education has a positive and marginally significant coefficient.

The study of parental education's effect in the Laguna sample can be amplified by looking at the other studies of data from the Philippines. Rosenzweig's 1978 study, using a national data set, shows that mother's and father's educaton is positively significantly related to the education of sons and daughters relative to a norm. This tends to cast some doubt on the extent to which the Laguna results can be generalized outside the rural area of the survey. Wery's study (1977) provides even more insight. His work shows, for example, that one does get different results for urban and rural areas.[9] Father's education has a positive effect on the completion of primary school for boys and girls in urban and rural areas. Beyond primary school, father's education ceases to be significant for sons in rural areas or at the tertiary level for sons in urban areas.

The result obtained for time spent in school in Botswana is surprising, but Chernichovsky (1981) offers an interesting suggestion: More-educated parents are more likely to send their children to school, but each child spends somewhat fewer hours there. Therefore, it appears that more-educated parents are more egalitarian in their education of children.

We can conclude that parent's education almost universally increases the education of their children. The only questions that need further explanation are the magnitude of the effect and the channels through which it operates. The magnitude of the effect is hard to summarize because of the wide variety of dependent and independent variables utilized. The studies can be grouped, however, and some generalizations are possible.

A number of studies have used years of school completed as the dependent variable. In these studies the effect of mother's education ranges from .05 to .52 depending on the age and sex of the child, the country, and the inclusion of other variables. Sanguinetty's (n.d.) study provides the best illustration of how maternal education's effect varies by the age and sex of the child (see figures 10–5 and 10–6). In general, the effect of mother's education increases with the age of the child, but this pattern is not completely uniform, especially for daughters.

Other studies that examine education's effect on school years completed show a narrower range of coefficients for mother's education, from .07 in Kenya to .26 in rural Brazil. Five of the eight values fall between .223 and .260 and seven of the eight between .152 and .260. This is a fairly narrow clustering given the wide range of methodologies used.[10]

Fewer studies incorporate father's education. Seven coefficients observed fell between .025 and .291, but there was little clustering of values. Either father's education has a less-consistent effect on the years of school completed or the measurement of its effect is far more sensitive to the methodology used—particularly the way in which income is controlled.

To estimate the effect of parental education on various dimensions of child schooling, elasticities can be calculated. Unfortunately, few studies include the necessary data for these calculations. The elasticities for wife's education show an even broader range than the coefficients, from .04 to 1.02. For husband's education, the values range from .01 to .22. It is difficult to generalize about the magnitude of the effect of husband's education relative to that of wife's. For the six cases in which elasticities

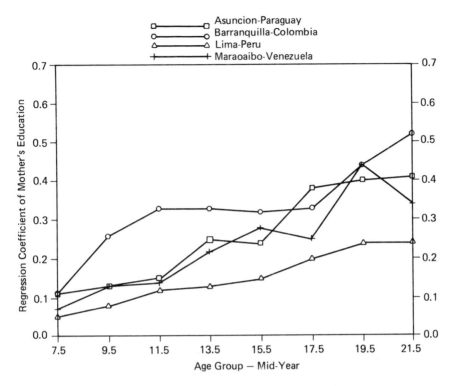

Figure 10–5. Effect of Mother's Education on Years of School Completed, by Age, for Sons in Four Latin American Cities

exist for both parents, wife's education has a much higher elasticity in three; in two, the values are very close and in one, the husband's is greater. Thus at this point we have too little evidence to make definite conclusions about the relative importance of education of the parents.

The effect of parental education on the education of children is not simply an income effect. In all but one of these studies cited, income, assets, parental wages, or landownership were controlled, but the effect of parental education on child schooling persists. Thus, this effect of education cannot be attributed to income or wealth effects. Alternatively, perhaps parental education is associated with access to schools. If access to schools is controlled, the coefficient on parental education was positive and significant in a greater percentage of the cases than if access were not controlled (84 versus 64 percent). The only five cases for which parental education was negative and significant occurred when there was no control for access to school. Thus the evidence seems fairly conclusive that parental education's positive association with the education of chil-

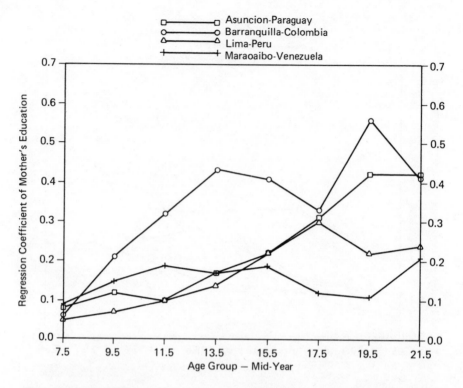

Figure 10–6. Effect of Mother's Education on Years of School Completed, by Age, for Daughters in Four Latin American
Cities

dren is not simply an income effect or a spurious result of associations
between the availability of schools in both generations. The specific
channels are still unclear but are probably related in part to other decisions
the parents make with respect to the number of children they have and
the investments they make in child health. The effect of first-generation
education on these two variables is reviewed in the following section.

Parental Education and Child Health

Parental education may alter child health in numerous ways. Most of the
effects of education on child health should lead to a positive relationship
between parental education and child health. The higher incomes associated with education should improve nutritional status and increase the
ability to afford healthy environments and modern medical care. The

improved knowledge and access to information provided by education should raise levels of sanitation in the home, increase the use of preventive medicine, improve the recognition of disease symptoms, and increase the use of curative medical care. The only possible negative effect of education on child health that has been suggested in the literature is that a wife's education will increase the market value of her time. If child health is intensive in mother's time, this might lead to a decrease in child health ceteris paribus (O'Hara 1980). An example of this possibility is the relationship between maternal education and breastfeeding. It has been widely documented that, as education increases, the practice of breastfeeding in developing countries decreases (see Cochrane 1979; Jain and Bongaarts 1980). This might have detrimental effects on child survival. Data show, however, that the net effect of maternal education on child survival is positive.

The negative relationship between maternal education and child mortality is shown in tables 10–2 through 10–5. These tables show consistent decreases in child mortality with increases in maternal education in 31

Table 10–2
Probability of Dying from Birth to Age Two, by Education of the Mother, in Selected Latin American Countries, 1966–1972

| Country | Year | Number of School Years Attended by the Mother | | | | |
		None	1 to 3	4 to 6	7 to 9	Over 10
Bolivia	1971–1972	.245	.209	.176	.110[a]	—
Chile	1965–1966	.131	.108	.092	.066	.046
Columbia	1968–1969	.126	.095	.063[b]	.042[c]	.032[d]
Costa Rica	1968–1969	.125	.098	.070	.051	.033
Dominican Republic	1970–1971	.172	.130	.106	.081	.054
Ecuador	1969–1970	.176	.134	.101	.061	.046
El Salvador	1966–1967	.158	.142	.111	.058	.030
Guatemala	1969–1970	.169	.125	.085	.058	.026
Honduras	1969–1970	.171	.129	.099	.060	.035
Nicaragua	1966–1967	.168	.142	.115	.073	.048
Paraguay	1967–1968	.104	.080	.061	.045	.027
Peru	1967–1968	.207[e]	.136[f]	.102[g]	.077[h]	.070[i]

Source: Eduardo E. Arriaga, "Infant and Child Mortality in Selected Latin American Countries," mimeographed (Washington, D.C.: U.S. Bureau of the Census, 1979), table 18.

[a]Seven years and over.
[b]Four to five years.
[c]Six to eight years.
[d]Nine years and over.
[e]Less than three years.
[f]Incomplete primary school.
[g]Complete primary school.
[h]Incomplete high school.
[i]Complete high school and over.

Table 10–3
Proportion of Children Dying by Age X, by Wife's Education for African Countries

		No school	Elementary	Above primary		
Ethiopia[a]	$0q2$	.179	.137	.012		
Gambia[a] (1973)	$0q2$	.275	.194	.118		

		No school	Primary	Postmiddle		
Ghana[b]	$0q1$	.1294	.1156	.0821		
	$0q2$	.1659	.1476	.1016		
	$0q5$	.2229	.1552	.1132		

		No school	Grades 1–4	Grades 5–9	From grades 1–4	Above grade 5
Kenya[a] (1969)	$0q2$	.160	.122	.090	.053	.033

		Illiterate	Literate			
Senegal[c] (1973–1977)	$0q1$	.1202	.0714			

		No school	Primary	Post-primary		
Sierra Leone[a] (1974 census)	$0q2$	.292	.217	.140		

			No school	Some education	Elementary	Higher
Sudan[a] (1973)	R	$0q2$	.212	—	.151	—
	U	$0q2$	.195	.114	—	.077
Tanzania[d] (1967)		$0q5$	.261	.192	.132	—

		No school	Grades 1–3	Grades 4–7	Secondary	
Uganda[e] (1969)	$0q2$	.181	.150	.108	.056	
	$0q3$	.206	.164	.119	.066	
	$0q5$	.242	.188	.146	.075	

		No school	Lower primary	Upper primary and above		
Zambia[a]	$0q2$	.174	.165	.093		

[a]Ramachandran 1979.
[b]Tawiah 1979.
[c]Republic of Senegal 1981.
[d]Egero and Henin 1973.
[e]Republic of Uganda 1976.

Table 10-4
Proporation of Children Dying, by Age of Mother and Education, in Selected Asian Countries

Country	Age	Year	No School	Some Primary	Upper or Completed Primary	Beyond Primary	Completed Secondary
Hong Kong	20–24	1971	.000	.000	.000	.000	
	25–29		.014	.005	.007	.000	
	30–34		.004	.009	.003	.016	
Indonesia	20–24	1976	.174	.171	.090		
	25–29		.164	.164	.112		
	30–34		.219	.199	.118		
Republic of Korea	20–24	1965–1966	.084	.064	.051		.00
	25–29		.110	.087	.058		.049
	30–34		.137	.104	.077		.054
Pakistan	20–24	1975	.231	.147		.136	
	25–29		.209	.172		.109	
	30–34		.213	.141		.086	
Philippines	20–24	1973	.103[a]		.066	.051	
	25–29		.083		.067	.043	
	30–34		.093		.088	.045	

Source: Constructed from several tables in Arriaga, 1979b.

[a]Includes grades 1–4.

Table 10–5
Proportion of Children Dying, by Mother's Age and Education, in Africa

		No school	Primary	Beyond primary		
Botswana (rural)[a]						
(1971 census)	20–24	.144	.109	.056		
	25–29	.176	.123	.068		
	30–34	.182	.141	.071		

		Illiterate	Read and write	Primary	Preparatory	
Cairo						
(1976)	20–24	.17	.13	.11	.09	
	25–29	.17	.13	.09	.08	
	30–34	.17	.12	.09	.07	

		No school	Some primary	Upper or completed primary	Beyond primary	Completed secondary
Kenya						
(1969)	20–24	.169	.127	.088	.048	.047
	25–29	.192	.132	.094	.061	.024
	30–34	.219	.146	.115	.059	.025
Nigeria[d]						
(Ibadan)	20–24	.108		.076	.056	.074
	25–29	.135		.112	.083	.062
	30–34	.183		.131	.089	.040

		No school	Primary	Secondary		
Zimbabwe[e]						
(1969)	20–24	.16	.10	.06		
	25–29	.18	.11	.05		
	30–34	.20	.13	.06		

[a]Republic of Botswana, 1971.
[b]Abou-Gamrah, 1980.
[c]Republic of Kenya, 1971.
[d]Sembajwe, 1977.
[e]Central Statistical Office, Rhodesia, 1971.

of 32 countries.[11] Even small amounts of education are associated with reductions in mortality. The strength of the relationship varies substantially, however. In Indonesia and Zambia, there is very little difference between the group with no schooling and those with some primary education, while the difference is 30–40 percent in Gambia, Pakistan, Peru, Senegal, and urban Sudan. The effect of higher education is, of course, even greater. The child mortality of the most educated mothers is one-half to one-tenth that of the uneducated.

Analysis of similar data shows that the effect of education on child survival will be greater the lower the level of literacy, life expectancy, and per capita expenditure on public health (Cochrane, O'Hara, and Leslie 1980). This suggests diminishing returns to the effects of education on child health as mortality falls and the possibility of reducing inequalities in life chances of children through public-health programs.

It appears clear that the effect of parental education on child survival is not just an income effect. There are relatively few multivariate studies of child mortality that include income or some proxy for income as well as education. Seven studies of this kind showed that male and/or female education was significant in six cases (see Sullivan, Cochrane, and Kalsbeek 1981). Income was significant in only two cases. The coefficients and significance of male and female education vary. In Nepal and Karachi, for example, female education was not significant, probably due to the small numbers of women who are educated (only 5 of 550 in Nepal). In other cases, the inclusion of endogenous variables makes it difficult to estimate the true effect of education. In a recent study of Brazil for 1970 (Merrick 1981), and in an earlier review of the evidence (Cochrane, O'Hara, and Leslie 1980), it was found that male education had about half the effect of female education. Brazilian data for 1976, however, showed that the effects of male and female education were much closer (Merrick 1981). Considerably more research on the socioeconomic determinants of mortality will have to be done before we can know why parental education has the effect it does on child mortality and why it varies.

Parental Education and Family Size

The effect of education on fertility is more complex than its effect on child health or child schooling because education's effect on fertility through some channels is positive while, through others, it is negative (Cochrane 1979). Education, particularly the education of women, has negative effects on fertility because it is associated with later ages of marriage, smaller desired family sizes, and better knowledge of family-planning methods. Education may have positive effects on fertility by improving maternal health and thus increasing the ability to conceive and carry fetuses to full term. Since education is associated with shorter periods of breastfeeding, the ability to conceive following the birth of a child probably returns earlier to more-educated women. Positive effects of education on fertility may also operate through the abandonment of traditional behavior that restricts fertility, such as prolonged postpartum abstinence. This is particularly important in parts of Africa.

The net effect of education, therefore, tends to vary depending on the level of development and the demographic stage of the country. In

very poor, highly rural, highly illiterate environments, fertility is frequently higher for women with some primary school than for those with
no schooling. At higher levels of education, fertility usually begins to
decrease. In more-developed environments, fertility is inversely related
to education over the entire range. These two patterns have been documented in Cochrane (1979).

Since new data are constantly becoming available, it is necessary to
constantly update material to see if the earlier observed patterns persist.
Table 10–6 summarizes data from 20 World Fertility Survey (WFS)
studies reported at the 1980 WFS Conference in London. These data
confirm the patterns found in Cochrane (1979). For all Latin American
countries, Korea, Malaysia, and Jordan, fertility falls as education increases. In the rest of Asian countries and Kenya, fertility rises with
education and then falls at higher levels. These patterns differ, however,
depending on which women are included in the analysis and on whether
male or female education is examined. Female education has a more-
negative impact on fertility than male education as shown by the average
values. For example, Korea, Malaysia, the Dominican Republic, Guyana,
and Peru all show that fertility falls consistently with female education
but that it rises with small amounts of male education.

Unfortunately, Kenya was the only African country for which WFS
data were available in 1980. However, a recent attempt to pull together
survey and census data for Africa has permitted us to verify these patterns.
In ten of the thirteen cases shown for Africa in table 10–7, age-controlled
fertility is higher among those with a small amount of education than for
those with no schooling. In two cases, Sierra Leone and Senegal, the
evidence is mixed; for Gambia, fertility is marginally lower for those
with some schooling than for the uneducated. In all cases, the fertility
of those with more than primary education is lower than that of those
with primary schooling. Thus, the patterns for these African countries
conform to what would be expected given their income levels, literacy
levels, and lack of urbanization.

The channels through which the positive and negative effects operate
have been documented in Cochrane (1979). Education apparently has a
fairly systematic negative effect on fertility through its effects on desired
family size and on knowledge and use of contraception. Education's
effect on the number of children a women can potentially bear during her
reproductive life seems to vary substantially. A major effect of education
is to raise the age of marriage of women. This has a negative effect on
the biological supply of children. This effect is offset, however, by the
fact that education is associated with better maternal health and the abandonment of behavior patterns that traditionally kept fertility low. Part of
education's effect on fertility is in fact an income effect. This is partic-

Table 10-6
Effect of Education on Predicted Completed Fertility

Country	Total Fertility Rate (All Women) Woman's Education				Adjusted for Marital Duration (Ever-Married Women) Wife's Education				Adjusted for Marital Duration (Ever-Married Women) Husband's Education			
	No School	Lower Primary	Upper Primary	Secondary	No School	Lower Primary	Upper Primary	Secondary	No School	Lower Primary	Upper Primary	Secondary
Bangladesh	6.2	6.5	6.9	5	6.2	6.6	7.1	6.1	6	6.9	6.6	6.8
Fiji					4.8	5.2	4.8	4.1	4.9	5.3	4.7	4.3
Indonesia					4.9	5.5	5.6	5.4	4.5	5.4	5.3	5.7
Korea	5.8	5.2	4.5	3.3	6.2	5.5	5	4	6.1	6.1	5.5	4.5
Malaysia	5.2	5.1	4.6	3.2	6.3	6	5.4	4.6	5.9	6.3	5.8	5.1
Nepal					6.1	6.5	6.1	2.8	6.1	5.4	6.2	5.4
Pakistan	6.6	(5.9)	(5.7)	3.6	7	6.7	7.1	5.8	7	6.6	7.3	6.8
Philippines	5.2	6.9	6	3.8	6.4	7.1	6.6	5.3	6.5	7.2	6.6	5.5
Sri Lanka					5.3	5.1	5.3	4.8	5.4	5.3	5.2	5
Thailand					5.5	5.7	5.3	3.6	5.1	6.8	5.5	4
Colombia	6.4	5.5	3.5	2.5	6.7	5.9	4.1	3.3	6.7	6.1	4.3	3.3
Costa Rica	(4.9)	4.5	3.3	2.7	5.2	4.5	3.4	3.3	4.7	4.5	3.6	3.3
Dominican Republic	(6.6)	6.4	4.1	(2.3)	6.9	6.7	4.9	3.7	6.6	7.1	5.1	3.5
Guyana	—	5.4	5.3	4	6	5.1	4.8	4.4	4.6	5.3	5	3.9
Jamaica	—	5.4	5.1	3.2	6.6	5.3	5	3.4	6	5.4	4.9	3.4
Mexico	7.6	6.6	4.7	3.3	7.4	7.2	5.5	4.6	7.6	7.2	5.9	4.7
Panama	—	6.1	4.3	2.9	6.7	6.2	4.5	3.6	6.6	6.2	4.5	3.7
Peru	7	6.4	3.7	3.4	7.7	6.9	5.4	4.5	7.2	7.4	6.3	5.1
Jordan	9.2	6.8	5.4	(3.6)	9.3	7.7	6.7	5.6	9.3	9.1	7.9	6.8
Kenya	8.4	8.9	8	5.5	7.4	8.1	7.7	7.8	7.2	8.2	7.9	7.8
Average all available countries	6.6	6.1	5	3.5	6.4	6.2	5.5	4.5	6.2	6.4	5.7	4.9
Average countries in total fertility rate	6.6	6.1	5	3.5	6.8	6.4	5.6	4.7	6.5	6.6	5.8	5

Source: Rodriquez and Cleland, 1980, Tables 4, 7, A–2.
Note: Parentheses indicate samples of size < 500.

Table 10–7
Age-Controlled Fertility, by Maternal Education, in Africa

		No school	Primary	Secondary	
Botswana[a] Standardized Mean Parity (SMP)		3.18	3.59	2.18	

		No school	Read and write	Elementary completed	Secondary and higher
Egypt[b] SMP	1960	4.21	4.53	4.26	3.59
	1974/1975	4.21	4.37	3.66	2.80

	No school	Primary	Secondary
Gambia[a] SMP	3.28	3.22	2.51

	No school	Elementary	Secondary	University
Ghana[a] TFR	6.2	6.4	2.9	4.1

Kenya		0	Grades 1–4	Grades 5–8	Secondary	
(1978–1978)[c]	35–44	7	7.6	7.1	3.3	
	45+	7.7	(8.7)	(8.3)		
	TFR	8.75	9.04	8.14	7.29	
(1962)[d]	35–39	4.99	5.89	5.67	4.65	3.03
	40–44	5.52	6.77	6.03	6.56	2.95
	45–49	5.82	7.38	6.58	3.89	4.67
	50+	5.19	6.93	6.10	3.13	

		No school	Primary	Some secondary	Secondary and higher
Nigeria[e] (Ibadan) CEB of women 38+	Moslems	4.66	4.50	(5.57)	(3.67)
	Christians	5.31	5.72	5	4.93

		Illiterate	Literate
Senegal[f] (1978) Married women	Number of children	4.18	2.83
	Duration adjusted	4.03	4.05
All women	Number of children	3.85	1.76
	Age adjusted	3.69	3.07

		No school	Primary	Secondary and higher
Sierre Leone[a] SMP	Western	3.41	2.83	1.68
	Northern	3.11	3.12	2.81

Table 10–7 continued

		No school	Primary	Above primary	
Sudan[a]					
SMP	Urban	3.1	3.4	1.8	
	Rural	3.2	3.6		
		0	*Grades 1–4*	*Grades 5–8*	
Tanzania (1967)[g]					
	30–34	4.2	4.6	3.8	
	35–39	4.8	5.1	4.4	
	40–44	5	5.6	4.6	
		0	*Grades 1–3*	*Grades 4–7*	*Secondary*
Uganda (1969)[h]					
		5.32	5.80	5.81	4.82

[a]Ramachandran, 1979.
[b]IBRD estimates.
[c]Republic of Kenya, 1980.
[d]Republic of Kenya, 1971.
[e]Sembajwe, 1977.
[f]Republic of Senegal, 1981.
[g]Egero and Henin, 1973.
[h]Republic of Uganda, 1976.

ularly true of the positive effects. It is difficult to disentangle the income effects from the pure education effects using existing studies. An important part of future research will be disentangling education's effect on fertility through higher wages and incomes from its effects through knowledge and attitudes.

Interactions

In this chapter we have been treating family size, child survival, and the education of children as if they were independent. In fact, as figure 10–1 suggests, these variables are probably jointly determined—that is, decisions parents make regarding one factor are related to, and may be affected by, decisions they make about others. In developed countries, for example, where the cost of raising children is high (because mothers may need to leave the labor force and because education is costly) parents appear to substitute quality of children for quantity—that is, they spend more on the health and education of one or two children rather than having many children. In developing countries, quality and quantity may be substitutes or complements, depending on circumstances. Other interactions are more obvious, such as the facts that healthier children probably stay in school longer and that frequent pregnancies may increase the risk of child deaths. The magnitude and, in some cases, the direction of these interacting effects are undoubtedly different under different economic, social, and cultural circumstances. Though considerable theoretical work has been done on the nature of these interactions, applied work, particularly in developing countries, is still rare. The results on which we have reported provide a streamlined and simplified picture. The interactions are more difficult to isolate and test, but really only in their web can the complexity of life in rapidly changing developing economies be illustrated.

Conclusions

Virtually all the applied work on which we have reported is based on analysis of cross-sectional data, but the story of development is really one of change over time. The magnitude of particular effects may be greater or less depending on both the interactions among household decisions we have hardly discussed and how changing circumstances over time alter the environment, which in turn is bound to alter the whole set of decisions.

Bearing in mind these cautionary notes, three points can be made to summarize this chapter. First, though there is some evidence that children are more likely to go to school where schools are more accessible, this is not a consistent result, either because of difficulties in measurement of school availability (particularly the paucity of work on the effects of school quality) or because the noneffect is real—that is, in some circumstances, children stay home regardless of school accessibility and quality. One of these circumstances is probably that parents do not perceive returns to schooling (for themselves or for their children) sufficient to make the investment worthwhile.

The second conclusion is more straightforward. Educated parents, especially mothers, are on average more likely to have healthier and better-educated children. This is true even taking into account income differences.

The third conclusion is that, contrary to conventional wisdom, education is not related to fertility in a simple inverse manner in all circumstances. In very poor rural environments, fertility may be higher for those with a small amount of education than for those with no schooling. This small positive association between education and fertility may be the result, at least in part, of the effect of improved health resulting from higher incomes associated with education, which is not offset by behavioral changes unless individual or aggregate education increases somewhat more.

Notes

1. This is in contrast to the more-standard investment models (Mincer 1974), in which the individual makes choices about education, taking into account the increase in the present discounted value of his or her future income stream due to an increase in education. This approach has been applied in the developed countries, where much of the variance in amount of schooling among individuals occurs after age sixteen, an age after which the foregone income costs of schooling can be reasonably attributed to the individual, rather than the family. Even for older-age children in developing countries, additional schooling may be more the family's than the individual decision, if family ties imply a longer period of sharing of income.

2. Parents, of course, face some uncertainty about children's future income since other factors besides schooling, including luck, can affect earnings. Parents can also leave physical assets to children, and these may be distributed among children to compensate for differences in human capital. See Becker and Tomes (1979) and Tomes (1981). The model described here is presented more formally in Birdsall (1981).

3. The model involves several simplications. First, we do not take into account the option parents have to invest in physical capital. This is not unrealistic for most households in LDCs. Assuming diminishing returns to investment in school (and other forms of human capital), and that the rate of return on a small investment in human capital is higher than in nonhuman capital, parents investing litle in their children would then invest entirely in human capital, and investments in nonhuman capital would occur only when the rate of return fell to the constant rate of return of investment in nonhuman capital. Second, investments in nonschooling forms of human capital are ignored. The model can easily be extended to take nonschooling investment more explicitly into account. At the margin, the returns to all forms of investment (for example, in formal schooling, in nonformal education, in physical capital to bequeath) should be equated, given prices of each.

4. Even if presence of a school had a consistently positive effect on enrollment, it would not always be clear why. There are two possibilities: one is that children are more likely to attend school if the school is nearby, but the other is that the central government builds schools first where they are most likely to be used. The presence of schools, in other words, may be itself endogenous.

5. See Gould (1978). He discusses the results of case studies undertaken in connection with a research project on school-location planning sponsored by the International Institute for Education Planning.

6. For comparisons across countries including developed and less-developed, see Inkeles (1977).

7. Welch (1970) showed this for farmers in Iowa. See also Jamison and Lau (in press).

8. The unemployment rate (but not relative wages by schooling level) has been shown to affect enrollment in the United States (see Lerman 1972; Corazzini, Dugan, and Grabowski 1972).

9. Wery's study is not strictly comparable to the other two because mother's education is not included. Quizon's (1981) analysis of the Laguna data does not include father's education.

10. The outlying value is found for Kenya where only oldest child's education was measured. This may be less dependent on maternal education than that of the average child in the household.

11. The only exception is Hong Kong where mortality has achieved such low levels that the number of deaths in each group is so small that the statistical significance of the patterns is questionable.

References

Abou-Gamrah, Hamed. "Fertility and Childhood Mortality by Mother's and Father's Education in Cairo, 1976." Paper presented at the Seminar on the Demographic Situation in Egypt, Cairo University, December 1980.

Arriaga, Eduardo E. "Infant and Child Mortality in Selected Latin American Countries." Mimeographed. Washington, D.C.: U.S. Bureau of the Census, 1979a.

———. "Infant and Child Mortality in Selected Asian Countries." Mimeographed. Washington, D.C.: U.S. Bureau of the Census, 1979.

Becker, Gary S., and Tomes, Nigel. "An Equilibrium Theory of the Distribution of Income and Intergenerational Mobility." *Journal of Political Economy* 87 (December 1979):1153–1189.

Birdsall, Nancy, "A Cost of Siblings: Child Schooling in Urban Colombia," *Research in Population Economic* 2 (1980):115–149.

Birdsall, Nancy. "Child Schooling and the Measurement of Living Standards." Living Standards Measurement Study Working Paper No. 14. Washington, D.C.: World Bank, February 1982.

Birdsall, Nancy. "The Impact of School Availability and Quality on Children's Schooling in Brazil." Mimeographed. Washington, D.C.:

Population and Human Resources Division, World Bank, March 1982.

Central Statistical Office. *Rhodesia, 1969 Population Census, Volume II: The African Population.* Salisbury, Rhodesia, February 1971.

Chernichovsky, Dov, and Smith, Christine. "Primary School Enrollment and Attendance in Rural Botswana." Mimeographed. Washington, D.C.: World Bank Population and Human Resources Division, 1979.

Chernichovsky, Dov. "Socioeconomic and Demographic Aspects of School Enrollment and Attendance in Rural Botswana." Discussion Paper No. 81-47. Washington, D.C.: Population and Human Resources Division, World Bank, October 1981.

Clavel, Carlos, and Schiefelbein, Ernesto. "Factores Que Inciden en le Demanda for Education." Mimeographed. ECIEL (Estudos Conjuntos Sobre Integracion Economica Latinoamericana), Chile, 1977.

Cochrane, Susan H. "Education and Fertility: What Do We Really Know?" World Bank Occasional Paper No. 26. Baltimore: Johns Hopkins University Press, 1979.

Cochrane, Susan H.; O'Hara, Donald J.; and Leslie, Joanne. "The Effects of Education on Health." Working Paper No. 405. Washington, D.C.: World Bank, July 1980.

Cochrane, Susan H., and Jamison, Dean T. "The Determinants and Consequences of Educational Achievement in the Rural Chiang Mai Valley." Discussion Paper No. 81-61. Washington, D.C.: Population and Human Resources Division, World Bank, December 1981.

Corazzini, Arthur J.; Dugan, Dennis J.; and Grabowski, Henry G. "Determinants and Distributional Aspects of Enrollment in U.S. Higher Education." *Journal of Human Resources* (Winter 1972):39–59.

Datta, G., and Meerman, Jacob. "The Educationally Deprived in Peninsular Malaysia." Mimeographed. Washington, D.C.: World Bank, June 1980.

Egero, Bertil, and Henin, Roushdi A. *The Population of Tanzania, An Analysis of the 1967 Census.* Dar es Salaam: BRALUP and the Bureau of Statistics of the Government of Tanzania, 1973.

Evenson, Robert E., and Banskota, Kamal. "Fertility, Schooling and Home Technology in Rural Philippines Households." Mimeographed. n.d.

Gould, William J.S. "Guidelines for School Location Planning." Working Paper No. 308. Washington, D.C.: World Bank, November 1978.

Harrison, David Selwyn. "Household Decisions about Fertility and Children's Education: The Case of Malaysia." Ph.D. dissertation, Department of Economics, University of California at Los Angeles, 1980.

Inkeles, A. "The International Evaluation of Educational Achievement," *Proceedings of the National Academy of Education* 4 (1977): 139–200.

Jain, A.K., and Bongaarts, J. "Socio-biological Factors in Exposure to Childbearing: Breastfeeding and Its Fertility Effect." Paper presented at the World Fertility Survey Conference, London, July 1980.

Jamison, Dean T., and Lau, Lawrence J. *Farmer Education and Farm Efficiency*. Baltimore: Johns Hopkins University Press, in press.

Knowles, James C., and Anker, Richard. "Economic Determinants of Demographic Behavior in Kenya." Working Paper No. 28. International Labour Office, Dec. 1975.

Lerman, Robert I. "Some Determinants of Youth School Activity." *Journal of Human Resources* (Summer 1972):366–379.

Lewis, Gwendolyn L. "A Model of Turkish Adult's Educational Aspirations for Their Children." Mimeographed. Pittsburg, Pa.: University of Pittsburg, September 1978.

Lockheed, Marlaine E., and Jamison, Dean T. "Participation in Schooling: Determinants and Learning Outcomes." Mimeographed. Washington, D.C.: World Bank Population and Human Resources Division, June 1981.

Makhija, Indra. "Adult and Child Labor within the Household and the Quantity and Quality of Children: Rural India." Ph.D. dissertation, Department of Economics, University of Chicago, 1980.

Merrick, Thomas W. "The Impact of Access to Piped Water on Infant Mortality in Urban Brazil, 1970 to 1976." Discussion Paper No. 81-52. Washington, D.C.: World Bank Population and Human Resource Division, August 1981.

Mincer, Jacob. "Schooling, Experience and Earnings." Chicago. National Bureau of Economic Research, 1974.

O'Hara, Donald J. "Toward a Model of the Effects of Education on Health." In *The Effects of Education on Health*, edited by Cochrane et al. Working Paper No. 405. Washington, D.C.: World Bank, July 1980.

Paqueo, Vincente B. "A Household Production Model of School Enrollment: A Probit Analysis of the 1978 Bicol Multipurpose Survey Data." Discussion Paper No. 81-31. Washington, D.C.: World Bank Population and Human Resources Division, June 1981.

Pearse, Richard. "The Quantity of Education Demanded in a Developing Peasant Society: The Case of East Java." *Asian Survey* 19 (November 1979):1093–1109.

Peek, Peter. "The Education and Employment of Children: A Comparative Study of San Salvador and Khartoum.'' Population and Employment Working Paper No. 33. Geneva: International Labour Office, March 1976.

Quizon, Elizabeth K. ''Child Schooling and Time Allocation in Philippine Rural Households.'' Paper presented at the Population Association of America Meetings, Washington, D.C., 26–28 March 1981.

Ramachandran, K.V. ''Fertility and Mortality Levels, Patterns and Trends in Some Anglophone African Countries.'' Expert Group Meeting on Fertility and Mortality Levels, Patterns, and Trends in Africa and Their Policy Implications, UNESCO, Economic Commission for Africa, Monrovia, Liberia, November 1979.

Republic of Botswana. *Report on the Population Census, 1971*. Gaborone: Central Statistical Office, August 1971.

Republic of Kenya. ''Mortality and Population Growth,'' vol. 6. Report on the 1969 Census. Nairobi: Central Bureau of Statistics, 1969, chap. 5.

Republic of Kenya and the World Fertility Survey. *Kenya Fertility Survey, 1977–78*, vol. 1. Nairobi: Central Bureau of Statistics, Ministry of Economic Planning and Development, 1980.

Republic of Senegal. *Enquete Senegalaise sur la fecondite, 1978*, vol. 1. Dakar: Minestere de L'Economie et des Finances, July 1981.

Republic of Uganda. ''Mortality—African Population.'' Report on the 1969 Population Census, Volume IV: The Analytical Report. Kampala: Statistics Division, President's Office, January 1976.

Rodriguez, German, and Cleland, John. ''Socio-economic Determinants of Marital Fertility in Twenty Countries: A Multivariate Analysis.'' World Fertility Survey Conference, Substantive Findings Session No. 5, Wembley Conference Center, London, 7–11 July 1980.

Rosenzweig, Mark R. ''The Value of Children's Time, Family Size and Non-Household Child Activities in a Developing Country: Evidence from Household Data.'' *Research in Population Economics* 1 (1978):331–347.

————. ''Household and Non-Household Activities of Youths: Issues of Modelling, Data and Estimation Strategies.'' Paper prepared for ILO Informal Workshop on Children and Employment, Geneva, 10–13 October 1979.

————. ''The Wage Structure and the Intrafamily and Intergenerational Allocation of Resources.'' Paper prepared for the International Union for the Scientific Study of Population Seminar on Individuals and Families and Income Distribution, Honolulu, April 1981.

Rosenzweig, Mark R., and Evenson, R. ''Fertility, Schooling and the

Economic Contribution of Children in Rural India: An Econometric Analysis.'' *Econometrica* 45 (July 1977):1065–1080.

Sanguinetty, Jorge A. ''Determinants of Years of Schooling in Individuals: A Study in Three Latin American Cities.'' Mimeographed. ECIEL (Estudos Conjuntos Sobre Integracion Economica Latinoamericana), Chile: n.d.

Sembajwe, Israel S.L. ''Fertility and Child Mortality Levels and Differentials among the Yoruba of Western Nigeria.'' Ph.D. dissertation, Research School of Social Sciences, Australian National University, September 1977.

Sullivan, J.M.; Cochrane, S.H.; and Kalsbeek, W.D. ''Procedures for Collecting and Analyzing Mortality Data in LSMS.'' Mimeographed. Washington, D.C.: World Bank Population and Human Resources Division, November 1981.

Tawiah, E.O. ''Some Demographic and Social Differentials in Infant and Early Childhood Mortality in Ghana.'' Expert Group Meeting on Fertility and Mortality Levels, Patterns and Trends in Africa and Their Policy Implications, UNESCO, Economic Commission for Africa, Monrovia, Liberia, November 1979.

Tomes, Nigel. ''The Family, Inheritance and Intergenerational Transmission of Inequality.'' *Journal of Political Economy* 89 (October 1981):928–958.

Welch, F. ''Education and Production.'' *Journal of Political Economy* 78 (January/February 1970):35–39.

Wéry, René. ''The Demand for Education and Employment.'' Working Paper No. 51. Geneva: International Labour Office, March 1977.

About the Contributors

Nancy Birdsall received the Ph.D. degree in economics from Yale University and is currently on the staff of the Population and Human Resources Division of the World Bank's Development Economics Department. She worked for the American Council on Education and the Smithsonian Institution prior to joining the World Bank. She has written extensively on population and development, including "Population Growth and Poverty in the Developing World," in the *Population Bulletin, 1980* of the Population Reference Bureau; on fertility and child schooling in developing countries; and on women and development. She is currently doing research on the market for schooling and school policy in LDCs.

Carmel Ullman Chiswick is visiting associate professor, Department of Economics, Northwestern University, on leave from the University of Illinois at Chicago Circle. She is the author of numerous scholarly papers on human resources and economic development, both historically in the United States and contemporaneously in the LDCs. Professor Chiswick has worked as a staff economist at the World Bank, specializing in problems of income distribution and employment in LDCs, and as a consultant to the Industrial Labor Organization. Before that she worked at the United Nations as a specialist in the social aspects of economic development and at the Agency for International Development.

Susan Hill Cochrane is senior economist at the Population and Human Resources Division, World Bank. Dr. Cochrane received the Ph.D. in economics from Tulane University in 1969. In 1976 she joined the bank as a Brookings Policy Fellow and in 1977 became an economist on the bank staff. Since then she has worked on both reviewing existing literature and collecting and analyzing new data in Nepal, Thailand, and Egypt. Prior to joining the bank, she taught at the University of South Carolina, the University of Texas at Austin, and the University of Melbourne. Her major publications include *Fertility and Education: What Do We Really Know?* (1979); "Children as By-Products, Investment Goods and Consumer Goods: A Review of Some Micro-Economic Models of Fertility" in *Population Studies* (November 1975); "Population and Development: A More General Model" in *Economic Development and Cultural Change* (April 1973); and "Structural Inflation and the Two-Gap Model of Economic Development" in *Oxford Economic Papers* (November 1972).

Nat J. Colletta is currently with the World Bank as a program officer in the Indonesia Country Division, East Asia Pacific Programs Department. Mr. Colletta has written extensively on education and development issues and has consulted widely on various aspects of formal and nonformal education. He coauthored a volume on nonformal education entitled *The Use of Indigenous Institutions in Non-Formal Education and Development* (in press).

Gary S. Fields received the Ph.D. in economics from the University of Michigan in 1972. He is currently professor of labor economics and economics at Cornell University. Professor Fields also serves as advisor to the World Bank and to many government agencies. He is the author of *Poverty, Inequality and Development* (1980) and many scholarly articles.

Philip Foster is professor of education at the State University of New York at Albany. He was formerly the director of the Comparative Education Center, University of Chicago, and head of the School of Education, Macguane University, New South Wales. His principal publications include *Education and Social Change in Ghana* (1975), *Fortunate Few: A Study of Secondary Schools and Students in the Ivory Coast* (1966), and numerous articles in books and professional journals.

Stephen P. Heyneman is a senior sociologist on the staff of the education department at the World Bank and has participated in the assessment of project effects in Asia, Latin America, and Africa. He has published articles in eighteen journals and has written monographs on the politics of curriculum, the planning of educational opportunity between regions, and the evaluation of human capital.

Donald B. Holsinger received the Ph.D. from Stanford University. Dr. Holsinger was assistant professor of education at the University of Chicago and associate professor at the University of Arizona before joining the faculty of the State University of New York at Albany in 1981. He has recently returned from a two-year assignment with UNESCO as research advisor to the Indonesian Ministry of Education. His research interests are in the area of sociology of education, and he has published and edited extensively in the area of the relationship between schooling and value formation and the effects of schooling on occupational attainment. He is coeditor of *Education and Individual Modernity in Developing Countries.*

Marie Thourson Jones is assistant professor of education at the University of Chicago. She received the Ph.D. in politics from Princeton in 1979, having done complementary work in Near Eastern studies. Her recent writings have concerned the making of social policy in Tunisia, education of girls in the Middle East, and higher education in North Africa.

Ransford W. Palmer received the Ph.D. from Clark University and is currently graduate professor of economics at Howard University. Dr. Palmer's numerous professional publications include *Caribbean Dependence on the United States Economy* (1980) and ''Equality, Incentives and Economic Policy'' in *American Economic Review* (May 1980).

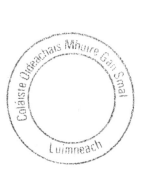

About the Editors

Lascelles Anderson is currently associate professor of education in the graduate school of education at Harvard University. Dr. Anderson received the Ph.D. in economics from the Graduate Faculty of the New School for Social Research, New York, in 1971. Before joining the Harvard faculty, Dr. Anderson was senior institutional research analyst with Bache & Co., and taught urban and quantitative economics at the University of Akron in Akron, Ohio. His current research interests include the economics of education, and education and development; and he has consulted in the Republic of Liberia and the Republic of China (Taiwan) in these areas.

Douglas M. Windham is a professor of educational administration and policy studies at the State University of New York at Albany and coordinator of the Program in International Educational Planning and Administration. He received the Ph.D. in economics from Florida State University and has been employed by the Ford Foundation and the University of Chicago. He has authored numerous articles, essays, and books on the economics of education, higher-education finance, and macroeducational-planning systems. Professor Windham has worked extensively in developing nations and has served as a consultant to the United States Agency for International Development, UNESCO, and the World Bank, as well as to various national governments in Africa and Asia.